Henry James's Ultimate Narrative

Henry James's Ultimate Narrative

THE GOLDEN BOWL

R.B.J. Wilson

University of Queensland Press
St Lucia•London•New York

Typeset by Press Etching, Pty Ltd, Brisbane
Printed and bound by Hedges & Bell Pty Ltd, Melbourne

Distributed in the United Kingdom, Europe, the Middle East, Africa, and the Caribbean by Prentice-Hall International, International Book Distributors Ltd, 66 Wood Lane End, Hemel Hempstead, Herts., England.

National Library of Australia
Cataloguing-in-Publication data

Wilson, R.B.J. (Richard Bartley Joseph), 1924-
Henry James's ultimate narrative.

(The University of Queensland Press scholars' library,
ISSN 0159-8856; 2).
Bibliography.
ISBN 0 7022 1593 7

1. James, Henry, 1843-1916. Golden bowl. 2. James, Henry, 1843-1916 — Style. I. James, Henry, 1843-1916. The Golden bowl. II. The Golden bowl. (Series)

813'.4

Contents

Acknowledgments

During some thirty years of interest in *The Golden Bowl*, I have incurred debts to many who have helped with memorabilia, texts, advice, facilities and encouraging criticism. The late Professor A.J.A. Waldock and Professor H.J. Oliver first aroused my interest in this work during my undergraduate years at the University of Sydney and my postgraduate work on Henry James's development was directed by Professor G.A. Wilkes during visits to him at Merton College, Oxford, and encouraged by Professor Wesley Milgate.

I record here my gratitude to the late Miss Theodora Bosanquet, one-time amanuensis to James, for the privilege of a highly informative interview with her in London in 1955 and for arranging a visit shortly afterwards to the late Mr Burgess Noakes in Peasemarsh, Sussex, for many years in James's service. Mr Noakes made most profitable my visits to Lamb House, Rye.

I am exceptionally indebted to the late Mrs Eleanor Green of Sydney, good friend, distinguished scholar and life-long Jacobite, and to the late Mrs Hilda Pratt of London, both of whom bequeathed to me their James libraries containing rare unrevised editions of the three major works, as well as the memory of invaluable discussions. Among other services rendered to me, are those by the old and new Fisher Libraries of the University of Sydney, the Mitchell Library, Sydney and the Central Library of the University of Queensland; also those by the British Museum Reading Rooms (including the Colindale Newspaper Annexe); and by the Serial Sections in the Senate Library of the University of London; and by Miss Carolyn Jakeman of the Houghton Library, Harvard, custodian of the James Family Papers.

Throughout 1965 in England, I benefited from stimulating seminars with Professor Barbara Hardy at Birkbeck College, a visit to Dr Miriam, and Professor Kenneth, Allott at Liverpool, and to Mr Douglas Jefferson at Leeds, and a sustained discussion in London with Dr Dorothea Krook. During 1973, when investigating how my own inquiries into the vexed question of the later style might profit from those of the linguistic schools of criticism, I had brief but helpful encounters with Professors Seymour Chatman at Berkeley and M.A.K. Halliday at Stanford and experience of post-graduate teaching by Dr David Lodge and Professor Frank Kermode at respectively the Universities of Birmingham and of London.

My most immediate gratitude naturally goes to those who have materially helped me to produce the following pages: to Professor A.C. Cawley who, while in Australia, acted as my first supervisor; to Dr Jane Novak my more recent one, who has brought to the whole project the authority of the University of Chicago Circle critics as well as her personal insight into what I was attempting and her invaluable tact, enthusiasm and candour as to whether I was achieving it; to my wife who typed early drafts and to Ms Elaine Greensill, Carmel King and Sandra Gough who patiently typed and retyped successive later ones; to Mrs Alma West for as patiently adding her checking of this final one to my own; to Miss Marilyn Bitomski who helped transfer some of the bibliography to cards; to Miss Sally Krimmer for having an unrevised James essay xeroxed for me recently in London; to Mr and Mrs Willis Haenke for so generously lending me a quiet working-place on Stradbroke Island; to many, many of my students, chiefly to Mr Ian Sibley, whose own work, amply attesting his keenness of eye and ear for felicitous English, I am later to cite; to Mrs Rosanne Fitzgibbons for her expert help in turning into a book a dissertation allegedly written as a book; and to Professors K.L. Goodwin and P.D. Edwards, who somehow kept the Research Committee of the University of Queensland patient with my long candidature.

I hope that my thanks to my daughters Susan and Katharine for their encouraging faith and for patiently sharing their lives to this date with Henry James may take the form of their being helped one day by this work to read the one it is designed to serve.

R.B.J. Wilson

A Note on Citation

References in parentheses within my text — for example (I, 290) and (II, 160) — are to pages in volumes I and II of the definitive (revised) "New York Edition" of *The Golden Bowl*, in which the novel appeared as volumes XXIII and XXIV of *The Novels and Tales of Henry James*, 24 vols., (New York: Charles Scribner's Sons, 1907-1909).

When making similar parenthetical references to chapters, I avoid Scribner's complicated division of them — for example (II.IV.iii) — which has never been repeated in any other edition and I refer to the more popular single-sequence used in the first English edition (London: Methuen Co., 1905) where the same chapter would appear thus: (xxvii).

My necessarily close argument upon the text often demands a series of brief quotations and when these cluster within my paragraph they are cited in sequence in brackets at the end of it.

To simplify further, I make full citation of the very numerous critical commentaries, not immediately after first mention but after quotation or reference, which soon follows. If a commentary is quoted several times within the same paragraph of my text and no other is introduced there, an index number appears after the last quotation and a single footnote consolidates the respective page references in their order of appearance in that paragraph.

All notes are numbered consecutively throughout each of the five chapters.

Words italicized by James appear in normal italics; words to which I wish to draw attention appear in bold italics.

R.B.J.W.

1

Introduction

In pursuit of all the "different responsible agents"

> The thing "done", artistically, is a fusion, or it has not *been* done — in which case of course the artist may be, and all deservedly, pelted with any fragment of his botch the critic shall choose to pick up. But his ground once conquered, in this particular field, he knows nothing of fragments and may say in all security: "Detach one if you can. You can analyse in *your* way, oh yes — to relate, to report, to explain; but you can't disintegrate my synthesis; you can't resolve the elements of my whole into different responsible agents or find your way at all (for your own fell purpose). My mixture has only to be perfect literally to bewilder you — you are lost in the tangle of the forest. Prove this value, this effect, in the air of the whole result, to be of my subject, and that other value, other effect, to be of my treatment, prove that I haven't so shaken them together as the conjurer I profess to be *must* consummately shake, and I consent but to parade as before a booth at the fair."
> From Henry James's Preface to *The Awkward Age*

I begin with those challenging remarks by James because they strike to the heart of the problem his major art generally presents and they may help me share my convictions as to why *The Golden Bowl* in particular so richly rewards the patient reading it persistently demands. The idea of the fusion of form and meaning by making all parts relevant to the whole would be obvious enough in any primer of any craft or art, but there is in James's thrusting statement an excited and exciting sense that he has sought and finally achieved these qualities to a degree that is indeed total and that his jaunty, defiant mention of the perfect and the consummate are witty gestures not to the figurative but to the literal. All critics of his work must have been aware of this notion and of this excitement; a few have responded by taking up one of the final three novels he completed and trying to relate a part of it to the whole of it. Yet, there remains an understandable itch to accept James's avowed premises and to try to discover what other kind of illumination results when one relates to the whole of any one of these works as many as possible of those parts which appear salient, either structurally, dramatically linguistically or whatever. How then might that one work further reverberate? How then might the phase that created it justify itself? Provided such a critic attended to "the thing 'done' " and not only to James's accounts of what he wanted to do or thought he had done, the criticism could suggest whether, in the chosen instance at least, he did make to the art of fiction a contribution that was commensurate with his half a century of dedicated application to it, and with his privately professed ambition of "splendid and supreme creation[1]."

Any such critical venture needs to be begun by someone whose minimum qualification is a conviction that these last three prodigious creations by a prodigious creator are deserving of such fullness of attention. I believe this attention can be amply justified, "in the air of the whole result", by the radically original vision *The Golden Bowl* gives us of the human adventure, of the social-solitary called man, of the nature of our knowledge, freedom and will, as well as of "the close connexion of bliss and bale"[2] that makes for "an awful mixture in things" (II,292), for a mystery that each of the human beings represented here personally confronts and discovers to be so strange. James may be seen to be asking himself as well as us if indeed wisdom can be held in a silver rod or love in a golden bowl. It may well be our increasing awareness of this elaborately asked rhetorical question and our responses to it that keep our attention such an excited and, I believe, such a rewarded one.

There are of course other obvious reasons for my choice of this novel. It comes at the end of the "major phase", which is first a phase of major production, accounting for the publication between 1902 and 1904 of three long, complex novels of increasing "difficulty". Probably the most debated, allegedly the most ambiguous, certainly the most elaborate of all James's works, it has commanded the increasing attention not only of Jacobite and anti-Jacobite critics but also of leading scholars and writers willing to acknowledge its substantial position in literature. Even if we see the "major phase" in wider terms, as, say, the final period extending from the late nineties to James's death in 1916, there are no other serious contenders: *What Maisie Knew* and *The Awkward Age* are experiments in the "dramatic" novel, *The Sacred Fount* was understandably excluded from the Scribner New York edition and *The Ivory Tower* and *The Sense of the Past* were never finished. But it is when we look closely at the "major trio" which manifests such a sustained application of James's characteristic mature powers that we see why the third work in it is so promising a choice, for each attains a difference in kind through a difference in the degree to which these powers are evidently applied, and the third may be seen as embodying his ultimate mode.

The "thing 'done' " so artistically in *The Ambassadors* produces rich, high comedy in the most sophisticated psychological realism then known to the English novel, and it remains essentially Strether's story. If there is a more qualified response engendered by the second most moving novel, *The Wings of the Dove*, it is not merely a case, as James put it, of "the makeshift middle"[3] but of each of the three different consciousnesses — Kate's, Densher's, Milly's — having been permitted to make its individual, unconcerted impact upon us. In the third work James is attempting and achieving so much more than in the preceding two that we do it scant justice if we lump it with them. He now takes that art of rendering a consciousness that he has so sophisticated and amplified in giving us Strether, Kate, Densher and Milly, and applies it to four principal and two minor characters while preserving, throughout, one kind of literary illusion, one pitch, one congruous whole, which, because there is no distinction here between form and meaning, expresses most eloquently the essence of his subject, his idea, his view of the human condition.

Another of my reasons is that, despite the critical industry that thrives on his later works, the full extent of James's radicalism as an experimenter in prose fiction has not been sufficiently recognized. Perhaps it has been overlooked, as Joyce's for instance could never be, because superficially *The Golden Bowl* resembles those James works immediately preceding it and can be mistaken for being merely different in degree from the work of James the First and James the Second rather than significantly different in kind. He is however not only renovating and refurnishing his house of fiction; he is concerned with an edifice much more commodious, one letting in much more light and commanding new vistas. If "attention of perusal",[4] (to use his phrase) does in fact reveal that he evolved during the Lamb House years a form of literary discourse affording empathetic understanding without permitting sentimental sympathy for, or exclusive identification with, any one character but relating, rather, all characters to human and moral absolutes without allowing those absolutes any didactic force, then he has clearly extended the frontiers of fiction. The provisions within the text of this novel testify to his having depicted the moral consciousness in ways that free that depiction from the moral simplifications that always threaten and sometimes overwhelm narrative, especially when it is in the third person.

Scrutiny suggests, in fact, his creation of a highly expressive scheme of narrative enabling him to simulate a poet's figurative intensity and a dramatist's scenic immediacy at a novelist's leisure. This mode keeps the reader at precisely that distance which ensures he will be kept busy. Denied omniscient explanations, confronted instead from point to point with the same vantage point shared by the author whose voice is constantly with him, the reader must deliberate on ambivalences within the given appearance of each figure and eschew moral judgment for moral cogitation. Like James, he is at once "down there in the arena", able "to rub shoulders" with each of the "more or less bleeding participants"[5] and also constantly aware of the passionate interest in the spectacle that all of them present not only from point to point but also retrospectively. The reader's cogitation increases its intensity in direct ratio to his willingness to sustain this vantage point from which all the difficult knowledge can be seen to be accumulating, the "scenario" scheme of composition keeping him aware of the context provided by the whole of the narrative that is antecedent to any one point in it. As James put it in the 1909 Preface: "We see very few persons in 'The Golden Bowl', but the scheme of the book, to make up for that, is that we shall really see about as much of them as a coherent literary form permits."[6]

It is in fact the role played by his notion of "scenario" that becomes one of the less obvious reasons for my choice of this novel for close appreciation. The 1895 Notebook entry developing the *donnée* of this novel is immediately followed by James's fervent recognition of this habit deriving from his so recently abandoned ambitions as a playwright. This "principle of the Scenario" is now called "divine" because it is seen to have such a "*singular value for a narrative plan too*", seen to be a "key that, working in the same *general* way fits the complicated chambers of *both* the dramatic and the narrative lock" and he ends the entry by adding: "But how much of the precious there may be in it I can tell only by trying."[7] By 1904 he is trying and is expressing his exultation to his agent,[8] Pinker, and I believe all this excitement can be justified by the account of the moral consciousness that the written book finally produces. It is when we analyze its structure into the "scenario" of its chapters that we see what this vaunted principle implies for James's evident effort to bring together the advantages of the literary credo responsible for Isabel Archer's solitary vigil by the fireside and the one serving Maisie's duologues with all who surround her.

The chief means of bringing together his notions of "picture" and "scene", notions evolved during his long development as an artist in prose fiction, is of course his notoriously mannered style of editorial discourse, and that rhetoric too achieves its greatest elaboration in his last completed long novel. Again, its link with all that the word "scenario" connotes for its creator becomes evident when we see what it owes to the *histrionique* of James's beloved *Comédie Française* for its heightened intensity and amplitude of expression through the play of tone. This discourse with its subdued editorial signals is the agent of unity that balances the scenario's "appeal to variety"; this is the constant source of control within which "the appeal to incalculability" can be made without forfeiting "a coherent literary form" and James can achieve his desired "handsome wholeness of effect". This agent of an artistic "fusion" that embodies James's final moral vision generates for us a relationship, with each character, of distanced empathy which holds our imaginative attention while postponing our moral judgment until everything has been shown and said. The language of this daunting piece of literature holds in tension all those "successive indirections" by which motive and consequence are so gradually unfolded and through which we are continually kept conscious of all four principal characters.

James's defiant " 'Detach one if you can' " rings often enough in my own ears as I set off in this study in search of the "different responsible agents" and argue my interpretation of a novel comprising two books (volumes), six parts and forty-two chapters devoted to those four principals, the "case" for each of whom James is clearly at pains to present and the development within each of whom is central to "the air of the whole result". But he himself had already precisely defined the necessary critical task when he defined, in a crucial passage of his Preface, the challenge he himself had accepted in writing the novel.

> That was my problem, so to speak, and my *gageure* — to play the small handful of values really for all they were worth — and to work my system, my particular propriety of appeal, particular degree of pressure on the spring of interest, for all that this specific ingenuity itself might be. To have a scheme and a view of its dignity is of course congruously to work it out, and the "amusement" of the chronicle in question — by which, once more, I always mean the gathered cluster of all the *kinds* of interest — was exactly to see what a consummate application of such sincerities would give.[9]

NOTES

1. Henry James, *The Notebooks of Henry James*, ed. F.O. Matthiessen and Kenneth B. Murdock (New York: O.U.P., 1947), p. 187. Hereafter *Notebooks*.
2. Henry James, *The Art of the Novel: Critical Prefaces*, ed. Richard P. Blackmur (New York: Scribners, 1950), p. 143. All eighteen of these, written for the "New York Edition", *The Novels and Tales of Henry James*, 26 vols. (New York: Scribner's 1907-1909), will be referred to hereafter as *Prefaces*.
3. Ibid. p. 302.
4. Ibid. p. 304. For James's continual pleas for his readers' cooperation, see "The Novels of George Eliot", *Atlantic Monthly* (October 1866), p. 482; "London Notes", *Harper's Weekly* (August 1897), p. 834 and *Prefaces*, p. 45.
5. James, *Prefaces*, p. 328.
6. Ibid. p. 330.
7. James, *Notebooks*, p. 188.
8. *The Letters of Henry James*, ed. Percy Lubbock. 2 vols. (London: Macmillan, 1920), II;15. Letter dated 20 May 1904. Hereafter *Letters* (Lubbock).
9. James, *Prefaces*, p. 331.

2

A History of Critical Response

The debate on ambiguity, ambivalence, multivalence, incalculability, text and context

The history of the critical response to *The Golden Bowl* makes lively reading. James's chagrin at the relative neglect of this novel could have been exceeded only by that he could have felt at its later being praised and blamed for what it was not trying to do; indeed the glacial slowness with which the critical controversy has in more recent years edged closer to his apparent concerns might well be taken as the critics' just revenge for the time James takes and the elaborate contortions he employs to embody his final vision in the novel itself. But intrinsic difficulties aside, the initial neglect was predictable enough. After the war that destroyed the world it depicted, the survivors were not interested in its subtleties that struggled to express what seemed no longer relevant. Then, in the thirties, those critics with proletarian sympathies studiedly ignored it; in the forties it was mentioned at the tired end of general studies reviving interest in an alleged master who, it seemed, was trying without much success to affirm heroic virtues in the Ververs; and in the fifties it was sometimes seen, on the contrary, as a very successful exposure of them.

It has been only in the 'sixties and 'seventies that impatience with such simplistic readings has caused more and more critics to wonder at not only the whole of the novel but the novel as a whole. The latest trend too in the use of external evidence has been away from surmise based on the public biographical "facts" of the son of the Swedenborgian, the brother of the philosopher and the cousin of Minnie Temple,[1] to the private history recorded in letter and notebook and to the distillation of his artistic credo available in his own critical commentaries, chiefly of course in his essays and prefaces. Most interesting in this seventy-five-year debate is the way, slowly but surely, the old predictable critical premises, often enough recognizable as irrelevant and insufficient, give way to new insights, sometimes documented and sometimes not, which suggest excitingly new premises altogether.

Those insights are made more often by poets than by fellow novelists, though Joseph Conrad and Graham Greene do join with T.S. Eliot, Ezra Pound, Stephen Spender and W.H. Auden in recognitions that are today proving increasingly significant. Virginia Woolf's review of "Mr Henry James's Latest Novel" asked for "unstinted" praise, while complaining about "a slight theme" and "a surfeit of words";[2] E.M. Forster felt all the characters of the later works had been "gutted of the common stuff that fills characters in other books".[3] But the creator of *Nostromo*, where the detail was in silver rather than gold, sensed James's radicalism and the further reaches it gave his fables: "the truthfulness of his art" is most evident in the endings, where "one is never set at rest . . . . It is eminently satisfying, but it is not final. Mr Henry James, great artist and faithful historian, never attempts the impossible."[4] Greene sensed it too and to limn the shadows he discerned so clearly, he borrowed from James's "Notes" for *The Ivory Tower* the reference to "the black and merciless things that are behind the great possessions".[5]

The poets emphasized this further reach. In his 1916 memorial note, Eliot paid tribute to the new territories James was opening up by his "mastery over, his baffling escape from, Ideas",[6] the suspect currency of ideology and intellectualism. Two years later, Pound recognized an attempt at "communication" that "is not a leveling", not a "elimination of differences" but rather a "recognition of differences, of the right of differences to exist, of interest in finding things different."[7] Spender reminded the decade of the thirties that "beneath the golden display of James's work, there lurk forms of violence and chaos" and that his "settings" are "vast and resonant".[8] Auden, meditating by the grave of the old ambitious artist, called him "stern proconsul of intractable provinces" and "poet of the difficult".[9] All these Moderns recognized the anguish in the imperative "Make it new" and, unlike Woolf and Forster, divined the proportionate measures to which an artist could be committed if he undertook, in the geography of the spirit, exploratory journeys that, while not being "impossible" ones, were still highly courageous and worthy of patient mapping.

None of these fellow-creators, however, offered to back his promising testimony with any kind of substantial detail and, when the more academic studies appeared, many of them tended to complicate the problem of discussing the novel without showing sufficient awareness of the complexity of the problem it presented. Writing in 1973, Mildred E. Hartsock reviewed the situation succinctly: "There are, in fact, three areas of what might be called 'unintentional fallacy' in critical writing about *The Golden Bowl*: the common use of invalid criteria; the frequently careless or inattentive reading of the text when that text is perfectly clear; the attribution of the critic's own incomprehension to an excessive ambiguity in James."[10]

Yet the vicissitudes in the debate were prompted only in part by the intimidating nature of its subject and ingenuity of its interpreters. A quarter of a century before this review, P.N. Furbank suggested that James "has had more ingenious critics than most novelists, but that is partly because he has told them what to look for";[11] to which, six years later, Jean Kimball rejoined that "he tells us *how* he has presented his story, but not what it is about".[12] Kimball is closer to the truth, yet the burden of the *Prefaces* is rather to tell us the kinds of stories he tried to write, why the earlier ones did not always come off, how he has tried to improve some and why it should be easy for us to recognize how the later ones usually came off very well indeed. We cannot blame James for the critical incomprehension: his own full commentaries on the latest stage in his art and on the perspective it gave to all his artistic endeavour were themselves subjected to invalid criteria and were inattentively read.

The parties to the controversy fall readily enough into three groups, each group gathering adherents concurrently throughout three-quarters of our century. In the first are those who see Maggie Verver and her father as the centre of James's attention and these critics argue about his success or failure in making this pair the centre of our interest. In the second are those who see Amerigo and his lover claiming a substantial part not only of the authorial attention but also of the interest, these critics also arguing about relative success. Both of these contradictory groups can be treated fairly summarily; it is the third group that most rewards our more patient sifting. It has swelled its numbers markedly in the past two decades and included major studies by John Bayley, Dorothea Krook and Laurence Holland, major chapters by Barbara Hardy and a masterly essay by Judith Chernaik, all of which help to advance the debate by showing that the issues involved not ambiguities but ambivalences. To try to match the necessary refinements of critical focus upon the text, I shall then conclude this brief account by reviewing the attention the final moments have received, especially the context James there provides for his stylized language.

The premises shared by the first two groups are predictable enough: James is at best a modified Puritan and his later artistic complexities are new ways of affirming old moral absolutes. These commentators are impressed by the first of the relevant Notebook entries: "The *subject* is really the pathetic simplicity and good faith of the father and daughter in their abandonment".[13] Ignoring that "pathetic", F.W. Dupee confidently declared that James "in the writing of the novel . . . seems to have tried to preserve this emphasis", adding as an afterthought, "unpromising as it would appear to be for a complex moral drama".[14] From 1918 to 1975, Maggie has been seen as the "victor" who "converts" Amerigo; she is the heroine, the heiress of all James's others, just as her creator is the heir of New England transcendentalism and that is what the novel is allegedly all about.

It is almost as if Maggie had become an inescapable first premise in any discussion of the novel of which she is but one important part. This habit has persisted despite James's long exile from the land of his spiritual fathers; despite his explicit personal disavowal of his father's beliefs; despite his always having artistically distanced his treatment of his cousin in his fiction; despite the obvious differences in his conception of Maggie compared even with his conception of Milly, her nearest fictive kin; and despite his having provided in the elaborate structure of the whole novel a context that would apparently deny her being either the centre of interest or the centre of attention. Obviously, for several generations of critics, she has been identified with an alleged didactic expression of a conventional moral stance which must strike many as having very little to do with this novel or with the documented interests of James's later years.

Much the same kind of assumption is made by the critics in my second group, those who agree that this is what James wanted to do but that he mismanaged things. As early as 1912, M. Sturge-Gretton wondered whether in all three major novels "their centres are living enough to carry the complexity their author lays on them".[15] Thirty years later, Ferner Nuhn was irritated by the "unexploited drama" and the "undealt-with matters that lie off stage" in this "great dream story".[16] F.O. Matthiessen complained shortly after that James had not found an " 'objective correlative' " and so credibility breaks down, for "love is not enough to redeem a world like Maggie Verver's" and her future life with her prince would be an "inevitably futile existence".[17] The reappearance two years later of the famous F.R. Leavis essay merely alleged this mismanagement with rancour: "Actually, if our sympathies are anywhere they are with Charlotte and (a little) the Prince";[18] and Marius Bewley declared that though James is aware of the implications of his showing Charlotte as "caged", his "attempt to explain them away is unsatisfactory enough to leave Maggie a pretty poor version of a charming, harmless heroine".[19] P.N. Furbank concluded that the reason why she and her father "come at last to look cruel and sullen" is because "James's irony gets the better of everyone".[20] In the 'sixties and 'seventies, the dissatisfactions remained but the outright rejections were fewer. When in 1960 D.W. Jefferson looked back over the two previous decades in which, on the one hand, Quentin Anderson had seen Maggie as Christ-like[21] and R.P. Blackmur had seen her as a Beatrice figure,[22] and, on the other hand, Joseph J. Firebaugh had claimed "the whole book . . . proves that James regarded Adam Verver as cold, inhuman and inadequate" and Maggie as "a heartless Machiavellian absolutist",[23] he remarked with classic temperateness: "the fact that it has given occasion for such violent differences of opinion seems to suggest something unresolved in the novel itself".[24] But what had not been resolved at this stage was the conflict between what critics expected and what James offered.

The most recent and most penetrating summary of this offering as an instructive failure was made in 1972 by Gabriel Pearson and I use his essay as a bridge to my third group of critics. He still talked predominantly about Maggie but he wondered too about the kind of fiction in which she is found. He noted how often one is tempted "to question the premises of the novel" and though he did not quote James's remark about trying to tell as much about the handful of characters as a coherent literary form permits, he showed a keen sense of the strains attending any such try. "As a structure," he argued, "it trembles on the verge of certain absurdities and artificialities, and James's talk has to be fast and rich and deep to stop it crumbling away." Pearson's essay impelled the whole debate into quite different critical territory, re-examining where James as author *is* at any point, whether Maggie has or has not his authorial sponsorship at the end and "whether the novel is in some sense a romance or about, and even a critique of, the romanticism of the Ververs".[25] All this shelved those kinds of reductive interpretations stemming from either Leavis's kind of "scrutiny" or from the doctrinaire application of Freud by Leon Edel.[26] The later James might not be merely fumbling certain conventions long embedded in the art of fiction, but might be challenging them altogether. His measures here may be not merely cosmetic. His radicalism could go deeper than his theory of "successive centres", and even his "divine principle of the Scenario" could be but one of the more obvious elements among many much subtler ones disciplining his discourse. Traditionally accepted notions of authorial control of "sympathies" might need reviewing and in the context of the novel as a congruous whole, reflex approvals and disapprovals of his characters by the reader might be being discouraged by the appeal of a much more sophisticated rhetoric. This big vexing book needed to be evaluated by criteria commensurate with the forces within it.

To my third and most interesting group of literati this was not news, vexed though most of them were with its ending. They accepted its challenge positively, shifting the discussion from its alleged ambiguities to its demonstrable ambivalences and of course soon prompting Maxwell Geismar's irascible attack upon the Henry James "cult".[27] Thus, from Pearson's stimulating dubieties we pass to the *aperçus* of all those writers in the 'sixties and 'seventies, who, teased by the apparently enigmatic, sought to resolve it by the "patience of perusal" James wished "at every point" to "absolutely invoke and take for granted".[28] Not that the book went entirely unnoticed. Perhaps the earliest and least calculable response (I cannot resist noting it in an aside) was the one accounting for three printings of the American edition in as many months in 1904 and justifying Frank Moore Colby's amusing guesses about what was really going on down there "behind that verbal hedge".[29] The style was really masking the attempt by James the decadent expatriate to undermine the public morals! One grows pensive imagining how much James's mixed reception by his fellow countrymen to his visit the following year,[30] when a fourth reprinting appeared, may be explained by that large number of readers who, as well as being burdened by a prurient interest in fiction, had found themselves burdened also by a massive tome that they had no doubt disappointedly abandoned.

Others among the earliest readers anticipated the response of those two modern novelists and four modern poets mentioned above. S.P. Waterlow pronounced the works of the major phase "genuinely difficult"[31] and Max Beerbohm, the fidelity of whose parodies of the major manner attest to his having given those works the requisite attention, encouraged readers less patient with such difficulty to conceive of reaches beyond *The Portrait of a Lady* and called for faith in these prodigious excursions into them. "Mr James," he said, "that very conscious and devoted artist, may be trusted, he especially, to have followed the right line of progress — to have got the logical development of his own peculiar gifts." "Max", the master of irony at one end of its scale, warning how a master at the other end of it expressed horror and reverence, personally recorded they were "a horror and a reverence that are never obscured for me by the irony of Mr James's way of writing".[32] But half a century was to pass before anyone even began the task of documenting such a case. That John J. Enck, however, had gone to the crux of the problem was signalled by the title of his 1958 essay, "Wholeness of Effect in *The Golden Bowl*",[33] and his emphasis bore this out.

As James's artistic performance, he said, "accomplishes

seemingly impossible feats with structure and idiom its uniqueness renders defining precisely what he achieves, quite apart from an evaluation, the more hazardous". Enck suggested the safer way of seeing it in relation to all the earlier James: "Although some passages sound so idiosyncratic that they verge on self-parody, the novel, if nearly a summary, does not recapitulate a balanced total from earlier titles. ***The familiar reveals heretofore undetected implications***; the new defies timeworn categories; the whole looks simultaneously constructed and irregular, designed and free." Enck saw why the debate had generated more heat than light: critics had "by extracting one strand, perhaps, forced themselves to distort these intricate proportions", and he took us back yet again to the *Prefaces*, to remind us how "James cautions the reader", and to quote one of the now most telling of his statements on this novel and its figures: "Their chronicle strikes me as quite of the stuff to keep us from forgetting that absolutely *no* refinement of ingenuity or of precaution need be dreamed of as wasted in that most exquisite of all good causes the appeal to variety, the appeal to incalculability, the appeal to a high refinement and a handsome wholeness of effect."[34]

Bayley made clear that he was not interpreting James's "appeal to incalculability" as an invitation to an unbridled subjectivism of response, and rightly so. If a work can mean "anything" it can mean "nothing" and can justly incur the negative connotation of "ambiguity". The incalculable is unpredictable and unmeasurable, certainly, and this is the essence of its *appeal*, but it is not necessarily infinite, as *response* can be. Responses too can be unpredictable and unmeasurable but because they are always potentially unlimited they can be contradictory and therefore pointlessly ambiguous. Bayley noted James's assumption that his kind of appeal was "an effect which in art should only be secured inside a strict adherence to form"[35] and this is exactly the kind of control that the complex art of *The Golden Bowl* can be demonstrated as supplying. That is why

Pearson could use one of Maggie's metaphors for her tense relationship with her father as such an apt description of the novel: "an exquisite tissue, but stretched on a frame" (II, 267).[36]

It was of course James himself who could supply also the phrase most nearly defining the effect he sought and which Bayley found awaiting him in the Preface: "an ambiguity of appearance that is not at the same time an ambiguity of sense".[37] When Bayley added that "it is the form that actually permits, and as it were controls, the incalculability",[38] he was really only recasting James's own well known but hitherto misunderstood statement as to how artistic provisions at all points determine "a discerned relation between a given appearance and a taken meaning" (I, 354).

The infinite, imaginative response of the sensitive reader to such a work becomes therefore a fitting context for the finite statement the work is embodying. That we may apprehend rather than comprehend this embodiment merely adds — to use still more of James's words that Bayley drew to attention — "the sharp taste of uncertainty to a quickened sense of life".[39] "Ambiguity" thus becomes a less helpful term than does "ambivalence" and that in turn eventually becomes a less helpful one than does "multivalence". Multiple values are by no means necessarily contradictory ones; as in chemistry, this kind of valency may be, rather, concerned with the combining potentialities of a variety of elements. James's own frequent reference to all his means as artistic "values" becomes indeed singularly appropriate for the kind of "fusion" he declared was his aim. Bayley's study thus insisted on a golden bowl as firm as it was full of a rich blended mixture (I, 286).

When Krook's monumental contribution appeared the next year, capped by two masterly chapters on this contentious fiction, she specified ingredients and their final flavour. She further modified her earlier concept of a sophisticated redemptive theme by suggesting Maggie as the chief agent of redemptive love and Adam as the executor of justice but she now maintained that this, like all else in the book, was deliberately left equivocal. She defined the ambiguity "as a huge, elaborate metaphor for James's experience of the unavoidable, unalterable mixed motive of all human action, and the consequent dual ('ambiguous') character of all human endeavour". Arguing that the selfless and the selfish manifested in each of the characters were not "merely conjoined but rather causally connected", she demonstrated that although all great writers have recognized and tried to render this, "James's distinction is that he invented a literary technique, the late style, which enabled him to render his sense of the fusion, or rather fusedness, of these co-existent and interdependent elements with a peculiar immediacy". As this "metaphor" is applied relentlessly, there is, in the end, never "really a question of alternative meanings", for "both the redemptive and the pessimistic meanings are possible"; just as, during Maggie's scene with her father in Regent's Park, "everything Adam says may mean nothing more than it appears to, or it may mean all that Maggie reads into it". It is rather, Krook concluded, that in "James's total vision . . . neither cancels out the other; and the ambiguity is intended to express precisely this experience of their permanent, inseparable fusion."[40]

I do not believe that this is what *The Golden Bowl* says or what the major phase is about. The redemptive and the pessimistic are simply incompatible and if James is offering us both he is guilty of an ambiguity as negative as the one with which Leavis and others charged him. This idea of their inseparability would mean not fusion *by* James but confusion *in* James and it may be shown that he is concerned with the fusion of form and idea, not with the fusion of two different ideas. Krook's kind of fusion would be reductive, producing a vision with merely two values in it, whereas James is apparently concerned with a far greater complexity. We know what everything Adam says to Maggie in that scene means to her, and my later analysis of James's presentation of these characters may show that we should be in no doubt whatsoever about what else Adam's words mean to him and to us. They have one value for Adam, another for Maggie and a third for James: for us they are assuredly multivalent. Here as everywhere else the complex style signals a complex perspective and we are apparently to be concerned in that scene with Amerigo and Charlotte as well as more directly with Adam and Maggie.

In the complex art of this novel, the dramatic mode rarely limits us to a consciousness of one character, even when it is ostensibly dramatizing only one and therefore Krook does not convince when she reads Maggie's self-doubts about her suspicions as the actual dramatization of life's inescapable ambiguity. What we have may prove to be the dramatization of Maggie at a moment when she is at the mercy of ambiguous appearances. Motives are shown as mixed in this story and so are consequences but the formal disciplines of structure and language distance them, never allowing either to become ambiguous, no matter how subtly the narrative is spun. What is "enacted" by the late style is not fusedness but coexistence; what it invites is a vivid awareness of what a single act means for all concerned in it, what the respective motive of each participant is and what the consequence for each will be. Even when the motives of any one participant are mixed they are never muddled, and the same is true of consequences: we remain clear as to what each one is, and as to when and why it changes. The constant referent that resolves ambiguity and promotes multivalence is the authorial vantage point: this is denied the bewildered characters but is constantly available to us if we are willing to cope with all it offers. To return to the chemical analogy: every other value relates to it as all elements relate to hydrogen.

Krook was right in asking us to entertain James's "total vision", just as Enck was right in describing this final novel as containing "the fascinations and puzzles which distinguish an *Alterswerk*".[41] But we must be sure we have the total; we must not mistake the fascinating and puzzling for the obscure when it may be the inevitably difficult; and all genuine puzzles have only one answer. I believe this novel itself rejects any notion of the redemptive not inclusive of each of the four principals and rejects too any notion of the pessimistic that does not include all of them. It does deal with the strange mixture of things and show how bliss and bale are two sides of one coin, but it deals with these matters more complexly, more variously and more comprehensively than Bayley or Krook respectively demonstrated.

In the continuing controversy, this alleged equivocal aspect received attention from many critics who posed questions that James would have been the first to ask if he has not in fact left us the novel to answer them. Barbara Hardy's two chapters on James in *The Appropriate Form: An Essay on the Novel* made well-documented suggestions as to how it could do so. She was the heretic in this debate. "All that we do not know is the detail of the future . . ." she asserted. "The important thing is not left doubtful — the moral issue is absolutely clear . . .. James is setting his story concentrated in . . . a world where there is no end to change and crisis. But the moral guarantee he does give us, explicity and completely." She insisted that any full account of "the merits and defects which make [James] significantly different from most other novelists" would have to include some discussion of "his symbolism, his dramatic prefiguration, his allusiveness, and his irony". Her close study of his "total relevance" warned that it was almost impossible to distinguish in any late work between "local effect and central relevance", a recognition echoing James's " 'Detach one if you can.' " What I am later to call "hypothetical utterance", she called the "remarkable short cut" of "intuition . . . exaggerated into telepathic communication between all kinds of people and in all kinds of circumstance".[42] Some of the well-known and much-disputed examples she cited of this latter experiment in vantage point had been cited by Sallie Sears, Philip M. Weinstein, A.R. Gard and C.T. Samuels[43] as examples of unqualified or confusing authorial guarantee, the "silken halter" passage being the signal instance. Evidently, much of what Hardy said still needed saying in the mid 'sixties.

Much, too, remains highly contentious in Hardy's own account of that guarantee. "James does not choose to speak in his own voice," she argued, "not at least when it comes to making explicit moral judgements, though he does not choose to leave these judgements to the reader." Both these statements are contradicted by the kind of novel James has written at this stage in his career, and thus Hardy's assumption that "James delegates his authorial summary to Maggie"[44] or indeed to anyone anywhere may be shown as untenable. One may accept, too, that there are finally no material ambiguities, without accepting that "the moral guarantee", which is in every sense given to us "completely", is in any sense given to us "explicity". Total effects, at least those on James's later scale, defy and would certainly be reduced by, any form of explication carrying so evident an authorial warrant.

While sharp disagreement about architectonics, especially about the vantage point of narration and "phantom spectators", continued to plague the debate, none of the contributors to it appeared to gain much help from, or even direct any attention to, the following sentence in the *Prefaces*: "Beset constantly with the sense that the painter of the picture or the chanter of the ballad (whatever we may call him) can never be responsible *enough*, and for every inch of his surface and note of his song, I track my uncontrollable footsteps, right and left, after the fact, while they take their quick turn, even on the stealthiest tiptoe, ***toward the point of view that, within the compass, will give me most instead of least to answer for.***"[45]

This has been usually read as referring only to those single, central reflectors, such as Strether, whom James tries hard to keep apparently single and central, but it can be read too (and without irreconcilable ambiguity) as referring also to *all* the characters among whom James stealthily tiptoes as he *continually* seeks the device affording the vantage-point and the kind of fulness that I have been arguing is his aim in *The Golden Bowl.* Within the one novel there is behind the apparent consistency of a fixed "centre", an actual authorial mobility; the provisions for an "appeal to incalculability" are thus reinforced by the provisions for an "appeal to variety," to interest of every kind in "a handsome wholeness of effect". The harmony in the congruous whole is achieved not only despite but also *through* the flux of all these authorial shifts which serve the amplitude and intensity of its final effect.

The recent debater who helps most in all these matters and on whose suggestions I shall now dwell at some length, the debater who, significantly, lets herself be helped most by James, both inside and outside his novels, is Judith Chernaik. Really grasping the nettle, she brought out the essential relationship between the late art and the late vision; she detected the nature of the complexity; she defined one function of the equivocal; she sensed the fuller range of the ironic and very cogently related all of this to the author of it. She followed farther than anyone else the leads of Krook and of Bayley. Speaking of those "endless minute corrections of error in vision" that should warn us against making the same mistakes the characters make, she again made Hardy's point but gave it more telling reasons. "To the extent that the critical decisions of the novel weigh right action against wrong, neither James's subject nor his perspective is particularly ambiguous". As for James's " 'morality' ", "the great commonplaces are always used dramatically", but this does not imply "an uncommitted moral relativism" for there is "the repetition of the same kind of conflict in novel after novel" which suggests rather "a consistent vision of life", in which James sees "openness, freedom, as the condition of right action".[46]

Contrast with George Eliot's characters brings out the determining difference, for where her "characters discover the complexity of what had hitherto seemed simple, James adds to the discovery that ***radical ambiguity*** which critics have so often noted, ***an ambiguity built into motive and act and consequence***". This is what *his* characteristic analyses "finally reveal", and "when", Chernaik continued, "ambiguity attaches to the fundamental moral imperatives, it challenges every romantic affirmation of love or morality". " 'Success' ", she emphasized, becomes "a terribly qualified term" in *The Golden Bowl*, where "the ambiguities are most unsettling" because "the fault is as evenly spread as is the good faith of all four . . . ."[47]

Uncommitted moral relativism is indeed prevented, and by the same artistic provisions as control the incalculability of effect, but I take issue with Chernaik on three vital points. Radical ambiguity is by definition not multivalence, and, as James generates the latter, they are demonstrably incompatible. Amid this sense of multivalence, the openness and the freedom are by no means so easily identifiable with right action, and the absolute advisability of such openness is questioned just as relentlessly as is the possibility, for human kind, of any freedom. Not only every romantic affirmation of love or morality but also every realistic one is consequently challenged by this novel.

Chernaik's most resounding perception, though, illuminating the dynamics of the irony, must be quoted in full.

> The novels leave us with the sense that ***an ironic view of life need not be reductive***, but can ultimately reveal possibilities which are closed to anyone who would deny reality (as Maggie attempts to do), who would deny that right action can only be based on knowledge. ***Irony is only narrow and exclusive in a narrow mind*** — a matter of saying that all dreams are mere self-delusion, all love mere egotism, everything good and lovely merely a rationalization for money and sex. The ironic vision in James, a self-confessed romantic — and a supreme

> realist — does not exclude romantic or religious experience, or study it only to lay bare its biological origin; ***it rather explores the relationship among all possible forms of experience and consciousness.***[48]

This really did advance the debate and when Krook returned to it the following year to review her own earlier deliberations in the light of extant research, she simply reaffirmed her notion of James having presented in *The Golden Bowl* a final ambiguity which invited the reader to follow Maggie's advice to her husband: " 'Find out for yourself!' " James is implying, according to Krook, that "by the light of our human observation and experience alone, we can *never* know with certainty what we need to know in order to make the 'right' decision or choice . . ." and that "there is in life 'no absolute measure — no supravision, above and beyond the individual vision' ".[49] I believe, for reasons stated above, that while there are involved no absolutes other than our commonplace moral imperatives, which remain merely a general referent, there is manifested in the artistically determined world of his last novel, however, a vision of human knowledge and nescience which has much more in common, rather, with the one Chernaik argues to be so consistently informed by the ironic (II, 203).

Chernaik demonstrated the crucial and obvious enough difference between James's private confessions and his works of art when she contrasted his *Notebook* recollections of his 1905 visit to the family graves in Cambridge ("I seemed then to know why I had done this; . . . It made everything right — it made everything priceless . . .. Everything was there, everything *came*; the recognition, stillness, the strangeness, the pity and the sanctity and the terror . . .")[50] with Maggie's climactic moment at the end of her story ("She stood in the cool twilight and took in all about her where it lurked her reason for what she had done. She knew at last really why — and how she had been inspired and guided, . . . how, to her soul all the while it had been for the sake of this end". It is of course the irony in the latter that determines the totally different value of each: Maggie, the romantic heroine, "is held in the inexorable grip of a plot which is thoroughly determined, and which [she] cannot fathom, and [her] experience is always qualified ironically by [her] ignorance"[51] (II, 367).

Chernaik did not choose to press further and indicate how in the grip of the elaborate frame supplied by this novel, *all* the principals try, as Maggie is patently trying, to fathom what it is that holds them where they then find themselves. Indeed, *all* of them are shown as not fully aware of how their experience is, to the last, qualified by an ignorance that underlines for us the irony of their attempts just as movingly as it underlines hers. This is part of the radical originality of *The Golden Bowl* and this is the fruit of what James was cultivating during those years in Rye. Every one of these characters is depicted as confronting the incalculable and we are shown, in their apparent and less apparent responses, just about as much as a coherent literary form can show, because James is cultivating there everywhere "the fine flower of the inferential".[52]

From these assessors of James's general ironic strategies, I now turn to the most important of those among my third group of critics who confronted his particular textual tactics. Laurence Bedwell Holland, revealing an authority won by saturation in the text, quoted its evidence with a persistence hitherto unparalleled. Presuming nothing, but resuming many key critical emphases, he noted H.G. Wells's notorious scepticism about the likelihood of *The Golden Bowl* and indeed any other novel ever justifying James's "presupposition that they can be made continuously relevant",[53] and he made two points of signal importance. They bear out, I believe, the insights of Conrad and of T.S. Eliot, the faith of "Max" and others, and the vital emphases of Bayley and Krook. They anticipated those of Barbara Hardy and of Chernaik and they exhaustively supported R.W. Short's declaration, made along the way, that "with

James no choices are accidental: he wills our attention to them all. Everything counts. The teacup is offered: Fanny lets the Prince see Charlotte."[54] Holland accepted all these critical ground rules. He saw why James "insisted on the close scrutiny which he demanded of his readers". Tacitly backing Enck, he argued of James that "the behaviour of his form in the finished work must take precedence over prior models in literature or patterns of meaning which lie outside his fiction, even when and if those precedent patterns were among his materials". He then added the crucial summation: "the formal novelistic 'arrangement' which created *The Golden Bowl* is confessed continuously in its style and in the deeds of the characters whose watchful provisions for each other implicate also the author who created and used them as the instruments of his craft".[55] I cannot hope to support satisfactorily my exegesis of what this novel can further yield unless I emulate the closeness of Holland's documentation.

As it is all a question of the reach of the detail, I shall conclude this survey of critical responses by choosing for my example that notorious tea-party in the final chapter in which Adam Verver and his wife pay their farewell visit to his daughter and her husband. The sentence that nearly all critics have discussed comes after Maggie and her father, moving towards the balcony, pause to admire a picture he had given her on her wedding, and after he has rhetorically asked her, " 'It's all right, eh?' ", they gaze around at their other material possessions in the room and eventually at the seated Charlotte and the Prince. "The fusion of their presence with the decorative elements, their contribution to the triumph of selection, was complete and admirable; though to a lingering view, a view more penetrating than the occasion really demanded, they almost might have figured as concrete attestations of a rare power of purchase." (II, 360).

Edward T. Bowden's comment that this suggests "the same old moral blindness"[56] of these two characters so ignored the antecedent account of their development in the long novel that he might almost have been seeing the chapter as a short story. Holland, ignoring nothing, saw how this sentence, like so many in the novel, reaches out to encompass all four principals at once and that Charlotte's and Amerigo's " 'contribution' was no more striking than the 'rare power of purchase' displayed by the fortunate Ververs in acquiring them".[57] This saw the sentence in the context of the whole scene, but not in that of the art of the whole novel, which can be shown to shift the emphasis from authorial comment of the kind Holland implies and from particular purchaser and purchased to the general act of purchase itself. For Frederick C. Crews, Adam's "objectification" of the other couple reveals him as thinking of them "only as they may serve or endanger Maggie".[58]

If the sentence were reporting, dramatically, the meaning which either Maggie or Adam takes, or even the one both take, from the given appearances, this argument might hold; just as it would gain in credence if taken as a statement emerging from "the muffled majesty of authorship".[59] Yet these words, neither dramatic nor authorial, are given to us indirectly, through the suddenly evoked phantom spectator. James keeps his distance and makes us keep it too, so that we may the better see the full proliferation of its effects as a sentence controlled by the "frame", the "system", the art this novel provides for it. Of those words "a view more penetrating than the occasion really demanded", Philip C. Weinstein said: "this coyness, or unwillingness, or confusion is what most grates";[60] yet they too function consistently with the same tight control. James's prose would no doubt be much simpler, in the pejorative sense, if we could rest, even if only momentarily, on a simpler, more overt authorial guarantee, but James's whole major art is only as simple as is compatible with his evident attempt to make clear the implications that interest him, and we cannot be indulgently subjective if we are to keep up with him and share his final perspective of them all. He would appear to want to share with us those effects which neither we nor the characters may have calculated on but which he evidently has seen manifest themselves with an ambiguity of appearance that is for him not an ambiguity of sense.

We need to go closer yet to this language, however, if we are to evaluate James's apparent attempt to extend its resources for his fiction. If, in the passage quoted above, he is trying not to make its words "round off" but "sound off", then we need to know what they reverberate against. H.K. Girling, writing in the mid 'fifties, was sceptical on this crucial issue. He saw James recognizing in slang "the possibilities of a poetic language" and devising "a form which allows the author to stand aside, as in drama, but still to remain present in every word uttered, as in poetry". But, argued Girling, just as Adam's " 'We're all right' " to Maggie in the garden at Fawns, as the climax of their agreement to part, is inadequate to bear the responsibilities James places on it, so too is Adam's " 'It's all right, eh?' " of the final scene. "In view of the immediate context of this phrase," he said of the first — noticeably choosing not to go beyond the immediate one — "and of the importance of the agreement, the words 'We're all right' are monumentally inadequate." When he did go beyond it, he made an assumption that James demonstrably does not share. "Insofar as the rightness of Maggie and Adam has been demonstrated by the whole novel, the phrase has meaning. Otherwise it indicates a completeness of communication between two people, . . ." This, if true, would of course be an inadequate function — would be even malfunction. What we really want here, he said, is "a sudden incision of poetic insight", whereas the words break down under "the most severe stress which James has imposed on any words". The reasons Girling offered reveal two more highly questionable assumptions. "Words in poetry cannot receive so much more from their context than they supply to it. 'All right' seems to depend so entirely on the context that a good deal of the necessary poetic penetration is lacking."[61]

The rejoinders are obvious enough. Do any words ever *supply* any context with much more than a dictionary gloss? How much or how little of "context" by which they could supply further meaning is being considered here in these two usages of that term? As for "insights", Maggie actually believes she does have one into Adam's state of mind at that moment but we would need to know more about James's rendering of the development, if any, in Adam before we could corroborate her belief. Besides, if we see this scene of theirs in the context of their Regent's Park one, and then see both of these in the context of the first one on that same sequestered bench at Fawns, "All right" might well imply "All wrong", but even after that we would have to consider whether in either case the "all" included also the other couple who are absent on all three occasions.

So when Girling moved on to the moment when father and daughter gaze around at their possessions and he suggested "the shade of irony which might adhere to the phrase 'power of purchase' is not felt in the context", we must continue to ask such questions. " 'Power' refers rather to the discrimination of the purchaser than to his capacity for acquisition as reflected by his bank balance." Why only the one and not the other, when each could clearly complement the other; and why could it not refer also to the original willingness of the other couple to *be* purchased? "The 'rightness', however, now refers to the perfection of their arrangements, just as the previous 'rightness' had applied to the perfection of their attitudes." Where is this particular "perfection" demonstrated? "Attitudes" to whom, when, where? Maggie's? Adam's? Their joint attitude? "As a final judgment, 'all right' is still inadequate; as before, James has placed the phrase with every care, but it seems not quite to have carried out the task he entrusted to it."[62] By now my questions must surely be clearly implicit and would still be asked if Girling had applied his principle to those even more formidable last words that are given to Amerigo by Henry James at the end of this final completed example of his art of fiction.

I must now examine how the structural frame supplied by his Scenario enables him to marshal his people into their various relationships. I must then try to trace amid the "high refinement" of his rendering of each character, from moment to moment, how their consciousness of their own and of others' motives develops, what each expects as consequences to his or her own, and to others', actions and how well or ill each knows what may be happening to them all. I must indicate where necessary what the stern proconsul of these intractable provinces may think of them all, just where exactly he or his reporting spy takes up his post among them, and whether or not he is explicit about anything other than his own apparent wonderment about them which he constantly assumes he shares with us. All this may determine whether James's "divine principle" is, in fact, a key that, acting in the same general way, fits both the dramatic and the narrative locks and may determine too what is thereby opened to us. The progression of scenes, the characterization going on among them and the intermittent glimpses of a somewhat more overt authorial activity should reveal whether these elaborate appeals to incalculability, to variety, and to high refinement are made to any significantly new purpose and whether the wholeness of effect, even if handsomely achieved, justifies such an ordeal of critical consciousness.

"So much, so *much*, hangs radiantly there",[63] James jotted in that notebook. Perhaps too much, perhaps a "quantity of truth" that did strain and even "burst" the "mould" his hands pressed so firmly at every point.[64] Perhaps Conrad was wrong and James did this once attempt the impossible, did reach for a finality of expression and perhaps this work testifies relentlessly to his presumption. Can any artist successfully undertake to share "a recognition of differences", as Pound put it, on such a scale, and, if he can, what might the resulting array of "values" mean? I suggest that James does share his vistas with us at the end of this difficult aesthetic journey but only after we and, I shall argue, *each of the four principal travellers*, have joined him on the eminence he selects and have looked back over the country traversed. By then his mode of rhetoric may suitably be only silence.

NOTES

1. Van Wyck Brooks, *The Pilgrimage of Henry James* (New York: Dutton, 1925); Quentin Anderson, *The American Henry James* (New Brunswick: Rutgers U.P., 1957); Alan Holder, *Three Voyages in Search of Europe: A Study of Henry James, Ezra Pound and T.S.Eliot* (Philadelphia: U. of Philadelphia P., 1966); Leon Edel, *Henry James: A Biography*, 5 vols. (London: Hart-Davis, 1953, 1962, 1963, 1969, 1972).
2. Virginia Woolf, "Mr Henry James's Latest Novel", *The Guardian*, 20 February, 1905, p. 339, cols. 2-3.
3. E.M. Forster, *Aspects of the Novel* (London: Arnold, 1949), p. 148. First published 1927. Hereafter *Aspects.*
4. Joseph Conrad, "Henry James: An Appreciation", *North American Review* (January, 1905): 102-8; quoted here from *Notes on Life and Letters* (London: Dent, 1925), p. 23. Hereafter *Notes.*
5. Henry James, *The Ivory Tower* (London: Collins, 1917), p. 287. Quoted in Graham Greene, "Henry James: The Private Universe", in *The English Novelists*, ed. D. Verschoyle (London: Chatto and Windus, 1936), pp. 215-28. Quoted here from *Collected Essays of Graham Greene* (London: Bodley Head, 1969), p. 39. Hereafter *Collected Essays.*
6. T.S. Eliot, "In Memory of Henry James", *The Little Review* (August 1918): 44-53; quoted here from *The Question of Henry James: A Collection of Critical Essays*, ed. F.W. Dupee (London: Wingate, 1947), p. 125. Hereafter *Question.*
7. *Literary Remains of Ezra Pound*, ed. with intro. T.S. Eliot (London: Faber, 1954), p. 298.
8. Stephen Spender, "Henry James", *The Destructive Element: A Study of Modern Writers and Beliefs* (London: Cape, 1935), pp. 1-10. Rpt. in part as "The Golden Bowl" in *Question* ed. Dupee, pp. 250-52.
9. W.H. Auden, "At the Grave of Henry James", *Partisan Review* 8 (July-August 1941): 266-70. Quoted here from *The Collected Poetry of W.H. Auden* (New York: Random House, 1945), p. 127. Hereafter *Collected Poetry.*
10. Mildred E. Hartsock, "Unintentional Fallacy: Critics and *The Golden Bowl*", *Modern Language Quarterly* 35 (1974): 273. Hereafter *Unintentional Fallacy.*
11. P.N. Furbank, "Henry James: The Novelist as Actor", *Essays in Criticism* 1 (October 1951): 404. Hereafter *Actor.*
12. Jean Kimball, "Henry James's Last Portrait of a Lady: Charlotte Stant in *The Golden Bowl*", *American Literature* 28 (January 1957): 449. Hereafter *Last Portrait.*

13. James, *Notebooks*, pp. 130-31.
14. F.W. Dupee, ed., *Henry James* (London: Methuen, 1951), p. 259. Hereafter *Dupee HJ*.
15. M. Sturge-Gretton, "Mr Henry James and His Prefaces", *Contemporary Review*, 101 (January 1912): 78.
16. Ferner Nuhn, *The Wind Blew from the East: A Study in the Orientation of American Culture* (New York: Harper, 1942), pp. 131, 136, 151. Hereafter *Wind*.
17. F.O. Matthiessen, *Henry James: The Major Phase* (London: O.U.P., 1946), pp. 104, 102. Hereafter *Major Phase*.
18. F.R. Leavis, "The Later James", *The Great Tradition: George Eliot, Henry James, Joseph Conrad* (London: Chatto and Windus, 1948), p. 160. First appeared in *Scrutiny* 5 (March 1937): 398-417. Hereafter *Great Tradition*.
19. Marius Bewley, *The Complex Fate: Hawthorne, Henry James and Some Other American Writers* (London: Chatto and Windus, 1952), pp. 92-93.
20. Furbank, *Actor*, pp. 413, 416.
21. Quentin Anderson, "Henry James and the New Jerusalem", *Kenyon Review* 8 (Autumn 1946): 557-58.
22. R.P. Blackmur, Introduction to *The Golden Bowl* (New York: Grove, 1952), pp. xx-xxi. Hereafter *Intro GB*.
23. Joseph J. Firebaugh, "The Ververs", *Essays in Criticism* 4 (October 1954): 401, 406. Hereafter *Ververs*.
24. D.W. Jefferson, *Henry James* (London: Oliver and Boyd, 1960), p. 111. Hereafter *Jefferson HJ*.
25. Gabriel Pearson, "The Novel to End All Novels: *The Golden Bowl*", *The Air of Reality: New Essays on Henry James*, ed. John Goode (London: Methuen, 1972), p. 332, 334. Hereafter *Novel to End Novels*.
26. Especially in Leon Edel, *Henry James: A Biography*. Vol. V. *The Master, 1901-1916* (London: Hart-Davis, 1972). Hereafter *Master*.
27. Maxwell Geismar, *Henry James and the Jacobites* (Boston: Houghton Mifflin, 1963).
28. James, *Prefaces*, p. 304.
29. Frank Moore Colby, "In Darkest James", *Imaginary Obligations* (New York: Dodd, Mead & Co., 1904), pp. 321-35. Rpt. in Dupee, ed., *Question*, p. 40.
30. See "Appendix II" on "James's Sales", *Henry James: The Critical Heritage*, ed. Roger Gard (London: Routledge and Kegan Paul, 1968), p. 557. Hereafter *Critical Heritage*.
31. S.P. Waterlow, "The Work of Mr Henry James", *Independent Review* 4 (November 1904) 236-43. Rpt. in Gard, ed., *Critical Heritage*, p. 367.
32. Max Beerbohm, Reviews of "The Doctor's Dilemma" 24 November 1906 and of "The High Bid" 27 February 1909, entitled "Mr Shaw's *Roderick Hudson* and Mr Henry James's Play". Rpt. in Beerbohm's *Around Theatres* (London: Hart-Davis, 1930), pp. 260-65,

323-26. Quoted here from rpt. in *Henry James: A Collection of Critical Essays*, ed. Leon Edel (New Jersey: Prentice Hall, 1963), pp. 24, 26. Hereafter *Critical Essays*.

33. John J. Enck, "Wholeness of Effect in *The Golden Bowl*", *Wisconsin Academy of Science, Arts and Letters*, 47 (1958): 227-40. Hereafter *Wholeness*.
34. James, *Prefaces*, p. 329; quoted in Enck, *Wholeness*, p. 227.
35. John Bayley, "Love and Knowledge: The Golden Bowl", in his *The Characters of Love: A Study in the Literature of Personality* (New York: Basic Books, 1961), p. 259. Hereafter *Characters of Love*.
36. Pearson, *Novel to End Novels*, quoted p. 354.
37. James, *Prefaces*, p. 324; quoted in Bayley *Characters of Love*, pp. 213-14.
38. Bayley, *Characters of Love*, p. 261.
39. James, *Prefaces*, p. 286; quoted in Bayley, *Characters of Love*, p. 246.
40. Dorothea Krook, *The Ordeal of Consciousness in Henry James* (Cambridge: U.P., 1962), pp. 313, 319, 320, 323, 324. Hereafter *Ordeal*.
41. Enck, *Wholeness*, p. 227.
42. Barbara Hardy, *The Appropriate Form: An Essay on the Novel* (London: Athlone Press, 1964), Chaps. i & ii, pp. 11-29, 20-50. Hereafter *Appropriate Form*.
43. Sallie Sears, *The Negative Imagination: Form and Perspective in the Novels of Henry James* (New York: Cornell U.P., 1968), pp. 170. Hereafter *Negative Imagination*; Philip M. Weinstein, *Henry James and the Requirements of the Imagination* (Cambridge: Harvard U.P., 1971), p. 176. Hereafter *Requirements*; A.R. Gard, "Critics of The Golden Bowl", *Melbourne Critical Review* 6 (1963), p. 108; and C.T. Samuels, *The Ambiguity of Henry James* (Urbana: U. of Illinois Press, 1971), p. 217ff.
44. Hardy, *Appropriate Form*, p. 45.
45. James, *Prefaces*, p. 328.
46. Judith Chernaik, "Henry James as Moralist: The Case of the Late Novels", *Centennial Review* 16 (1972): 108, 111, 112. Hereafter *Moralist*.
47. Ibid., pp. 116-119.
48. Ibid., pp. 120-121.
49. Dorothea Krook, "The Madness of Art: Further Reflections on the Ambiguity of Henry James", *Hebrew University Studies in Literature*, 1:i (1973): 33.
50. James, *Notebooks*, pp. 320-21.
51. Chernaik, *Moralist*, pp. 106, 120.
52. James, *Ivory Tower*, p. 216.
53. H.G. Wells, "Of Art, of Literature, of Mr Henry James", *Boon, The Mind of the Race, The Wild Assess of the Devil, and The Last Trump* (London: 1915), pp. 84-128; rpt. in *Henry James and H.G. Wells: A Record of their Friendship, their Debate on the Art of Fiction, and their*

Quarrel, ed. with intro. Leon Edel and Gordon N. Ray (London: Hart-Davis, 1959), p. 246. Hereafter *HJ and Wells.*

54. R.W. Short, "Henry James's World of Images", *PMLA* 68 (September 1954): 949. Hereafter *Images.*
55. L.B. Holland, *The Expense of Vision: Essays on the Craft of Henry James* (New Jersey: Princeton U.P., 1964), pp. viii, 337. Hereafter *Expense.*
56. Edward T. Bowden, *The Themes of Henry James: A System of Observation through the Visual Arts* (New Haven: Yale U.P., 1956), p. 113. Hereafter *Themes.*
57. Holland, *Expense*, p. 405.
58. Frederick C. Crews, *The Tragedy of Manners: Moral Drama in the Later Novels of Henry James* (New Haven: Yale U.P., 1957), p. 110, n. 4. Hereafter *Tragedy.*
59. James, *Prefaces*, p. 328.
60. Weinstein, *Requirements*, p. 194.
61. H.K. Girling, "The Function of Slang in the Dramatic Poetry of 'The Golden Bowl' ", *Nineteenth-Century Fiction* 2 (September 1956): 147, 145, 145-6, 146. Hereafter *Slang.*
62. Ibid., pp. 146, 146-47.
63. James, *Notebooks*, p. 188. Entry made between 14 and 27 February 1895.
64. James, *Prefaces*, p. 46.

3

The Strategy of the Structure

The principle of the Scenario, the centres of consciousness and the authorial stance

The principle of the Scenario

The general strategy of the novel, of what we are told, when, and how, is much more complex than James's summary of it in the Preface suggests; the tactical phantom spectators aside. True, Book Second is generally narrated from Maggie's vantage point; indeed, even the Assinghams have only one parley and otherwise Fanny herself appears only in Maggie's company. In Book First, however, there is far more mobility in the vantage point, and the Prince, who gives his name to these first twenty-four of the total forty-two chapters is, by comparison with Maggie in her book, by no means as persistently our point of vantage, nor even as steadily the centre of attention or the centre of interest. In Parts First and Third of his book he is the centre of attention but in Part Second, devoted to Adam, Maggie and Charlotte, he is present only in the telegram that concludes it; even in the other two parts it is clearly Charlotte who dominates our interest, and as well as Fanny sharing chapter iv with him, the Assingham have exclusive command not only of chapter xvi but also of the chapters concluding his book. There has thus never been any textual basis for the notion that James presented his novel mainly in terms of the figures who give their names to the two books into which it is disposed.

The point is of course more fully supported when we move from strategy to tactics. In Part First, only the first chapter is concerned with the Prince's nervous misgivings about the consequences of his just-completed interview with the lawyers. In the second, he learns from Fanny of Charlotte's arrival; by the third she has appeared; in the fourth the Assinghams are speculating on her relation with him and filling out details of a former stage in it; and the last two chapters are devoted to scenes between them that present Charlotte with a positive, attractive, interesting and even sympathetic force of which little is lost on Amerigo and nothing is lost on the reader. The burden of this part, then, is not "The Prince", or even his role as the future husband of Maggie, but his role as the former lover and present admirer of Charlotte. The part is concerned with these relationships and their implications; the emphasis is on the mixed motives behind Amerigo's becoming betrothed to Maggie and Charlotte's arrival at that moment. We already have by this point three figures claiming our attention.

Part Second, twenty months later in time, introduces a fourth, Adam, and though the first three chapters are concerned with his reactions as father, grandfather and father-in-law, the remaining three are taken up with his relationship with Charlotte, with the interest of her decision and the Prince's response to it. Among these four figures the reader's attention is divided in such a way as to make impossible any exclusive identification of sympathy or — and this is more significant — any choice of any one of these four figures as an exclusive vantage point from which to view the unfolding drama. The successive indirections of James's rendering of the narrative in these two parts of Book First keep us continually aware of all four figures.

This is still very much the case in the first three chapters of Part Third, when the Prince and Charlotte are actually doing "the 'worldly' " for Maggie and Adam at the Foreign Office ball. Throughout chapters xiv and xv, their dialogues with Fanny keep before us the absent *sposi* as does her fevered consciousness of all four principals during her (chapter xvi) homecoming in the brougham; Fanny herself thus forms more solidly a fifth element to be considered in the whole moral dilemma. In xvii and xviii, the afternoon-tea scene where the clandestine lovers make their pledge, their marriage partners — the ostensible subject of their talk — are ever present to the reader. Chapter xix, the pre-Easter dinner at Eaton Square, insists clearly enough on our awareness of all parties. By chapter xx where the Prince muses on Fanny's obvious concern at the situation and by chapter xxi where he discusses this with Charlotte at Matcham, their preoccupation with it is in itself a constant reminder that the authorial interest is always apparently in a quartet and never in duets (I, 318).

From here to the end of this part which ends Book First, James makes it difficult for readers to simplify the complexities that apparently interest him: though chapter xxii shows us the lovers frankly accepting the opportunity their Gloucester visit is to offer, chapters xxiii and xxiv are all Fanny's stricken anxiety from which there clearly emerges an implied admission that Adam and Maggie are as " ' "rum" ' " as the Colonel suggests and that they are responsible for any possible consequences through having virtually invited them. Fanny's endless speculations as to dangers and outcomes are less important than the vantage point she provides for the reader: by examining her consciousness, we are given, despite her sense of having been betrayed and her consequent partisanship, a view of the situation as it is, an understanding of how it evolved and a keen interest in how it will develop. This is as much as James is asking for. Moral judgment can still be held in abeyance as all parties are clearly guilty of contributing to the situation; moral interest is of course heightened (I, 374).

My analysis of Book First, of the general functions of its three parts and of their chapters, has suggested that the above effect has been sought by a variety and mobility of vantage point in the conducting of the whole discourse. In Book Second, with its three parts devoted respectively to the repercussions of Maggie's disillusionment, pretence of ignorance and acceptance of Adam's decision to return to

America with Charlotte, the provisions for keeping all four figures in our minds are still evident but the principle of the discourse changes. We gain in Maggie a constant referent. Except for chapter xxxi, the Assinghams' guilt-ridden conference, of which Maggie is the chief subject anyway, there is, in Book Second, no chapter in which she does not appear and in which she is not importantly influencing the action. James allows her to become and remain the centre of direct attention but she is not the only interest and certainly not the central one. She shares this equally with the other three who crowd her consciousness, which includes in fact every other figure, not the least of course being the Assinghams.

Whereas Book First kept Maggie, and her father, before us as members of a quartet by showing them most persistently in relation to the Prince and Charlotte, the Prince and Charlotte are now kept before us by being shown in relation to Maggie and to Adam but chiefly in relation to Maggie. There is still no encouragement, or even the presented means, for partisan projection by the reader into any one of the four chief figures. Any strengthening of empathy or sympathy or any tendency to identify with Maggie as a result of her being the consciousness chosen by James as a now constant referent is neutralized by the persistent and vivid reflection within that consciousness of each of the other figures.

The indirect attention thus given to the others does not in the least remove them from the centre of interest; rather, it ensures (under James's provisions) that the individual challenge of each to the narrator who is trying to avoid an over-simplified reader-response to a highly ambitious and complex discourse will be met and coped with without imperilling that discourse. The chief of the apparent reasons for the choice of Maggie as reflector and referent are not those that a student of James's long development from Daisy Miller through Isabel Archer to Milly Theale might expect; this can be left for later discussion. My concern now is to try to demonstrate that my impression of Maggie as a figure among four, all of whom are to be of equal interest, is the one that any close perusal of the text does produce.

Book First ends on the night of that day on which the Prince and Charlotte visit Gloucester and their adultery becomes for the reader an implied fact. Chapter xxv, that opens Part Fourth of Book Second, reveals James employing the further indirection that is offered by retrospection, for Maggie is here remembering, several days later, the Prince's return that night, and of her (unusually) awaiting him at Portland Place as a result of her increasing dissatisfaction with a quartet that had hitherto satisfied them all. Her preoccupation with the general relationship of the two couples would in itself keep us alert to the interest of parties other than herself, but the intensity of this interest is now increased by irony.

There are her general reflections that the Prince seems as if shut away from her as in a pagoda and that Charlotte, whose masterly taste in clothes she believes she can never hope to emulate, remains inscrutable when asked to comment on her friend's style. There is her wait itself, "while the absentees still delayed"; there is the implied fact that Adam, off in Eaton Square, also waits. There is the speech she hypothetically makes to Amerigo as she waits, expressing the intensity of her love for him. But most operative of all in the cause of taking up with the Princess as it were without losing contact with the Prince, is the provision for the scenic vividness of Maggie's sitting in her small drawing room, elaborately dressed for dinner, being counterbalanced by her report of Amerigo's expression and pause as he at last enters and encounters the fact of her so unusually awaiting him there. The irony continues in chapter xxvi when we are conscious of how her innocent enquiries about Charlotte and Gloucester cannot have failed to arouse Amerigo's anxieties; and the next morning at Eaton Square with Adam she notices the expression of the night before also in Charlotte's face. It is the awareness of some kind of collusion between her husband and her father's wife in relation to her that accentuates the solitariness she had sought to allay (II, 14).

The ironic reaches a new peak in xxvii. Maggie feels that as "a difference had been made in her relation to each of her companions", the planned trip to Spain with her father is now impossible but she fears his cancelling as a possible sign of his sharing reasons for agreeing with her. He cancels it after the Eaton Square dinner for the Matcham set where the whole concourse have been present, and the effect upon Charlotte and Amerigo is noted by her, and for us, as prodigious. Her efforts to put physical distance between these two begins on the homeward journey when, though outwitted by her husband, she for the first time resists his affectional domination of her. Adam and Charlotte, and what they represent as values and responsibilities to the occupants of the carriage, are virtually fellow passengers in it (II, 47).

James's apparent concern for equality of emphasis upon each of the four sides of the moral dilemma is evident in chapters xxviii and xxix where he brings Adam closer to the foreground again after having left him for some time in the middle distance. He is very much his daughter's main anxiety during the return of the Matcham set to dinner at Portland Place, where she, at once, wants to appear confident before Lady Castledean but also cannot risk too untypical a display of extroversion without arousing her father's suspicions and anxieties on her, and indeed on his own, behalf. When he calls without his wife and, finding Maggie without her husband, suggests a walk in Regent's Park, she is herself acutely aware as she prepares for the outing, that their *sposi* may be meeting elsewhere; she is whimsically happy that at least this frees her father and her for a renewal of their old intimacy, and she reflects that the present predicament results from his good intentions in marrying to prevent her thinking him neglected after her own marriage.

The burden of their conversation, beneath their filial badinage, is the immorality of their enjoying each other's company so often — on the old terms — at the expense of the other couple's social representation of them. They examine the notion of selfishness; and though Maggie's motives, in now preferring the more active social role that a gathering at Fawns would present, are clear to us, the whole duologue helps James keep us aware of the truth of this summary of their indulgence. The pathos of their imminent sacrifice of each other is balanced by its justice in the light of consequences, and consequence awaits them on the balcony, as they return home, in the form of Amerigo and Charlotte. The brief tableau of that encounter acts for the reader with the force of a pointer tapping a quadrilateral on a blackboard.

In chapter xxx Maggie breaks out with all directness to Fanny about her fears. She is explicit about her capacity to do anything for love — love absolute, not just for husband or father. In the context of the antecedent action, this profession cannot fail to bring to mind abundant evidence of Charlotte's willingness to do anything for love of the Prince. Fanny has to lie to Maggie that her fears are groundless; and the Assinghams, in xxxi, discuss how it will be necessary, throughout the forthcoming visit of all to Fawns, to lie for her by appearing as if all is well. The Assinghams' moral involvement with the quartet is emphasized: it is because Fanny did in good faith help the Prince into his marriage that she must now in good faith help Maggie retain it. But the major role of the stolid Colonel and his endlessly speculating lady is to range over all the relationships so far presented, to sharpen our awareness of the state each has now reached and to help us hover over the whole scene, keenly conscious of its present complexities and its imminent developments. These include Maggie's relationship respectively with her father, his wife and her own husband; her husband's with Adam and Charlotte and herself; Charlotte's with the Prince, with Adam and with Maggie;

Adam's with each of them individually; the Assinghams with all of them — individually and collectively; so the interest is thickly "bristling", "values" are multiplying, "differences" are being recognized.

Such a dramatized summary at this point in the novel has a function other than ensuring amplitude and clarity: it ensures that all this will continue to be correctly distanced; that we will not lose the all-inclusive viewing point even though an imminent change in key, to greater directness in rendering Maggie's responses and an acceleration of the action, might well otherwise imperil that vitally necessary viewing point. The change comes after xxxii, after Maggie, waiting with the Prince in London to later join the Ververs at Fawns, deliberates on the tone she must sustain with the Prince; after she has decided how she will choose to appear to Adam, how she will handle Charlotte, how she can use Mrs Assingham in all this; and after she has made accidental contact, during her visits to the Amerigo archives in the British Museum, with the antiquarian's shop near it.

Chapters xxxiii and xxxiv suggest a James who is apparently making a virtue of necessity. He has to make probable the extraordinary coincidence of its being the same shop visited years earlier by the Prince and Charlotte; he has to make plausible the shopkeeper's later conscience-stricken visit to her which results in her learning only now of her husband's earlier relationship with her old school-friend, now her mother-in-law. Actually, as I hope later to show, James successfully makes the extraordinariness the point, but this material is potentially melodramatic and the scenes of encounter between Maggie and Fanny and, especially, between Maggie and Amerigo are potentially Victorian theatre of the most morally oversimplified kind, the kind that could rivet attention to their particularity and reduce the whole novel to its latent absurdities. They are so dangerous indeed that James opts for a stylized "scene" that is perfectly in keeping with his stylized "picture" of Maggie's consciousness to that point. So, her pointing out to

Fanny the golden bowl on the mantlepiece, Fanny's handling of it, her smashing of it, Amerigo's entry at that moment, Fanny's exit, Maggie's inevitably symbolic carrying of the three fragments, her significantly finding that "she could carry but two [of them] at once", all give invaluable service to James's apparently sought-after aesthetic effect in two ways (II, 182).

Firstly, the actions-fraught-with-meaning, the scenes in which the connotations are unmistakably portents, rescue James's whole enterprise from a histrionic bathos. Secondly, the discourse, in becoming instead a form of solemn apologue that avoids, by its context, the elementariness of allegory or the arbitrariness of symbolism, now serves ideally James's continued provision for the reader of a point of observation that helps him look at everyone without focusing exclusively on anyone. Maggie's actions and words are dramatic in the usual sense that they express at this immediate moment her consciousness, that we have been long examining, but her actions direct our attention primarily to those acutely relevant other figures; and her final words to Amerigo, " 'Find out for yourself!' " in response to his anxiety as to how much Adam knows, directs him, and us, not only to Adam but also of course to Charlotte. What could have become and remained a fictive simulation of drama that began and ended with the interaction of two figures, does in fact concern us, still, with the far more complex interactions of five (if, as we must, we include Fanny). The ten chapters of this long Part Fourth thus end after establishing a mode of discourse that heightens intensity without simplifying interest (II, 203).

The five chapters of Part Fifth and indeed the remaining three that form the concluding Part Sixth, depend heavily upon that same mode. Chapter xxxv opens Part Fifth with a generalized account of the situation at Fawns and prepares for the impotant reintroduction of it in the following chapter, the terrace scene at Fawns, by balancing the impression we are gaining of Maggie with a potent though very indirect impression of Charlotte, who is to be her partner in that scene. James apparently felt that a re-entry of Charlotte into the foreground, after her presence as one of the principals had been attested persistently but obliquely, required the reinforcing for the reader of exactly how painful her position has been since Maggie's discoveries. For Charlotte has been kept in ignorance by the Prince of Maggie's having confronted him; so that if she does now come suddenly to the fore in this arena it is without having the advantage of knowledge. Maggie's impression is that the Prince's response to the crisis has been to leave it to her and Charlotte to resolve; by the nature of his assumed air of ignorance of this crisis, Adam must be doing the same. The disposition of the narrative up to this point makes evident that a direct encounter between these two women has been long anticipated.

It ensues in chapter xxxvi and it is the supreme test for James's chosen methods of narrative. We see it all reflected in Maggie's consciousness but her consciousness is by no means all we see. Her responses are fevered, painful — made brilliantly interesting — and we watch as she lies and kisses her way towards the right and true goal as she sees it, the preservation of " 'the bowl without the crack' ": James has no difficulty in presenting for our inspection her case (II, 217).

Nor does he fail to meet the difficulty of presenting Charlotte's, even though, inevitably, through the medium of Maggie's fearful, antagonistic responses to her. For we cannot deny that Charlotte is telling and seeking literal truth in their pregnant duologue. Any attentive reading of the novel up to this point would have made clear James's provisions — in modes of narrative, in scenic emphasis, in words uttered and in actions shown — for an understanding of how Charlotte is equally as trapped as Maggie is; trapped not only by desire but also by opportunity and the coercion of events in the general lapse of time. Maggie sees her as "the creature . . . out of the cage" but we cannot help also seeing her as the creature at bay. The two women fight very differently but the appeal of each is equal in its degree of interest. Against Maggie's chosen persona of fear and weakness and humility, there is Charlotte's "high elegance", her "inveterate completeness" and her "noble erectness" (II, 239,243).

Nor is there any moment in the whole immense complex and subtle narrative when we are more conscious of the fact that though we have dwelt long in the mind of the Prince, briefly inhabited the mental world of Adam, and are now firmly ensconced amid the imaginings and thoughts of Maggie; and though we have on several occasions visited the speculation factory of Mrs Assingham, we have at no point in Book Second enjoyed anything but an indirect account of how it has all been for Charlotte. The hints that James can now give us by implication, by imaginative omission and by the suggestive power of his mode of stylized drama, are all the more potent. James, who had long ago learned to reserve for the most difficult elements in his work the principle of successive indirection that rarely let him down, now employs for his presentation of this important, difficult and even (for his apparent plans) most dangerous member of his quartet, all the advantages of the indirect, not the least of which are the appeal to the incalculable in what Charlotte may be possibly thinking and feeling, and what she is probably thinking and feeling. The modes modify each other; neither is dominant, which is exactly what the art employed in *The Golden Bowl* to this point implies is James's aesthetic goal.

But the two women and the nature of their encounter are only half or (if we include as we should the Assinghams), only a third of the "values" with which James has to juggle. The whole of chapter xxxi is built on the social encounter of all six. It begins in the smoking-room with Adam, Fanny, the Prince and Charlotte settling down to bridge while the Colonel, at the other end of the room, writes letters, and Maggie, nearby, pretends to read a periodical. It ends with the others witnessing from the door onto the terrace, Charlotte and Maggie in embrace. This is the immediate, vivid, cogent context for the main business of the chapter, a context that would of itself insist on the presence, and the pertinence, of all the figures involved in it.

James makes further provisions on this count and, it would seem, wisely. "Cards after dinner" is given further portentous significance by the grave and hushed narration of how Maggie "rose from her place".

> Silent and discreet she bent a vague mild face upon them as if to signify that little as she followed their doings she wished them well; and she took from each, across the table, in the common solemnity, an upward recognition which she was to carry away with her on her moving out to the terrace a few minutes later. Her father and her husband, Mrs Assingham and Charlotte, had done nothing but meet her eyes; yet the difference in these demonstrations made each a separate passage — which was all the more wonderful since, with the secret behind every face, they had alike tried to look at her *through* it and in denial of it (II, 234).

The passage is immediately followed by one which makes abundantly clear how this union of James's fondness for reflecting the action in a single consciousness and his sophistication of the dramatic, scenic methods help him here to gain the best of both worlds. The account of Maggie's sense of responsibility for the safety of all of them is piercingly embodied without lessening our concern for each and every one of those others. "It all left her, as she wandered off, with the strangest of impressions — the sense, forced upon her as never yet, of an appeal, a positive confidence, from the four pairs of eyes, that was deeper than any negation and that seemed to speak on the part of each for some relation to be contrived by her, a relation with herself, which would spare the individual the danger, the actual present strain, of the relation with the others". Just as, in dreams, we see ourselves as a figure in them, so James, while populating Maggie's consciousness of the scene before us, ensures that she remains for us but one of the figures within it (II, 234).

It may be safe to infer from James's conducting of the narrative, immediately after the graphic expression in this scene of his inclusive attitude, that he felt he could safely devote attention of a relatively exclusive kind, first to Adam and then to Charlotte. Chapter xxxvii shows us Adam and Maggie tacitly agreeing that he take Charlotte to America, and the entire scene they enact on the same bench at Fawns where they years earlier decided in good faith to bring Charlotte into their world is eloquent with pathetic ironies. It is abundantly clear that Adam does know the real situation between his wife and his daughter's husband; it is also eloquently, though subtly, obvious that both father and daughter are painfully conscious of this move meaning the sacrifice of their own former, indulgent togetherness. The immense distance they have travelled since their former discussion is evident in Maggie's pronouncement on selfishness when she claims that even if Adam won't admit she is selfish he should and the Prince could. They recognize their parting is right; we are given opportunity, in the context of the novel, to recognize it is complexly inevitable.

Then in chapter xxxviii there is a vivid reminder, in every way equally as moving, of the painfulness implied for Charlotte by this transplanting to American City. Maggie and Adam exchange expressive glances about the girl's doomed state and though the metaphorical halter about her neck is a silken one it is still firmly attached to Adam. Again the evocativeness of the oblique rendering is sought by James and the swift, generalized glimpse of Charlotte's state as she conducts guests through the Verver collection is as poignant as is the way this brave parade acts upon the nerves of Amerigo and of all those who, knowing, watch or hear her. Again there is balance; the reader's sympathy, empathy and interest can be sustained equally for all.

Part Fifth ends with the extraordinary charade that Charlotte and Maggie act out in chapter xxix. It is the counterpart of their other charade on the terrace some nights before, when Maggie forced herself to pretend ignorance and Charlotte forced the Judas kiss. Now it is Maggie who seeks out Charlotte and in hot daylight they both speak more directly and explicitly than at any other point in the whole novel. They speak what they know to be lies and what we know to be essential to their respective natures. Charlotte must assert her dignity, persistently rejecting Maggie and claiming Adam for herself; Maggie must pretend to believe her, pretend to accept the charges of possessiveness towards her father and of hatred towards Charlotte, because she can through this renunciation of her own hatred and fear try, in the one act, to aspire towards the kind of love she professes and also pursue her pragmatic course. This way, both women are safe from any reference to the Amerigo they love in common and who is throughout the scene almost as palpably present as is Adam.

Part Sixth is evidently an attempt to bring the novel to a close on those terms that James has appeared to be striving so strenuously to preserve. It concerns all four figures all the time and it is apparently at pains to make clear that far from this conclusion being in any sense a resolution of conflicts, it relates how all four are losers and how each ends in solitariness. The note is struck in the opening of chapter xl, which finds Maggie and Amerigo arrested in stillness and inaction "in the desert of Portland Place" and "with the stale London September close at hand" (II, 321).

Maggie's own testimony as to where they all are is valid as far as it goes. She sees the Prince has been waiting for the Ververs to leave the country. She sees herself as helping him wait, of "seeing him through". She sees Adam as waiting in Charlotte's company at Fawns while his wife supervises preparations for the move. She sees Charlotte as being in torment, hiding her humilitation and therefore never venturing to accept the available opportunities of contacting her lover during her brief visits to London; she is eloquent about her rival's predicament and she speculates on what she or Amerigo could do about alleviating her torment. The "foredoomed ingenuities of her pity" even reach to an insight into the intensity of Charlotte's bitterness at the loss of what Maggie acknowledges to have been a " 'golden flame' " of passion (II, 322, 330).

We accept this much of her testimony because as witnesses we can corroborate it. But when she ventures so soon after this into judgment, she is instantly distanced. She and her father, she tells Fanny, are " 'lost to each other really much more than Amerigo and Charlotte are; since for them it's just, it's right, it's deserved, while for us it's only sad and strange and not caused by our fault". This "scene" neutralizes any tendency towards exclusive sympathy which the "picture" of her consciousness may have tended to generate. Charlotte, she says, is held by her ignorance as to how much Adam knows; the Prince is held, Maggie implies elliptically, at the close of the scene, by herself. The status quo — better the bowl without the crack — will soon be fully asserted, but the presentation of this chapter is thick with qualifiers (II, 333).

Every figure could at this point easily become the victim of Maggie's kind of moral simplifications. Adam, all powerful, dominates his wife by enigmatic silence; Amerigo cowers, actionless, in as close proximity to Maggie as possible, until the lover he has rejected has gone to her American " 'doom' ". Maggie herself is so complacent in the security of this newly reconstituted safety, convinced that justice has therefore been done. Charlotte is tormented by her own refusal to acknowledge even now the fact of Maggie's marriage, the fact of her own, and the fact that the Prince has acted, as he had long ago warned he would act, on his declaration that if ever she should take risks she would take them alone. But James subverts such simple judgments of these people and ensures the richer interest in all of them. In the context provided by the scenario to this point, Maggie's answers pose questions and we are kept asking them; and while we can still ask them of Maggie herself, we can continue asking them of everyone else (II, 288).

The language of James's discourse in this chapter carefully insists that we remain conscious of the whole scenario. When Amerigo tells Maggie that Charlotte is " 'stupid' ", it is the truth, and not he, that is brutal but this does not exhaust the quantity of truth evoked by the word, for it has a history which makes it echo, and not only against the once naive Maggie who hears it. We heard, long before, Charlotte herself promise him that for things she did not want to know he would find her " 'stupid' ". We heard too on another discriminated occasion, the Assinghams speculating about applying the same word to Adam and his daughter. On another, Maggie, when desperately seeking the truth of the lovers' relationship, asked Fanny: " 'You've only believed me contented then because you've believed me stupid?' " We listened to Amerigo opting for not this word but its companion, "idiotic", when marvelling that even the Ververs could imagine a *galantuomo* such as he going about with a woman such as Charlotte in a state of innocence. In a novel that is in part about various forms of human stupidity, the interest of such usage is not merely definitive or even merely dramatic but also richly speculative, comparative and inclusive (II, 348, I, 363, II, 135, 111-112, I, 335).

The same is true of the use of the word "terrible" in this second-last chapter of the long novel. It too triggers off a review of other occurrences of it emphatically placed throughout the scenario. After the visit with her former lover to the antiquarian, Charlotte applies it to the temptations and vulnerabilities implied by any innocence such as Maggie's. When Mrs Assingham has witnessed the loss of that innocence, she applies it to the ruthlessness for which Maggie exchanges it as she politically manipulates the lovers. When now Maggie, with her memory of her own pain as vivid to her as her compassion for Charlotte's, says that it's always terrible for women, Amerigo, from the new depths of his knowledge of what the whole adventure has meant for them all, makes the generalization explicit: " 'Everything's terrible, *cara* — in the heart of man' " (I, 102, II, 115, 349).

Approached thus, the final chapter can be seen to continue this kind of comprehensive attention. Though all four principal figures have appeared together before in such tableaux, they have never before *all* been such centres of so intense an interest nor had such sustained attention applied to their present collective situation. Each of them shares equally in the tensions of this farewell occasion and James affords the view that ensures our appreciation of this fact.

> . . . the note was struck indeed; the note of that strange accepted finality of relation, as from couple to couple, which almost escaped an awkwardness only by not attempting a gloss. Yes, this was the wonder, that the occasion defied insistence precisely because of the vast quantities with which it dealt — so that separation was on a scale beyond any compass of parting. To do such an hour justice would have been in some degree to question its grounds — which was why they remained in fine, the four of them, in the upper air, united through the firmest abstention from pressure. There was visibly no point at which, face to face, either Amerigo or Charlotte had pressed; and how little she herself was in danger of doing so Maggie scarce needed to remember. That her father wouldn't by the tip of a toe — of that she was equally conscious; . . . (II, 361).

James's directing of the action ensures that the dynamics of these final scenes will aptly reinforce those generated and sustained by the entire scenic principle. We are shown and we hear Maggie and her father together, Maggie and Amerigo together. Of Amerigo's parting colloquy with Charlotte we do not need to hear any direct word; nor do we need any more specific reference to a final encounter between the incalculable quantities that Maggie and Charlotte now represent. The fact that Adam has no word or sign for Amerigo needs only the subdued report that James gives of it. The indirect rendering, with its generalized — even stylized — treatment of such details is now invoked and we are kept at that distance from all the figures that will best help us appreciate their individual positions as, in these concluding moments, each of them is revealed as knowing, in isolation, a self-awareness that cannot contribute to a self-fulfilment.

As we look back over this novel to the disposition of books, parts and chapters, to their respective natures, their sequence and their total impact, it would appear that James sought effects that could be summarized, albeit crudely, in the following way. Book First will set out the origin and development of the crisis, Book Second will trace the course and nature of its resolution. Parts First, Second and Third will have ostensible and real subjects; the former will be, respectively, the marriage of the Prince, the marriage of Adam, the adultery of the Prince and Charlotte; the latter will be the implications of Charlotte's presence, marriage and exploitation of opportunity. Parts Fourth, Fifth and Sixth will have as their ostensible subjects, respectively, Maggie's enlightenment as to the real situation, her attempts to change it with Adam's tacit cooperation, and the coming together of Maggie and the Prince in a new relationship on the departure of the Ververs. The real subject of these last three parts will be the extra moral and emotional consequences her acts incur and implications for all the others with whom she is in relationship. The general effect will involve the reader in a consciousness, a very complex one, of the "felt"[1] lives of all these people, of their motives, their responses and of their ultimate frustration in a manner incalculably strange, given their high intentions, high intelligence, high civilization.

The centres of consciousness

The purpose of this kind of hit-and-miss summation of possible, even of probable, intentions apparent in this ambitious work of prose fiction is the recognition it provokes of how dense the interest really is at any point in the book as we actually read it and how strongly the final effect does reverberate. Such a reaction continues as we ponder James's selection of that variety of vantage points for the narration of Book First and his selection of Maggie's consciousness as the chief referent for Book Second, and the relation between the two.

The book has in effect four figures, each of whom could have provided, with varying but appreciable degrees of success, the central consciousness in which all interests were reflected. (We can too readily recognize the thinness of interest in any scheme that saw either, or even both, the Assinghams serving that function.) The abiding aesthetic effect of the novel would then have been, in every sense, that of a thicker version of *The Ambassadors.* There is one kind of Jamesian novel in the story of Charlotte Stant becoming Mrs Verver in pursuit of her former lover Prince Amerigo and being defeated by his wife, her long-time friend, Maggie, the daughter of her husband; but if James had ever wanted to write it, it would have to have been in the eighteen-seventies. There is another kind of opportunity in the adventures of Amerigo, the "innocent" abroad in Ververland which he discovers contains his former lover whom he renounces, after accepting opportunist pleasures, when he discovers for the first time the character resources of his wife; but that too would have been written by James no later than the early 'eighties.

There is easily imaginable the story of Adam Verver's quest for cultural riches in Europe after a financial career far surpassing Christopher Newman's, accompanied by a daughter for whom he first purchases a princely husband and for whom, out of further kindness, he himself later takes another marriage partner; then, when they both discover whom he has in fact married, he patiently pulls the silken halters in the background until he salvages everything by their renouncing each other. It is imaginable — but only from James's hands in the 'nineties. There is even a not inconceivable story involving a Charlotte, a Prince and a Maggie in the sort of narrative emphases that we find interesting James in *The Golden Bowl's* immediate predecessor, *The Wings of the Dove* — but at this point the game can cease because the reasons for the choices inherent in *The Golden Bowl* being as they are, should now be evident in the difference between the respective natures and function of Milly and Maggie. To have told the tale in terms of a Milly Theale, even of a Milly rid of fatal disease and possessed of an Adam and an Amerigo to live for, would have been to revert to Catherine Sloper of *Washington Square*, which James would not even include among his revisions for the definitive edition of his works, for there was a passiveness there, a lack of intellectual excitement; she had proved a dull reflector and, indeed, even Milly would have proved too limited a one for the novel he wrote in 1903-4.

What this brief speculative excurse drives home is that Maggie's Book Second is read in the context of a Book First that has for its reflecting consciousness characters who are essentially worldly, disenchanted, pragmatic and already conditioned by the numerous challenges of reality. Would not this serve as an essentially accurate summary of what the astute American industrialist, the poverty-stricken Italian nobleman, the cosmopolitan but penniless American beauty and the shrewdly social Assinghams have in common? Maggie offers the ideal consciousness in which to reflect, for more sustained perusal, these people and this world, a world in which she must herself become an effective agent. The sustained perusal will of course include Maggie and facilitate the difficulties of making credible her naive and intense faith and the nature of her love for her father as she progresses on her journey to fuller consciousness. Hers will by no means be the only journey of interest but, given her nature, it will be the longest. She later learns to work subtly but her paramount quality is a simplicity of moral vision which affords James the least inconvenience in his task of rendering for us indirectly, but with sufficient vividness, emphasis and means of empathy, the quite other minds and spirits and emotional evolutions that are also very much the point of the novel.

Her responses to husband, father and friend are at first total and fervent responses, in themselves dramatically revelatory, but always leaving James plenty of room to show us what she does not see. She never does see her father as James enables us to see him. Even when, alerted to a more deliberate concern for motive, she becomes more self-conscious in all her relationships and she changes her responses to Amerigo, Charlotte and Adam, the very intensity of her preoccupation draws the reader's attention the more markedly to those hints James sows that all this is, in her, exaggerated, almost over-compensatory. We can just as easily at such moments see her as the others see her and see their cases just as clearly, despite the obliqueness of their representation.

Perhaps the over-riding advantage of her serving as vantage point throughout the infinitely more difficult tasks that challenge James in Book Second is that though Maggie's idealism so approaches a transcendental absolute it is, as such, an exaggeration of a norm with which we are not totally unfamiliar and thus presents us with a single idea — a pure point of depature, as it were — for the elaborate, intricate and delicate moral territory into which that book takes us. The Princes's mixed frailties, the tarnished glibness of the Assinghams, the history of Adam's earlier materialist saga, can serve well enough as lens for a general introductory inspection of Bond Street, Cadogan Square, Portland Place, Eaton Square and Fawns but, for the necessarily microscopic focus upon the issues raised by James's quartet in the second book, we need the clear, intense magnifications afforded by Maggie if we are not to lose James's point.

The provisions built into the chosen methods of narration suggest very emphatically that it would be a mistake to regard Maggie as the "protagonist", however, even if only because the kind of fictive account that James is now evidently entertaining renders that term obsolete. That it inaccurately describes Maggie's role because it places it out of proportion, is clear: I hope to have already demonstrated that she is not the chief figure in this drama. She is neither the person to whom all the important things happen nor the person who initiates all of them. If the role as initiator of action were the criterion for "protagonist" or for even "deuteragonist" or perhaps even for "antagonist", then it would apply equally to the three other figures. What of Amerigo who woos and wins Maggie and who collaborates so completely with Charlotte in Gloucester? What of Charlotte herself who gambles on that expensive trip to him on the eve of his marriage, who marries Adam and who manipulates so adroitly the arrangements for all clandestine encounters and exploits every opportunity, from that rainy afternoon with the Prince in Portland Place, to the extra overnight stay at Matcham and the following afternoon at Gloucester? What of Adam, who provides not only all the venues from London and Fawns to American City but who also sustains his old relation with Maggie after her marriage then, for Maggie's sake, marries Charlotte and finally takes her off the scene with him?

All four figures are responsible for actions which vitally influence the creation, development and "resolution" of the whole dramatic action. Even if we fancy the notion of the Prince and Charlotte working together against Adam and Maggie we arrive at one pair of deuteragonists in opposition to another pair. But what James's handling of Maggie's role in Book Second discourages altogether is any such a notion of sets of pairs; the notion encouraged is that the reason why everything is terrible in the hearts of men and women is that each remains eternally isolated. If in defiance of James's art here we choose to blame or praise any of these men and women, we must blame or praise all or none. If we agree to respond to his plea for "attention of perusal"[2] of the given textual evidence, we neither blame nor praise any and we compassionate all within a final, distinctly original vision.

Maggie is not the chief character but she is the chief element in the delicate artistry of the highly adventurous undertaking that Book Second constitutes. As I have tried to demonstrate, she remains one referent and part of the total point without getting in the way while that point is being made. There may well be another reason, an extra-textual one, why James thus uses her. She helps him make a virtue of necessity - in two senses. Within the novel, she is the only suitable candidate: the inadequacy of the Prince's moral vision and its potential for development are two of the main points made in Part First and it is only in Part Sixth that he shows any growth in this quarter; Adam Verver is portrayed for four of the six parts as being obsessed by one idea, his cultural enrichment of American City, and by one love, Maggie. The only other candidate would then be the brilliant Charlotte, but James knew, (one not too wildly speculates) from his experiences in trying to keep control of Kate Croy for the benefit of *The Wings of the Dove* that if in addition to suggesting as much as would be necessary of the passional life of such a "splendid shining supple creature", he also bestowed on her the potential advantages — for sympathy and empathy — of being a sustained centre of consciousness, he would have no chance of making room for, much less keeping a balanced interest in, all three of the others. Indeed, he would have immense difficulty in presenting any adequately ironic view of Charlotte herself. As it is, in the novel (a point already remarked on) we are rarely allowed for long anything approaching a direct view of her consciousness; it is usually refracted through the others. So it is this that could be the negative reason for James's preference for Maggie's mind and soul as his main mirror (II, 239).

The more positive reason must already be obvious to any reader of James's canon. He had devoted forty years of busy writing life to the creation of her predecessors, in the male line as well as the female. There is in the long gallery of his portraits no figure more recurrent. Daisy Miller, Madam de

Mauves, Isabel Archer; Longmore, Rowland Mallett, Strether; from the heroes and heroines of the earliest stories to the studies of Fleda Vetch and Milly Theale the genealogy is long. It was because this was the kind of figure he knew best how to handle that he could the more confidently attempt to depict it when it was to be depicted fully and finely — though not, in the old sense, centrally — and when that depiction was to make irrelevant, through irony, any suggestion of his being concerned with either heroes or heroines. He knew ways of tracing in such a consciousness the journey that could be made from innocence to experience without a loss of integrity and with a gain in moral insight. He had been developing over those many industrious years an art of editorial intrusion which awaited only the development of a commensurately subtle and multivalent prose style for its successful application to his most ambitious undertaking and it is the operation of that editorial style in *The Golden Bowl* which I now foreshadow.

The authorial stance

It has already been noted that James, whose dedication to the dramatic presentation of his story and to his theory of centres did not succeed in thereby drawing attention away from his authorial presence, remained in fact "the old intruder".[3] The point is of course valid but it springs from post-Joyce discussion of fiction techniques and in fact its suggestion of intrusion is a misleading one in discussions of James. It is as false to speak of him intruding into his story as it is to speak of Thackeray's commentary in *Vanity Fair* being anything other than central to the purpose of that novel. The editorial in a James novel is constant in the style and remains, throughout, the reader's vital referent. It is not an editorial element that exploits personality in Thackeray's or even in Fielding's sense of a persona addressing "dear reader", but it is there; it permeates; it is always a distancing signal and it transcends in importance the function of the theory of "centres", the "focusing" and the "reflecting" techniques, if only because it controls them. The relation of James as editor-narrator to his other elements — drama, scene, picture — is of course subtler than in Thackeray's case, where indeed, there are far sharper transitions from commentary to scene: James evidently hopes that the style of his editorial will make all transitions imperceptible and the novel will be, as he said, "all one and continuous".[4]

In the major phase, the strain placed upon the editorial manner becomes prodigious, for while the style has to indicate constantly James's apparent detachment from his character, it must also learn a variety of "voices" by which each character's view of himself or herself or of themselves in their relationships can be fully and fairly, empathically and arrestingly, evoked. Appreciation of the nature and function of these "voices", or rather of the significantly different "tones" in the one editorial "voice", places upon the resources of literary criticism strains not markedly lesser than those no doubt experienced by James himself. It is now indeed that his challenge quoted at the beginning of this study is most clearly recalled: "My mixture has only to be perfect literally to bewilder you — you are lost in the tangle of the forest."

Yet the critic who wants to take the mixture whole has (to mix the metaphor) to do no more than any other reader and attentively peruse the signals James gives while conducting each bewildered character steadily through the tangle. Sometimes the signals are given by his spies or ghosts along the way; sometimes they are merely a matter of our being prompted by the scenario to cast a long backward glance and to contrast where we have recently been with where we now find ourselves; more often it is a new tone in the voice of our discreet guide as he uses the same word to describe some new interest; and always along each path there grow the fine flowers of the inferential. It is the *quality* of our attention that is important if we are really to emerge from the forest with James. We must learn how to watch each different traveller while listening to this same guide in a way that ensures we never forget any of them.

It is an attention calling for an inclusive empathy, not for a exclusive sympathy; it calls for an awareness of the relationships appearing among several variables. The variables are not "Ideas": T.S. Eliot may be proved right. They are the artistic "values" that derive from the spectacle of human beings, each trying to "make" his or her own life and, because they are multivalent and in continual flux, any ample and intense record of them demands not only the utmost attention but also constant percipience. James works his readers hard — from that first moment in fact when he introduces us in Bond Street to the bewildered Prince Amerigo.

Just how hard may become more evident when I apply to the first paragraph something like the kind of scrutiny that Ian Watt applied to the first paragraph of *The Ambassadors*, where he demonstrated what James is there demanding of his prose and what is consequently demanded of us.[5] We are worked even harder from the first words of the later novel. Strether is set at exactly the distance best affording the intrinsic appeal of his character and circumstances as well as James's lightly ironic play with both. But the earlier novel is designed primarily to give us the impact of all the ensuing European adventures upon this wondering ambassador from Woollett. The Prince, however, is merely the first of several who are to wonder among adventures in which he is but one figure. Although the younger and the older man might possibly be able to exchange meaningful glances in the similar territory each eventually reaches by such different paths, the scale of development is altogether more ambitious in the later novel and James can be seen in its opening words moving already "on stealthiest tiptoe, toward the point of view that, within the compass, will give [him] most instead of least to answer for".[6] The strategy of the structure is reproduced in the tactics of the sentence; the compass of the Prince's consciousness and of

Bond Street itself must be transcended. We must learn immediately to anticipate, to discriminate — to accept, in short — the demanding stance James is inviting us to share not with the Prince but with himself. But before setting out on the path leading from that West End encounter, I must note how other cartographers have mapped it.

NOTES

1. James, *Prefaces*, p. 45.
2. Ibid. p. 304.
3. John E. Tilford, "James the Old Intruder", *Modern Fiction Studies* 4 (Summer 1958): 157-64.
4. Henry James, "The Art of Fiction", *Longman's Magazine* 4 (September 1884): 502-21. Revised version quoted here from *Partial Portraits* (London: Macmillan, 1888), p. 392. Hereafter *Partial Portraits.*
5. Ian Watt, "The First Paragraph of *The Ambassadors: An Exlication*", *Essays in Criticism*, 10 (July 1960), 250-74.
6. James, *Prefaces*, p. 328.

4

The Tactics of the Characterization

A. The Prince and the prose of suspension

Very few such cartographers of this Amerigo's journey have considered that a fine nib or brush was needed for their task. Only recently, as part of the trend to look more closely at each of the characters, have many attended to much of the evidence James from the first supplies or acknowledged by their responses any appreciable complexity in it. That the Prince might have at first a moral simplicity and yet not be the subject in the novel of simplistic treatment has been acknowledged most explicitly by Carl Maves[1] who saw the altogether unsimple final position to which it leads him. It is after all he who then tells Maggie that everything is " 'terrible' " in the heart of man; and when he tells her that Charlotte is " 'stupid' " — an epithet by which he has alienated many critics — he is only reminding himself again that she had more knowledge, and less excuse, than he. He is also recognizing and indeed implying that he too is not wholly exempt from such an epithet, though for him it is not also an epitaph. Both epithets show moral mileage.

This recognition of the nature and function of Prince Amerigo has come later than it should, mainly because, despite James's provisions to the contrary, critics allowed him to be eclipsed in their interest by Charlotte in whom they perceived a more spectacularly active agent, or by Maggie, whose victim, they decided, she became. Yet he has for long deserved closer reading. James's portrait of him is consistent and shows a development that highly illuminates one facet of his many-faceted theme. As well as representing a basic passional force against which we see in truer perspective the forces which motivate Adam and Maggie, he represents, as an outsider — foreign to all the American inhabitants of this English scene — the reader's first view of those inhabitants. Except for the blunt Colonel, who understands him earlier — and better — than anyone else, he is the only figure whose relative poverty, simplicity and clarity of vision reassure us, confronted as we are with the awesome wealth of Adam's world, the self-defeating febrility of Fanny's mind and the exaltation with which Maggie rejoices in fatal ignorance, that we are not alone in finding these people at first so disturbingly remote from realities more familiar.

Accompanying him as he learns to take the Verver world on its own terms, as he is thrown more profoundly upon his deepest insights and as he more clearly sees Maggie's response to knowledge, we become aware of the full distance traversed. The sharpest of all the ironies that he must experience, though, is that his own greatest accession of knowledge derives not from his final view of Maggie, whom he realizes he did not know, but from his final view of Charlotte, whom he thought he did know. Ever alien, he is finally as solitary as is each other figure. But I must now go back, to precisely how James does introduce us to him in Bond Street, to where he takes him and us from there and to how our stance is determined by the seven sentences comprising the first paragraph of the novel.

> [1] The Prince had always like his London, when it had come to him; he was one of the Modern Romans who find by the Thames a more convincing image of the truth of the ancient state than any they have left by the Tiber. [2] Brought up on the legend of the City to which the world paid tribute, he recognised in the present London much more than in contemporary Rome the real dimensions of such a case. [3] If it was a question of an *Imperium*, he said to himself, and if one wished, as a Roman, to recover a little the sense of that, the place to do so was on London Bridge, or even, on a fine afternoon in May, at Hyde Park Corner. [4] It was not indeed to either of those

places that these grounds of his predilection, after all sufficiently vague, had, at the moment we are concerned with him, guided his steps; he had strayed simply enough into Bond Street, where his imagination, working at comparatively short range, caused him now and then to stop before a window in which objects massive and lumpish, in silver and gold, in the forms to which precious stones contribute, or in leather, steel, brass, applied to a hundred uses and abuses, were as tumbled together as if, in the insolence of the Empire, they had been the loot of far-off victories. [5] The young man's movements, however, betrayed no consistency of attention — not even, for that matter, when one of his arrests had proceeded from possibilities in faces shaded, as they passed him on the pavement, by huge beribboned hats, or more delicately tinted still under the tense silk of parasols held at perverse angles in waiting victorias. [6] And the Prince's undirected thought was not a little symptomatic, since, though the turn of the season had come and the flush of the streets begun to fade, the possibilities of faces, on the August afternoon, were still one of the notes of the scene. [7] He was too restless — that was the fact — for any concentration, and the last idea that would just now have occurred to him in any connexion was the idea of pursuit (I, 3-4).

Ostensibly, the seven sentences give us first the patrician and the modern Roman, then the young man, his instincts, his preoccupations; actually they give us that idea of him which James chooses we should entertain at this point. It is a complex idea, arrived at by successive statements and qualifications. The opening declaration has its significant rider: he likes what he can receive and then he takes possession. The reason for this preference of his, shared by many of his contemporaries, reaches far back into their common past and is edited to become general and abstract: "truth" and "state" edge us away from particular detail in the two contrasted epochs; the rivers become centres of power. Already time and space are parts of the idea.

The second sentence obtrudes even more considerations between him and us, which James just as assiduously helps us to marshal. This Prince recognizes "the real dimensions of such a case"; that is, an imperial capital to which everyone is subservient and makes obeisance. But this unattractive truth about him must be ameliorated, for our antipathy would inconveniently blur and reduce the idea, as would undiscriminating sympathy, so though the syntax gives the fact the emphasis afforded by the close of the sentence, the diction diminishes the impact. "Case" is surely neutral enough; "such a scale" generalizes it almost to abstraction; "real" honestly includes the revealing adjective but in the phrasing it is applied to the bland and pluralized "dimensions". Denying the pleasures of less complex responses, the prose encourages us to join in busy contemplation with an author whose account of matters is neither disinterested nor judgmental.

There is in fact almost no need in the third sentence for the careful reminder that all this the Prince "said to himself": we have our distance and we can keep it, not even needing for our continued reading any authorial jog stronger than the reference to the bridge to the centre of London's gold and the one to the Corner famed for pragmatic politics and casual encounters. James, however, makes sure and his sustained use of the past perfect in the long fourth construction provides for the whole account to be further cooled by retrospection, while parts of speech and syntax that usually serve their supportive adverbial and adjectival functions are not subordinated beyond effectiveness. Thus the rhythm of the whole gives its emphasis to "indeed" and arouses interest in the Prince's motive for his choice of direction. Yet there is a further refinement needed even here. "After all sufficiently vague" modifies the force of "indeed", suggesting merely that his negative preferences are stronger than his positive ones. "At the moment we are concerned with him" is a brief exchange between James and us but bears also the overtone that at other moments our Prince might direct his footsteps more purposefully to either of these previously mentioned objectives. "Simply enough" connotes "simply enough for innocence" and also reiterates the idea of his being at a loose end, as does "now and then".

"Working at comparatively short range" is the phrase in which James's prevailing light irony comes closest to candid disparagement of its object; as well as its literal description of window-shopping, it hints at an imagination limited to a preoccupation with the windows' contents, but even this pejorative note is modified by "comparatively". The pejorative is sustained with less mitigation in the ensuing account of these luxuries, where, as well as being carefully blurred by plurality and generality, sheer tasteless quantity is stressed in "massive and lumpish"; "uses" is accompanied by "abuses"; "tumbled together" suggests an avid, hasty grabbing; "insolence of the Empire" is surely derogatory enough and so is "the loot of far-off victories".

These final three phrases show us James also foreshadowing subsequent accounts of the Prince's grabbing of the Verver millions, his patrician acceptance, on all occasions, of personal tributes, and the second paragraph's details of his own much more immediate victory with Maggie. The prose insinuates the necessary idea of plunder without slipping into a photographic naturalism or "realism" that would swamp the given idea of him beneath an evocation of surfaces, or reduce him to a type. We are in Bond Street clearly enough and we have been appraised of this character's preoccupations but we can also still hear James. The concrete does not imperil the concept; the characteristics resist being simplified; the idea of him clarifies and fills.

Nor are the relevant physical particularities allowed to sabotage the even trickier task of imparting details to us about the Prince's susceptibility to attractive women. That they are a greater source of distraction than silver and gold is signalled in "not even, for that matter". For this fifth sentence, he has to become "the young man". Further, that he "betrayed no consistency of attention" is atypical yet very much a reality, and a source of his interest for us; his capacity to be confused and preoccupied despite the presence of immediate appeals to his susceptibilities is what rescues him from the class of cheap adventurers. James treats the distraction, to which on this occasion the Prince proves immune, with an indirection that is directly proportional to the literary hazards in this part of his subject. He evokes not sensuousness but the quintessential idea of it and the exact degree of the young man's response to it. The passage is as a consequence foreshortened to within an inch of its life: "proceeded from possibilities in faces shaded, as they passed him on the pavement, by huge beribboned hats" is not impresssionism but a formulation of it. Again plurality, abstraction, indirection and synecdoche have given the necessary shadow without the inconvenient substance. "Or more delicately tinted still under the tense silk of parasols held at perverse angles in waiting victorias" similarly does much in little: this connoisseur appreciates the finer delicacies of the flesh; he is interested enough to be frustrated by the "perverse angles" of those parasols and, in this context, "tense" and "waiting" heighten the sense of opportunity and anticipation.

In the paragraph's penultimate sentence, James rallies for the main point of it. The tendency is towards a summary: "though the turn of the season had come and the flush of the streets begun to fade" underlines again the Prince's more usual and even habitual indulgence in pleasures social and sensuous; "flush" links easily with his attention to "shaded" and "delicately tinted" complexions and generalizes from them. "Still one of the notes of the scene" ("still" insisting on the continuity of this preoccupation) breaks down this information in a manner similar to that employed earlier, for a different subject, in "the real dimensions of such a case"; the potentially graphic and erotic is fragmented and transmuted into an idea allowed, with reluctance, to pass right through his mind.

The ultimate sentence explains why he lets it pass; the symptom is traced to its cause; the restlessness is announced as a fact. James almost "states" it! He can now afford to; by now we have learned enough to see it in perspective. More significantly, James has withheld it until we could appreciate and adopt his own attitude to this present centre of attention. But of course that fact, and indeed, any other, is not nearly as important as the impact of the paragraph itself, wherein the prose, in a manner almost fugal, suggests, modified, varies, qualifies, holds to our notice two or three notions "at once", satisfies with its sudden precision our need to comprehend it, stimulates too with its velleities our subtler pleasure in apprehending it, and is in all its items excitingly recognizable as an ambitious attempt to represent a complex idea in the process of further complicating. It defines the kind of attention needed by negating the kind such details would usually arouse. We are evidently meant to be more concerned with the reasons for his restlessness and generally atypical behaviour than with his materialism, sensualism or candid appraisal of his long heritage and his present opportunities. The whole passage generates an appeal that the discipline of James's presence prevents becoming either stereotyped response or subjective guess. Its irony is non-reductive.

We learn in the next paragraph that after an effort unprecedented on his part he has just achieved a goal and is now somewhat less steadily pondering consequences. We have met him shortly after the lawyers have caused him to think of keys crunching in strong locks and as he reflects on his future father-in-law's "easy way with his millions", his own notion of reciprocity is expressed in a sentence that declares ideal intentions while suggesting real limitations. "If there was one thing in the world the young man at this juncture clearly intended it was to be much more decent as a son-in-law than lots of fellows he could think of had shown themselves in that character." When, in his recall of discussions with Maggie as to what she and her father expect of him, the talk is of his dark antecedents, her American romanticism and of moral values, he is even more at sea and there is an heroic quality in his attempt to reach shore through a candid discussion of such notions as faith, hypocrisy, dissembling, lying and deception. This merely embarrasses Maggie and further confirms his impression of a discomforting Verver innocence, of a limitedness of experience that offers him little solace in his frank and candid quest (I, 5).

James, in his authorial capacity, carefully admits the superficiality of this thinking but emphasizes the occasion, the motivation and the understandable humanity of it. "Something of this sort was in any case the moral and the murmur of his walk. It would have been ridiculous — such a moral from such a source — if it hadn't all somehow fitted to the gravity of the hour, that gravity the oppression of which I began by recording." He has established as credible and interesting the fact of the Ververs' extravagant degree of idealism, the rather vertiginous expectations it implies and Prince Amerigo's very understandable responses to all this at such a decisive moment. The Prince feels he is lost in a white mist such as encountered by Poe's explorer Pym, and though it is undeniably white and pure, it could rather terrifyingly deprive any man of his bearings. It causes this man to reach for the hand of Fanny Assingham, who is a little nervous in admitting the exact degree of her collusion with him in the making of his marriage and who compounds his own nervousness by announcing Charlotte's return. Her subsequent entrance, his itemized response to her present physical charms, his past passional knowledge of them, his apprehensions as to the motive of her return and his tense effort to rally resources to face up to her in a manner compatible with his so newly-won status as a man legally affianced, make him less a subject of amused spectatorship and generate interested compassion. When James immediately places us in relation to the history of their former relationship, through the duologue in which Fanny's anxiety is tempered by the Colonel's scepticism, the details of the perversity that attended the former lovers' circumstances can only reinforce that interest and compassion (I, 18).

Throughout his first re-encounter with her in Cadogan Place, throughout the subdued-toned dialogue but quite electric undercurrents of their exchanges in Hyde Park and at the antiquarian's, he is just as straight with Charlotte as he is vulnerable and responsive to her appeal and charm. When, at Fanny's, his former lover speaks of the question of her own possible marriage, he steadily returns to her, " 'My dear friend, . . . it's always a question of doing the best for one's self one can — without injury to others.' " In the park, at the end of their discussion of how Verver good-faith-and-decency spoils people by inviting them to abuse it and thus places the Ververs beyond help, he insists, " 'We *can* [help] — we always can. That is' he competently added, 'if we care for them. And that's what we're talking about.' " In the Bloomsbury shop he firmly refuses to accept any gift, as from her to him rather than to both him and Maggie; and as he afterwards vehemently admits that superstition drives him to refuse a bowl with a crack, he spells out for her that he is afraid for, and therefore frankly protective of, *his* happiness, *his* " 'safety' ", *his* " 'marriage' " — of in fact everything that concerns himself. He could not at this stage be franker to Charlotte; these thoroughly dramatic scenes attest in action the evidence of that good faith he avows on entering the Verver world, in accepting its advantages and in determinedly renouncing that "lost time" of his and Charlotte's of which a flawed bowl would have been less a *ricordo* of their past than an omen for his future (I, 58, 103, 119, 114).

The language of Part First is artistically faithful, in a very inclusive sense, to an authorial responsibility that will not flinch from implying, by the facts given, that the Prince we meet in Bond Street is aware of his moral fragilities; that the arrival of Charlotte Stant in Cadogan Place severely tests them; and that his two subsequent interludes with her test them further. It is faithful also to a rendering of the young man's consciousness of these unaccustomed moral vistas, this unexpected arrival and these intractable demands on his integrity, that includes also an unsentimental, precisely-defined tracing of his rallying to meet them. James lets both kinds of facts, or rather, as many relevant facts of all kinds as he can coherently include by statement, implication and innuendo in a delicately graded and timed discourse, speak for themselves. The result is an unfolding that prompts speculation and that in no way simplifies, neatly classifies or glibly interprets but, rather, invites by its very nature that we too postpone judgement and continue in pursuit of understanding.

James does not give us another direct account of Amerigo, an account that is not filtered through the impressions of some other character, until well into Part Third. We have by then therefore had our own encounter with Adam Verver, been privy to his conference with Maggie about the wisdom of his marrying, and watched him woo and win Charlotte, with whom we have our first direct relationship at the beginning of this part. She is seen dealing with a Fanny Assingham alarmed by the decision to remain on at the Foreign Office ball after Maggie and her father have left it. In terms of our observation of the Prince now as he too deals with the accusatory Fanny, three years and some eight months have elapsed, but even here in chapter xv, the second of this part, James is more concerned with Fanny herself than with confiding fully the Prince's new attitude to her, and we are not supplied with any explanation as to the difference, the greater degree of assurance, in his deportment of himself, or why he is content to tease her high seriousness by emphasizing her complicity in his present, more complex, domestic situation.

It is not till we are treated to another of Fanny's self-scarifying sessions with her Bob that James allows us to learn one account of the extraordinary developments that have manipulted Amerigo and Charlotte into such close proximity. He begins chapter xvii with the ironic sentence, "It appeared thus that they might enjoy together extraordinary freedom, the two friends, from the moment they should understand their position aright"; and he thereafter limits himself to authorially reporting what these two make of it, sometimes rendering Charlotte's initiatives, sometimes the Prince's, frequently rendering for us their joint decisions and conclusions. It is she, not James, who concludes: "Nothing stranger surely had ever happened to a conscientious, a well-meaning, a perfectly passive pair: no more extraordinary decree had ever been launched against such victims than this of forcing them against their will into a relation of mutual close contact that they had done everything to avoid." We are now given the contents of the telegram which Amerigo sent to her on hearing of her forthcoming marriage and which she offered to show Adam: *" 'A la guerre comme à la guerre then . . . We must lead our lives as we see them; but I am charmed with your courage and almost surprised at my own.' "* They declare they had done what they could to prevent the situation. It is he, not James, who summarizes it for us. "What had happened in short was that Charlotte and he had by a single turn of the wrist of fate — 'led up' to indeed, no doubt, by steps and stages that conscious computation had missed — been placed face to face in a freedom that extraordinarily partook of ideal perfection, since the magic web had spun itself without their toil, almost without their touch" (I, 288, 289, 290, 298).

"Almost". The prose keeps them both transparent by jogging our knowledge, and the revisions help by moving that important "extraordinarily" from after, to before, "partook", and by eloquently insisting not on "the freedom" but on "a freedom".[2] That they earlier enjoyed yet another freedom, that involving the choice of revealing or not revealing their Roman time to their partners before marrying them, is the moral imperative that need be recalled now no more firmly than by the irony informing not only the first sentence, quoted above, of this chapter but the remainder of it. On the rainy afternoon when boredom makes him vulnerable to the opportunity that it gives her and they seal their " 'sacred' " pledge, our own conscious computation, missing none of the steps and stages that have brought them to this moment of sensual release, includes also their partners, whose contributory characteristics are sounded clearly enough in that irony. "The whole demonstration, none the less, presented itself as taking place at a very high level of debate — in the cool upper air of the finer discrimination, the deeper sincerity, the larger philosophy" (I, 312, 300-301).

When James does venture on another direct account of Amerigo alone, on the Matcham terrace, he opens it with a comparative view of the avidity that drives Adam Verver, collector of pictures and princes, for it was "as if the whole place and time had been a great picture, from the hand of genius, presented to him as a prime ornament for his collection". The prose continues to stress the ironic and comparative while reporting that "what marked it especially for the highest appreciation was his extraordinarily unchalleged, his absolutely appointed and enhanced possession of it", thus again reminding us that it is a gift issuing from Verver purblindness (I, 350).

Like Merton Densher, who found himself in "the circle of petticoats",[3] he is aware of how Lady Castledean, Maggie, Fanny and Charlotte serve his opportunity, but we learn this not in James's original form of words, where these people were felt to "combine and conspire for his advantage"[4] but in his revision, where they were "trying to outdo each other in his interest", in which the emphasis falls not upon his special benefit but upon their various motives and not upon the concerted and rational but upon the hecticly competitive. Unlike Merton Densher, he does not yet enquire into this, nor even yet into the English dislike for "*les situations nettes*", though James evidently hopes that we will do so and that we will not soon or so unluckily succumb to discouragement. "The enquiring mind, in these present conditions, might, it was true, be more sharply challenged; but the result of its attention and its ingenuity, it had unluckily learned to know, was too often to be confronted with a mere dead wall, a lapse of logic, a confirmed bewilderment." Too often for Amerigo, evidently; not too often for the mode of enquiry that the major manner is here conducting into such apparent incalculables (I, 351, 354, 354-55).

This is the last time we see the Prince other than through indirect report of him in the consciousness of his wife and in the intense ratiocinations of Fanny. We see him uneasily coping with Maggie on the night of his return from Gloucester; we see him attempting, unsuccessfully, to allay her strange new alertness by his embrace of her in the carriage after the dinner for the Castledeans. We glimpse him with Charlotte on the balcony at Portland Place looking down at Maggie, Adam, the Principino and the nurse returning from Regent's Park; we see him enter to confront the smashed bowl; we hear his responses to his wife's accusations. We are conscious of him as a dramatically significant quantity amid the social occasions involving them all: he is one of the witnesses of the Judas kiss enacted by his wife and his mistress on the terrace of Fawns that night of the game of bridge. We learn of his inability to remain at Fawns where, according to Maggie's plausible theory, he is vulnerable to the suffering he has himself enforced on Charlotte by remaining silent as to what his wife knows, whom she has told and why he and Charlotte are now sundered.

Our most potent glimpse of his probable state of mind at this later point is given with extreme indirection in Maggie's speculations about his way of life up in their London home. His excuse for going there had been to unpack books newly arrived from Rome. "She saw him in truth less easily beguiled — saw him wander in the closed dusky rooms from place to place or else for long periods recline on deep sofas and stare before him through the smoke of ceaseless cigarettes. She made him out as liking better than anything in the world just now to be alone with his thoughts." Her hypothetical scene forcefully prepares us for the actual one James has given us, in the penultimate chapter of the novel, where she takes to him Charlotte's telegram announcing her arrival with Adam for a farewell tea. By then "his 'own' room where he often sat now alone", has become for her "his prison", where "he struck her as caged" and as "in his more than monastic cell" (II, 293-294, 337, 338).

Though we cannot accept Maggie's impressions as authoritative and must not select from them only evidence that is interpretatively convenient, we would be obtuse not to evaluate them. Maggie is making calculated guesses about her husband's moods, motives and manners and though these guesses are not conclusive they do constitute informed testimony. She may sometimes be right about effects and wrong about causes; she may even be partially right about some causes. James's emphasis upon it suggests that her consciousness of her husband requires our discriminating attention. Thus, context suggests that she is right in her assumption that he chooses isolation in a need to be alone with his thoughts: that is obvious enough. She is right, too, when she says he finds her ideas "queer". But she is right only about the simpler of two quantities when she speaks of his having been trying over the past months to find out how much Adam knows of his relationship with Charlotte. The greater quantity in all his mental preoccupation has clearly been made up of much more than this: of the whole adventure that his foray among the Ververs has become; the superficiality of his earlier assumptions about moral responsibility; the banality of his notion that "others" could be carefully protected; the strangeness of his wife's access to powers he had never guessed her as possessing or achieving; the necessity to be cruel to the woman he has passionately enjoyed; and the need to express to his wife his new awareness of her value (II, 344).

My point is that while Maggie has come thus far through their ordeal by exercising the relatively simple moral principle of putting the bowl back together again, he now stands at a point of vantage from which he sees not only far more than could ever be seen from Bond Street or from the Matcham terrace but much more than Maggie can or will. She is no longer innocent but her new experience, though sophisticating her means of achieving her goal, does not sophisticate her conception of that goal. She is still naive enough to want to believe, apparently, that clocks can be turned back; he knows they cannot.

Proceeding carefully, then, with Maggie's view of Amerigo — in our pursuit of James's implied view of him — we do find agreement on some details. We can accept her notion that "Taste in him as a touchstone was now all at sea", if only because it is evident from his reported conduct that he has no touchstones now at all and is himself manifestly at sea. We can accept too from the evidence of his dialogue alone if not from her attendant commentary that ushers it to us, that he does not understand her or know her " 'even yet' "; she is still only intermittently discernible for him in that "white mist" which has from the first obscured his view of her. But in two other exchanges we need to qualify and see distinctions between what she hears the Prince say and what we hear. I have already noted in an earlier section that his pronouncement, " 'Everthing's terrible, *cara* — in the heart of man' ", plumbs far deeper than her comment on Charlotte, on herself and on women in general. In their exchanges following this, she probes to discover why he has remained in isolation and silence, whether he accepts that she knows of his relation with Charlotte, whether he admits it and how much of her knowledge he will admit as true. When she persists that " 'it's only a question of the quantity of truth' ", his reaction is far deeper than her statement warrants in itself and an essential reach of it is lost on her. " 'Oh the quantity of truth!' the Prince richly though ambiguously murmured" (II, 345, 348, I, 23, II, 349, 350).

In the context of his Roman background, of his first experience of the Ververs, of his earlier as well as his more recent experience of Charlotte, of his most recent experience of Maggie's emergence as a new force and his evident fresh consciousness of himself, how can we read this other than as a personal response to vistas traversed, as a deeply moving personal response to all he has glimpsed of what the general human condition can manifest? But Maggie, mainly conscious of her own vistas, glimpsed from different peaks, acknowledges his very briefly; she is concerned mainly with his response to *her* and she comes back to the moral absolute by which she has simplified and by which she has tried to hold the bowl together. The quantity of truth? " 'That's a thing by itself, yes. But there are also such things all the same as questions of good faith.' " It wrenches him back into direct relation with her and with moral schemes that he now acknowledges as necessarily salient in his own vistas. " 'Of course there are!' the Prince hastened to reply. After which he brought up more slowly: 'If ever a man since the beginning of time acted in good faith —!' But he dropped it, offering it simply for that." This second part of his response, of an altogether different tone, speaks eloquently to us who, because we are capable of a disinterestedness denied to Maggie, and because we have long enjoyed a vantage point of spectatorship that commands *all* vistas, can admit that his avowal of good faith is indeed just part of the quantity of truth. Our relativism keeps us attentive to *both* figures and to the values of *each* (II, 350).

Maggie's response is intimate, conjugal, passional; she interprets his words as a profession of love. "For that then when it had had time somewhat to settle like some handful of gold-dust thrown into the air — for that then Maggie showed herself as deeply and strangely taking it. 'I see.'

And she even wished this form to be as complete as she could made it. 'I see.' " James is quite explicit on her taking it "for that" and not for something else, something which in the Prince's mind included "that" but was not limited to it. She takes it for "that", James says, "deeply" and also, he tells us, "strangely", which is why the Prince has an understandable hesitation before responding to the "completeness" of her commitment to him. "The completeness had clearly after an instant struck him as divine. 'Ah, my dear, my dear, my dear —!' It was all he could say." And it is precisely this emotional declaration, leading as it directly does to a different level of communication between them, that again demonstrates that their togetherness is more apparent than real. James signals this in the immediately subsequent line: "She wasn't talking however at large" — and she presses deeper in her concern with personal contact: " 'You've kept up for so long a silence —!' " (II, 350).

But again it is the reader, not she, who is aware of the range of the Prince's feelings. He is clearly torn. He is coming back to her, yes, but it is apparently as much for refuge as for love, and he is emphatic as to when. Rattling quickly over the inessentials, he now faces the extra quantity and provides for dealing with it. " 'Yes, yes, I know what I've kept up. But will you do,' he asked, 'still one thing more for me?' " She, oblivious of the extra quantity that is for him still a complication, is shaken into incredulity that their togetherness cannot be all. "It was as if for an instant it had with her new exposure, made her turn pale. 'Is there even one thing left?' " And still he, conscious of his not being in a position where he can speak all, can only proffer further fervent endearments, while James's comment explains why. " 'Ah, my dear, my dear, my dear!' — it had pressed again in him the fine spring of the unspeakable." James then spells out the difference of their positions. "There was nothing however that the Princess herself couldn't say. 'I'll do anything if you'll tell me what.' " He does tell her. " 'Then wait'. And his raised Italian hand, with its play of admonitory fingers, had never made gesture more expressive. His voice dropped to a tone —! 'Wait,' he repeated. 'Wait.' " (II, 350-51).

Yet he does not tell her why; he merely allows her to understand the obvious reason as the real one. "She understood, but it was as if she wished to have it from him. 'Till they've been here, you mean?' " This is, in one obvious sense, reason enough. " 'Yes, till they've gone. Till they're away.' " Without realizing she is stressing even further only the obvious inference when there is another, she goes on. "She kept it up. 'Till they've left the country?' She had eyes on him for clearness; these were the conditions of a promise — so that he put the promise practically into his response. 'Till we've ceased to see them — for as long as God may grant! Till we're really alone.' 'Oh if it's only that —!' " James reminds us that it cannot be "only that". The Prince very evidently wants time. He is genuine in his desire for an appreciation of his wife but he will not be sufficiently free of Charlotte until her husband has actually taken her away and as this is literally "unspeakable", he must let Maggie content herself with the more obvious inference in his " 'really alone' ". He is being passionate about two things at once. He does put — as far as he can — the promise into his response, but the revealing qualification is there in the "practically". He does want to be free of his passion for Charlotte: there is surely vehemence enough in his " 'Till we've ceased to see them — for as long as God may grant!' " (II, 351).

The condition he imposes is therefore as inevitable as it is inexorable; and the irony offered for our appreciation is Maggie's serene contentment with what we know to be the less vital element of what is patently a partial explanation. That the Prince is in this scene torn is attested in the action a moment later when, his own feeling for her mounting in intensity, it is she who has to say " 'Wait!' " and the form of words James gives her are richly ambivalent, serving not only her impression of Amerigo but also our impression of them both. "It was the word of his own distress and entreaty, the word for both of them, all they had left, their plank now on the great sea" (II, 352-53).

This penultimate scene thus contributes essentially to the effect James apparently seeks in the final one, an effect which, as I have tried to show in my earlier treatment of it, is very much concerned not with two couples but with four individuals, with their apparent togetherness as couples, and their actual isolation as four human beings. Awaiting the Prince's return from delivering the Principino to Miss Bogle, Maggie sees this moment as the reason for her campaign of reconstituting the bowl as all golden still and without the crack, but she is assailed by premonitions perfectly understandable by the reader. All her discipline "had been for the sake of this end. Here it was then, the moment, the golden fruit that had shone from afar; only what *were* these things in the fact, for the hand and for the lips, when tested, when tasted — what were they as a reward?" She waits to find out and when he stands before her again, she becomes terrified "she must strike him as waiting for a confession".She is further horrified by her consciousness that "his acknowledgement hung there, too monstrously, at the expense of Charlotte, before whose mastery of the greater style she had just been standing dazzled". James then shows her eventually facing some of the inevitable consequences of her success and she at first tries to dismiss them (II, 367, 368).

> "Isn't she too splendid?" she simply said, offering it to explain and to finish.
> "Oh splendid!" With which he came over to her.
> "That's our help, you see," she added — to point further her moral.
> It kept him before her therefore, taking in — or ***trying to*** — what she so wonderfully gave. He tried, ***too clearly***, to please her, — to meet her in her own way; but with the result ***only*** that, close to her, her face kept before him, his hands holding her shoulders, ***his whole act enclosing her***, he ***presently*** echoed: "See? I see nothing but *you.*" And the ***truth of it*** had with this force ***after a moment*** so strangely lighted his eyes that as for

pity and dread of them she buried her own in his breast (II, 368-69).

The only word italicized by James in this final paragraph is the " '*you*' " of " 'I see nothing but *you*' ", which in every sense emphasizes the multivalence that is the point, the informing spirit, of the whole novel. Amerigo has been "trying to" take in what Maggie offers; he has tried "too clearly", and Maggie, to whose consciousness we have more direct access at this moment is well aware of this evidence of effort; she even finds herself enclosed by what is evidently with necessity, an "act" in both senses of that word. For he finds that these, "only", are the words which he is now capable merely of echoing. He is abstracted, preoccupied, as "presently" and "after a moment" reveal. When he discovers that he has said, in effect, that he sees only her, as a literal fact, and also her only and not Charlotte, he too has his reaction on facing "the truth of it" (II, 368-69).

James's Prince Amerigo, presented "as consistently a foredoomed, entangled, embarrassed agent in the general imbroglio[5]," can hardly be also Oscar Cargill's[6] hollow man, Daniel J. Schneider's[7] sensualist, Tony Tanner's[8] statue, Dupee's[9] child, much less the simple wrongdoer miraculously redeemed by Christof Wegelin's[10] or Blackmur's[11] Maggie. Nor is he Krook's[12] insolubly ambiguous Prince; he is much more akin to the complexly developing one glimpsed by Bayley, Pearson and Maves.[13] Girling[14] did not reach back far enough into the rich context provided for what characters say in this novel. Amerigo's words to Maggie about Charlotte's " 'making her life' ", reach back, via her father's to her about how " 'we're working it, our life, our chance' " to those he spoke to Charlotte at Fanny's before the marriage: " '. . . it's always a question of doing the best for oneself one can — without injury to others' ". Like all the other words he speaks at the end, and especially his last, they appear to give scant comfort to this figure whose solitariness here has little to do with his foreignness, which can indeed now be seen to pertain not only to the national and the social but also to the domestic and deeply personal (II, 349, 92, I, 58).

Nothing is rounded off with the neatness of which Hardy[15] complained; rather, as Chernaik[16] argued, no formulation of the knowledge known is possible — and, as Conrad insisted, Mr James never attempts the impossible. I suggest that my account of his linguistic tactics bears out the intention apparent in his structural strategies: that this character has his case, as does each of the other characters, and that as it is embodied in nothing less than the total impact of the whole novel, it must constantly be seen in relation to all these other cases.

I therefore move on to the second of the figures so interestingly delineated from the earliest pages of it, Charlotte Stant.

NOTES

1. Carl Maves, *Sensuous Pessimism: Italy in the Work of Henry James* (Bloomington, Indiana: Indiana U.P., 1973), pp. 146, 138. Hereafter *Sensuous Pessimism.*
2. James, *The Golden Bowl* (London: Methuen, 1905), p. 203. Hereafter *GB* (Methuen).
3. James, *The Wings of the Dove.* 2 vols. XIX and XX. *The Novels and Tales of Henry James.* (New York: Scribner, 1907-9), II, 289.
4. James, *GB* (Methuen), p. 349.
5. James, *Prefaces*, p. 329.
6. Oscar Cargill, *The Novels of Henry James* (New York: Macmillan, 1961), p. 391. Hereafter *Novels HJ.*
7. Daniel J. Schneider, "The Divided Self in the Fiction of Henry James", *PMLA* 90 (May 1975): p. 453. Hereafter *Divided Self.*
8. Tony Tanner, "*The Golden Bowl* and the Reassessment of Innocence", *The London Magazine* 1:2 (November 1961): 44. Hereafter *Tanner GB.*
9. *Dupee HJ*, p. 264.
10. Christof Wegelin, "The 'Internationalism' of *The Golden Bowl*", *Nineteenth-Century Fiction* 2 (December 1956), p. 180. Hereafter *Internationalism.*
11. Blackmur, *Intro. GB*, pp. xx-xxi.
12. Krook, *Ordeal*, p. 257.
13. In Bayley, *Characters of Love*, Pearson, *Novel to End Novels* and Maves, *Sensuous Pessimism.*
14. Girling, *Slang*, p. 137.
15. Hardy, *Appropriate Form*, p. 46; commenting on *The Ambassadors.*
16. Chernaik, *Moralist*, pp. 106, 120, 121.

B. Charlotte and distanced empathy

The characterization of Charlotte, has occupied a major part of critical attention. This is partly because those seeing her as a villainess have had to compete with a day and age taking a less theatrical view of adulteresses, partly because critical emphasis has swung from her "sin" to her "punishment"; but it is mainly because the problems presented by James's apparent conception of her are further compounded by those of his increasingly indirect rendering of her. She is "off" for much of Book Second, and throughout the ceremony of farewell we hear directly no word from her. She is the subject of the other characters' discussion but she is never permitted to become at this point the exclusive object of the reader's immediate attention.

R.W. Short, Krook and Maves[1] released the issues of debate from confinement to "bad" Charlotte and "poor" Charlotte and tried to look at more of what James has given us about her. What Charlotte does is too clear to need any gloss; it is *why* she consciously and deliberately wills herself to reply to Fanny as she does, to *appear* to be morally insensible, and *how* she can so persistently sustain such an appearance, that seems to be the interest James wants us to cultivate. Like Kate Croy, who declared she was a person who could do things she did not like, Charlotte the worldly sophisticate can see realities and refuse them. We may be being treated to something much more breathtaking than her refusal to recognize her guilt; we seem to be being shown her refusal to recognize the impossibility of her successfully fulfilling her conscious will with *that* lover in *those* circumstances. Driven by a profound passion of which her pride is an incidental expression, she would seem well beyond the redemption Krook believes in; and James's text appears less concerned with asserting the great moral commonplaces than with showing the pathetic courage of her clearly futile attempt to manoeuvre among them.

When Elizabeth Owen considered Charlotte's "given appearance"[2] she did not see that it might be given in a way that so strongly implied not only the "apparent life" but also "the unapparent [life], in which things *really* happen to us"[3] — as James put it in that letter to Edith Wharton. Thus, "a taken meaning" neglects the full "quantity of truth" in it unless we remember that here, as always in this major manner, any "given appearance" is itself given the context first of the authorial ushering and ultimately of the whole novel. Miss Owen argued that James relies on how Book First opens our "blind eyes" to Charlotte as Maggie has hers opened in Book Second, but our eyes may be opened to much more in both books. True, Charlotte does use " 'straightness' " as a weapon, just as she manipulates and contrives her "effect"[4], and James ensures that we see and hear all this. But, as a characterization within this major mode she is not an actress of the English stage at the turn of the century; she is an actress trained in the far subtler *histrionique* of the *Comédie Française* of that day and this is what James is simulating by all that makes his "principle of the Scenario" so "divine" to him. The result keeps her actions vivid, their consequences more ominous than she will admit and the motives behind them the most arresting and moving part of her role in the whole drama (I, 354, II, 350, I, 354).

This is why Maves's subsequent remarks about her avowed willingness to be found stupid do not take us far enough; "Charlotte for all her fine flexibility, cannot adjust her pride to circumstances that require an admission of ignorance". It is, for those around her, apparently her pride that prevents her adjustment; for us, I shall argue, it is her passion that creates the inflexibility most fatal to her. The appearance of *all* we are given suggests that it is not an admission of ignorance, of what the others may or may not "know", that is beyond her but an admission to herself of what we know. She has no trouble giving any appearance any meaning she wishes, but James always helps us take the full meaning of it. So when Maves says that "life is a game she can only play offensively; experience at first stimulates, but finally baffles her, for she cannot let it alter the fixed idea of her triumphant superiority",[5] he ignores the entire later part of the novel in which she is patently aware of being not triumphant and where what she cannot let life alter is her fixed idea not of her superiority but of her passional priority with Maggie's husband.

The way in which James may want us to accept his characterization will depend on the kind, the timing, the reliability and the full quantity of the information he gives us about her from point to point in his narrative and it is to this that I now turn.

My account of the characterization of the Prince suggests that James is apparently interested in that young man's initial uncertainties, his vulnerability to manipulation and the way he develops too a new though still divided state of mind. Any interest in Charlotte, like her impact on the other characters, would seem to derive from exactly the opposite condition: she knows precisely what she wants to do, why she wants to do it, how she believes she can do it. She knows these things vividly from the first and for three-quarters of the narrative; right up to the point, in fact, when she is confronted with quite other courses and it is only then that she knows the bitterness of division. There is in her characterization thus no gradual development to depict, merely a sustained singleness of purpose and a crisis with painful consequences, and she is shown as not being able, or not being willing, to alter her purpose.

She is for these reasons a much simpler character to discuss, for though she is shown in relation to all the other characters all the time, there is nothing in the least incalculable about her motives, for she has only one: the capture of her lover Prince Amerigo. She is the only character who is herself concerned with only one relationship and, for as long as she can entertain the illusion of this being sustained, we can have little difficulty in knowing her as she things she knows herself: that is why James can, after her crisis, safely depict her with extreme indirection (necessary for other reasons) without fear of our misreading her even then. She is not one of this novel's complex values; she is its most intense one.

The textual evidence for this view falls very compactly into six stages matching the six parts of the novel. In the first she comes back to the Prince, patently obsessed with the need to assert in one way or another her possession of him. In the second she deliberately, in every sense, puts herself into proximity with him and in the third she works for and achieves with him the closest of physical relationships. In the fourth she remains determined to continue this intimacy as carefully as Maggie's new consciousness of them both will allow; in the fifth she fights, first defensively, then aggressively, always hampered, to cling to him; and in the sixth she is sundered from him.

We see, in all this, Charlottes other than the one who loves the Prince: we see the social ambition that coexists with her passion; we see her acknowledge pressures that could, if she permitted them, deflect her from the fulfilment of that passion; we see a thoroughly credible woman and not a "humour"; and we see it all clearly and immediately from point to point. The structure as well as the text would seem in short to be continually implying that James's interest in her lies not in her adventuress or adulteress aspects, for these are patently obvious facts, nor in vilifying or commending her for them, but in illuminating the consequences, not only for others but also for herself, of her reponse to life as she finds it and tries to make it. The resulting characterization is not in the least simplistic for its having been informed, chiefly, by one over-riding motive.

James ensures that she and her motive enter the novel together. " 'Has she come with designs upon me?' " the Prince humorously asks Fanny Assingham when he goes to her from Bond Street that afternoon on the eve of his marriage. We learn that the "handsome, clever, odd girl" who can ill afford trans-Atlantic crossings, has come straight to London from Southampton and has already spent an hour with Fanny, who, knowing the pair's history, is as a consequence as nervous as he. When she comes in we see ample reasons for all these things. "She could have looked at [Fanny] with such straightness and brightness only from knowing that the Prince was also there" and "that immediate exclusive address to their friend was like a lamp she was holding aloft for his benefit and for his pleasure". He makes a lover's enumeration of all her charms, attesting her success in so holding her lamp, seeing her as having "the sylvan head of a huntress", then seeing her becoming for him "a muse" and "when she did turn to him it was to recognize with her eyes what he might have been doing". Her first words are " 'You see you're not rid of me. How is dear Maggie?' ". But it is her timing and facial expression and not her banter that are most revealing, as when he tells her he and Maggie are going to America. In the original text, "She hesitated;"[6] but in the revised, with significant deliberation:

> ***She waited***: "But now? — Immediately?"
>
> "In a month or two — it seems to be the new idea." ***On which there was something in her face*** — as he imagined — that made him say: "Didn't Maggie write to you?"

When he speaks of the probability of her having seen her way to marrying, "she looked at him an instant, and, during these seconds he feared for what he might have spoiled".

She replies steadily " 'To marrying whom?' " (I, 40, 43, 44, 45, 46, 47, 56, 57).

The whole of this first re-encounter at Fanny's reminds us how sharply and how often we may need to discriminate between what is said and what is shown. Between the Prince's earlier conception of her as needing his help in arranging appearances as "the twentieth women" and her actual arranging of him here exactly where she wants him, is one instance. Dramatic description as well as dramatic dialogue gives us other such differences: between her steely determination and his uneasy response to it; between the image he has given us shortly before of his bride-to-be and the image we receive through him of this lover; between the innocent "niceness" of the young American girl's background and the polyglot origins of this experienced loner. There are also the different precautions she takes when Fanny is present and when Fanny is not. They all signify in her a mastery informed by passion and disciplined by intelligence to one end.

Even her veiled indulgences confirm its intensity, as when, Fanny's banter turning upon the Prince's obligation to bring off a marriage for her, the girl has her revenge: " 'And you must help, dear,' Charlotte said unperturbed — 'as you've helped, so beautifully, in such things before.' " Nor does her bland reference to penny bus rides as her alternative to carriages allow any escape for the young man about to become a millionaire. We are to remember much later her dislike of America and her remarks about " 'mere existence' ", but now these harbingers, like all the talk of " 'omens' ", are details in a scene dominated by what drives Charlotte Stant. In Fanny's report of it to Bob the shock waves are still evident, both in her well-founded anxiety, and in his taciturn conviction, about Charlotte's motives for returning. This Assingham interlude, in providing the history of her Roman time with Amerigo, makes significantly clear that once they had decided to part, she had ensured that the width of the Atlantic must separate them (I, 59, 57, 59, 63-88).

Her walk with him from Green Park to Marble Arch makes equally clear that she has crossed it again with the intention of using every minute of the " 'one hour alone' " together that the excuse of the present-hunting has provided. Knowing her Prince, she knows his unease, so she successfully gives him the overt demonstration that will allay it: "What she gave touched him, as she faced him, for it was the full tune of her renouncing". Thus, the Prince reads her. But she has a moment earlier "read . . . in his face" his consciousness of how this rendezvous evokes their Roman past. James shows her doing what Amerigo expects, precisely because he expects it: she declares her love in words but always with "her eye on him" to mark their effect, and though he can "take it for amusing that she reaffirmed, and reaffirmed again, the truth that was *her* truth", James keeps our eyes and ears alert to every sign that she wants to make it *his* truth, too. " 'I wanted you' — she kept it up, slowly, softly, with a small tremor of voice but without the least failure of sense or sequence — 'I wanted you to understand. I wanted you, that is, to hear. I don't care, I think, whether you understand or not' " (I, 89, 95, 97, 96, 97).

Only after she has given this "a few minutes to sink in" does she add: " 'You may want to know what I get by it. But that's my own affair.' " We can not only reject the words as patently ingenuous protestation: the tumult and turbulence implied behind them testify to her total commitment. Read in the context of the narrative so far, they are telling him that it took only the news of his own impending commitment to someone else to prove to her satisfaction that the parting did not, will not, work and that she is willing to ignore now the logic, the financial detail, that prompted it. He hears them well enough, as he hears too her later remarks about Maggie which she makes "with a serenity of appreciation that was odd, certainly, as a sequel to her words of ten minutes before": and he hears her develop the subject of Maggie's character. "She had spoken thoughtfully, her eyes on her friend's; she might have been talking, preoccupied and practical, of some one with whom he was comparatively unconnected." When suggesting that Maggie's absolute unselfishness imposes strains that " 'nobody . . . is decent enough, good enough, to stand' " without extra spiritual resources, she pointedly adds: " 'certainly . . . such people as you and I are not' ". Though he resists these tacit pleas for identification with her, she consistently implies their oneness and she merely simulates agreement with his rejoinders about their consequent obligations by finally replying, we are told, "reasonably" (I, 98, 100, 101, 102, 103).

James very evidently takes care to preserve the interest of this knife-edge balance of hers throughout the time at the antiquarian's where, as they can find no trinket for Maggie, the Prince asks her if there is anything for herself. It makes her start and she looks not at the objects but "for an instant very directly at him" before refusing. Any such *ricordo*, he carefully explains, would be " 'of this little hunt' " and not of any earlier time and so she responds as challengingly as she can: " 'A *ricordo* from you — from you to me — is a *ricordo* of nothing. It has no reference' ": and she later underlines her appeal: " 'You don't refer . . . *I* refer' ". When he in turn refuses to accept anything from her, we learn that "She exhaled a long breath that was like a guarded sigh" (I, 108, 109).

The shock of discovering that the antiquarian has understood their Italian makes it for Amerigo altogether too much the old Roman time. When the produced bowl is seen by him to be cracked, he escapes to await her in the street, while she, "frankly charmed with the cup" which she can so readily identify with him, gives us, indirectly, her musings on how she may still reconcile her relationship and his marriage. She is "unsatisfied, mystified". Holding the bowl, she is holding for her what is most precious. " 'I want it. But I must decide what I can do.' " It is in fact Amerigo who decides. Though, outside again in Bloomsbury with him, she offers it to him, even lying about the price by reducing it by two-thirds in case the money should be his reason, he emphatically rejects it, confronting her with his deep-rooted superstition and, more devastatingly, with his concern for *his* " 'happiness' " and " 'safety' " which he identifies with his " 'marriage' " and with " 'everything' " (I, 114, 116, 117, 119).

It is a turning point for her, and James ensures that it is also the interest of her reaction as well as that of her partner's that can here command our attention. His condition for accepting any gift for himself is that he not keep it *to* himself. "Well, she looked, before him there, at the condition — then abruptly, with a gesture, she gave it up. She had a headshake of disenchantment — so far as the idea had appealed to her. It all appeared too difficult." His promise to give her something when she marries patently pushes her too far. "She took it from him, but it determined in her the only words she was to have uttered, all the morning, that came out as if a spring had been pressed. 'To make you feel better?' " Thus is Charlotte Stant shown as losing this first round — attesting her passion but not having it at this stage acknowledged by the object of it (I, 120, 121).

In Part Second she is shown as having given away that fight in order to fight again in a new way. Though she is seen at a distance in the first five of the seven chapters in this part, James's having permitted her to dominate the former one ensures that we remain aware not only of her but also of her chief preoccupation. Her nature as we essentially know it is thus what prevails when we encounter the irony of Maggie's describing her as " 'brave and bright' ", to an Adam amusedly bringing his daughter's idealized sketch closer to reality. We are in a position better than Adam's to appreciate the irony of her effusions about Charlotte's " 'courage and her cleverness,' . . . great imagination, . . .

great attitude . . . great conscience . . .'." Not unexpectedly her father responds to this naive effusion with irony of which she remains unaware. " 'She *was* . . . the one of your friends I thought the best for you.' " When, still serving our double vision, they discuss whether Charlotte's " 'condition' " is " 'that of having loved so intensely that she's . . . "beyond everything" ' ", James of course lets them reveal much about themselves but he is not letting us forget the altogether different levels of reality, and intensity, on which we have already known Charlotte and what drives her (I, 180, 180-1, 181, 182, 188).

A month later, after Charlotte has arrived and rid Fawns of the Misses Lutch and Mrs Rance, Adam learns even less about her from the fatuous Mrs Assingham than he did from Maggie. He conceals his amusement by merely repeating everything she says. Our own ironic view, different from Adam's, is served rather by Fanny's asinine " 'I don't pretend to be sure in every connexion of what Charlotte knows' " and her opinion, regarding the ridding of the other guests, that Charlotte simply " 'saw how effectively she could work' ". She must indeed rid the scene of those whose life-style resembles so closely the homeless wandering state we have just heard Maggie describe to Adam as Charlotte's own (I, 194).

We see how effectively she works with Adam himself when the young couple go off to Rome and she becomes the sedulous letter-writer reporting the health of the Principino, becomes in fact "a domestic resource", plays for him each evening "his 'favourite things' . . . with a facility that never failed, or that failed but just enough to pick itself up at a touch from his fitful voice". During the visit to Gutermann-Seuss she makes sure she enjoys a popular success and throughout the purchase of the Damascene tiles proves "capable . . . of the right felicity of silence". The girl we see working so purposefully in the middle distance is ever the one we have known earlier in the foreground, to which, during the Brighton and Paris interludes, she returns (I, 201, 202, 215).

During both, the Prince is more present to her than is her suitor. When the proposal is made, she dismisses the disparity in their ages; when asked if she can " 'face such a union' " she literally does so: "She had another pause, and she might have been felt as facing it while . . . she met his eyes without evasion" — thus she is shown as avoiding a negative rather than as affirming a positive and her response echoes her discussion with the Prince at Fanny's when she had pointedly asked him, " 'You think I ought to argue for more than mere existence?' " Now she more steadily tells Adam: " 'I should like to have an existence' ". Adam continues to misinterpret her diffidence and if his apologetic account of himself as a person who is far from the " 'natural, . . . ideal' " match for her does not sufficiently evoke for us the Prince, his "dim vision of some objection in her mind beside which the one he had named was light, and which therefore must be strangely deep", surely does (I, 219, 57, 219, 220).

Her obvious hesitancy and preoccupation when he speaks of having " 'known' " her strike him as "oddly conscientious" and " 'very, very honorable' ", but clearly she is not asking Adam questions to which she does not already know the answers. She knows full well what Maggie means to him; just as she knows that his idea of putting Maggie at ease is insufficient reason for her to accept this proposal. She continues silently to extrapolate. When he asks " 'Isn't a man's idea usually what he does marry for?' ", "Charlotte, considering, looked as if this might perhaps be a large question, or at all events something of an extension of one they were immediately concerned with". Charlotte, very sure of Amerigo's "idea" in not marrying her and in marrying Maggie, listens to Adam's further argument about his marriage giving the other couple greater freedom together, and James is precise as to how she listens. "Charlotte ***appeared to examine for a minute, in Maggie's interest,*** this privilege — the result of which was a limited concession. 'You've certainly worked it out!' " (I, 221, 222, 224).

It is also a very limited response, consequential only to his words and not at all to her thoughts. But there are sharper thoughts yet to be confronted. When he suggests, " 'We'll go straight to Paris to meet them' ", we learn: "Charlotte, at this, rose with a movement that was like a small cry; but her unspoken sense lost itself while she stood with eyes on him . . .". During this remarkable proposal scene in which neither of the parties is primarily concerned with the other — the man being explicitly solicitous of his daughter, the woman being implicitly conscious of another man she greatly loves — her unspoken sense of complexities dominates it to the end (I, 225).

In Paris they intensify. Adam cannot plumb her: "she made him fidget". She keeps looking at him harder than seems warranted, and when he hands her Maggie's telegram, he senses in her look "a dim shy fear", but he concludes, ironically, this means "that — as a man, so to speak — he properly pleased her". He mentally notes that on reading Maggie's words of " 'love and joy and sympathy' " she does not say they are "enough — though he saw the next moment that her silence was probably not disconnected from her having just visibly turned pale". He cannot know the strain his plan for a rendezvous of the foursome in Rome places on her. "This seemed to hold her — as he had previously seen her held, just a trifle inscrutably, by his allusions to what they would do together on a certain contingency." She can barely conceal her emotion when he regards Amerigo's possible wishes, also, as totally subservient to Maggie's: "His tone made her for a moment meet his face . . ." (I, 229, 230, 231, 232).

But Adam's mystifications, which further focus attention on Charlotte's conflicts, turn to frustrated impatience as she stalls for time — while pretending that that is what Maggie is doing — and James's figurative account of the scene itself generates in the hotel court, "overarched and glazed", a suffocating atmosphere at once exotically hothouse and clinically portentous. It is heated, gilded and draped, "muffled against loud sounds and guarded against crude sights" but it resembles too "some 'dental', medical, surgical waiting-room, a scene of mixed anxiety and desire, preparatory, for gathered barbarians, to the due amputation or extraction of excrescences and redundancies of barbarism". Here in Adam's pampered, indulged world, Charlotte will make decisions based on a false private assumption and having immense repercussions for all of them (II, 232, 233).

From this figure onward Amerigo is brought, metaphoricaly and literally, even closer to Charlotte's side and thus to our even closer attention. When Adam asks if it is incredible to her " 'that when a man is still as much in love as Amerigo' " he should want to comply with his wife's wishes, her reply is for us, ambivalent enough. " 'No — nothing is incredible to me of people immensely in love.' " He promptly enough rejoins: " 'Well, isn't Amerigo immensely in love?' " and we are told that "she hesitated but *as for the right expression of her sense of the degree* — but she after all adopted Mr Verver's. 'Immensely.' " Charlotte believes she knows with whom he is so immensely in love, so she hesitates while finding an acceptable form of reminding Adam that Amerigo " 'has never seen [Maggie] do anything else' " but what her father wanted. Then James introduces the word for which the elaborate exotic-surgical figure has so recently prepared the way.

" 'To what catastrophe will he have observed such a disposition in her to lead?' " Adam asks, to which she promptly replies: " 'Just to *this* one.' With which she struck him as rising straighter and clearer before him than she had done even yet. 'Our little question itself?' Her appearance had in fact, at the moment, such an effect on him that he could answer but in marvelling mildness. 'Hadn't we better wait a while till we call it a catastrophe?' " (I, 233, 234).

The whole remarkable scene is indeed one of "mixed anxiety and desire", the anxieties of each being as different as are the desires of each. The mixture is of course greatest for Charlotte, who is already growing painfully aware of the consequences of her so soon getting what she wants and who can see so much more truly the form and reality of the immediate future. During the high banter which Adam initiates about a possible telegram from Amerigo and in which she only appears to participate, he tells her that Amerigo will not telegram: " '*He* doesn't know you're morbid.' She just wondered — but she agreed. 'No — he hasn't yet found it out. Perhaps he will, but he hasn't yet; and I'm willing to give him meanwhile the benefit of the doubt.' " The painful turning of the ironic screw continues remorselessly, mainly by Adam's unconscious hand. He reminds her that " 'naturally' " Maggie will speak for Amerigo and when she "had a demur" at the word, he talks about her *new* relation to Amerigo. " 'About its making me his stepmother-in-law — or whatever I *should* become?' Over which for a little, she not undivertedly mused. 'Yes, there may easily be enough for a gentleman to say to a young woman about that.' " There is a half-turn more to be made; he *explains* him to her.

> And then as the girl, with one of her so deeply and oddly, yet so tenderly critical looks at him, failed to take up the remark, he found himself moved, as by a vague anxiety, to add a question. "Don't you think he's charming?"
> "Oh charming," said Charlotte Stant. "If he weren't I shouldn't mind."
> "No more should I!" her friend harmoniously returned (I, 233, 236, 237, 238).

This proves to be the final intolerable twist and she breaks out in a speech that is the companion of the passionate declaration to her lover in the Park; she makes it *about* him, in a sense *to* him; she makes it in another sense about and to herself. It is as passionate as, but more interesting than, her former cry, because now her situation makes so many more demands on her. We are much later to hear yet other Charlottes but we never hear so directly a more beleaguered one. She speaks here of all that makes her distant from Adam's world, Adam's daughter and that daughter's situation and she defines herself for us in the most arresting dramatic terms that signal how, in these two interludes with Adam, her emotions will trace out the same kind of trajectory they did in the earlier ones with Amerigo. These will end as those did, in a defeat that is sounding already in her voice:

> "Ah but you *don't* mind. You don't have to. You don't have to, I mean, as I have. It's the last folly ever to care, in an anxious way, the least particle more than one's absolutely forced. If I were you," she went on — "if I had in my life, for happiness and power and peace, even a small fraction of what you have, it would take a great deal to make me waste my worry. I don't know," she said, "what in the world — that didn't touch my luck — I should trouble my head about" (I, 238).

Nothing could better serve James in his "case" for Charlotte than the appearance *it* — not only she — is given here, and nothing could better serve that case's function among all the others in the novel as a congruous whole than the immediate context of this scene, which stresses entrapment, isolation, differences. The ways in which it reveals Charlotte as limited, as possibly "wrong", in her view of what constitutes " 'happiness and power and peace' " are only less interesting than the ways they reveal her as possibly, partly, perceptive and "right". We understand her, we "share" her emotions, but the further, the distinctive, aesthetic value she contributes is that because she is so consistently distanced, she transcends her particularity, not only as a character in this novel (she is but one for whom a case is made) but as a characterization of an individual human being. The dramatic poetry generates here that general reach and universal reference for which Krook so praised the later prose.

In the former interludes she had eventually to admit herself defeated and there was that "headshake of disenchantment"; this time, as her lover's telegram commits her to telling Adam that she will give him what he asks, she does use the word Adam had expected of her in vain when Maggie's approving missive had been received. Adam says, " 'Then it's best of all' "; she says, " 'It's enough' ". He asks if it is " 'funny' ", for that, we recall, was one of the alternative forms of it he foresaw; James's scenario supplies: "Thus, finally, she again dropped her eyes on it, drawing in her lips a little. 'No — I call it grave.' " She has got what she wants but not on her own terms. This is the most direct account we have so far received of the solitariness she feels but refuses to accept (I, 121, 240, 241).

I have tried to show in my interpretive analysis of this scene that from speech to speech, indeed from phrase to phrase, the implications for motive and consequence multiply, while figurative language such as the "waiting-room" image supplies, informs our cogitation with a vivid and emotionally potent summary of the diversity of emotions that are relevant to any justly full appreciation of it. We are kept by James at precisely the distance which should ensure we see it clearly and see it all. We are active participants in an effort at understanding the data that the scenario is endlessly embodying, synthesizing, formulating. None of this can smother Charlotte as a unique fictive person, for James provides for our seeing and hearing and thinking with her; all of it prevents us from doing that only.

The word "interesting" is the safest word to use to describe that attention we direct to her at this moment, just as it proved the least cumbersome one to describe the kind we direct to the Prince and may, as I hope later to show, serve well to describe the appeal of Adam, of the Assinghams and of Maggie. "Compassionate" is too close to "sympathetic" and that in turn is too close to those stances we are asked to take up in relation to some other characters in some other novels: to Dorothea Brooke, say, or even to Natasha Rostov, whom we certainly know as intensely. "Interesting", which may seem too cold a word, is really the most compendious one, subsuming these others, connoting the intimacy of our knowledge of Charlotte and the detachment with which we ponder its context. It is at least a word that precludes the relatively simpler, directer sort of nexus established for us with Emma Bovary or Anna Karenina; just as it precludes the kinds of literary "value" inherent in James's own earlier characterization: Madame Merle remains merely a manipulator; even the machinations of those who surround Nanda and Maisie can be classed and pigeon-holed much more readily. To begin to do justice to the originality of *any* of the characters in *The Golden Bowl*, we must, keeping well within the major period, consider Madame de Vionnet and then ponder Kate Croy. Immediately, *then*, we recognise, in the literary experience we have of these true kinfolk of Charlotte's, a higher degree of the same very special kind of literary attention with which James renders her for our appreciation. This is a rendering faithful at once to her individuality, to her multiple motives, to her modulation among many kinds of desire and to all the relationships making up her predicament and bringing pressures to bear upon her. We cannot help seeing her as she is; we cannot possibly see only her. Acutely conscious as we are of her particular conditions, we are kept just as conscious of the more general human conditions we share with her.

James's major sophistication of the nineteenth-century novel enables it to generate, here in the new century that was to know the Joycean "epiphany", a way of experiencing character that is obviously similar but importantly different. Both methods evoke creations that "bristle" with suggestion; both solidly specify all the relevant conditions, keeping the context faithfully dense. But the Jamesian strategies, and chiefly among these the Jamesian language, prevent the luxury of simple identification or even the richer luxury of enjoying at the level of spiritual empathy and recognition a sort of literary Mass, a common oneness.

His whole art insists that as well as identifying with all the characters all the time, we think hard about what their common predicament precisely implies. It insists that we continue exercising our intellects (as well as our imaginations and emotions) on these challenging implications which it is constantly causing to ramify for us in profuse detail.

The "scenic" component of the "divine principle of the Scenario", ensures that this art of fiction will approach the simultaneity of presentation that the stage dramatist enjoys, whereby we remain aware in the one instant of all the characters present. The "histrionic" component, deriving from the authorial "focus" on significant pause, silence and action, ensures that we remain aware also of those absent and of the significant consciousness those present have of them. So James keeps us very busy: he gives us Charlotte here but that means he gives us also Amerigo; he gives us Adam but that means he gives us Maggie, too. We cannot avoid having to conjure with all four all the time. If at any given moment our attention is drawn to motive, then the motives of all become relevant; just as, if the issue be consequences, then the consequences for all become relevant.

There is nothing ambiguous about this multivalence; the rendering achieves its comprehensiveness without losing its important particulars. The motives for Charlotte's deciding to marry — and the motives for her hesitation — are spelled out very clearly, even enumerated. They are very different from Adam's, which are frankly enough explicated. What of the Prince's? The witnessed discussion of these reveals, under the scenario system, that they are read quite differently by Adam, by Charlotte and, it is implied, by Maggie. Further, Maggie's motive for marrying the Prince is unmistakable, as are those for her encouragement of the marriage of her father and her friend. There is thus for a reader during this scene just such a buzz of cogitation and calculation. As concurrently as the temporal art of fiction will allow, we are committed by this art to cogitate also upon the consequences that have resulted from Maggie's marriage and which could emerge from this one to which Charlotte has just committed herself. They are consequences such as she, rather than as Adam or Maggie or even Amerigo, can envisage them, but certainly the lives of all will be inexorably affected. This "major" art makes clear that while Adam is mainly aware of his responsibility to Maggie, Charlotte is at this point aware of the responsibilities she incurs for all of them.

Charlotte fails to win from Amerigo's telegram the response she wants; she succeeds, by her impending marriage, only in putting herself in proximity to him. Henceforth she is to attempt to exploit her achieved advantages, first boldly, then cautiously; and ultimately she is to face defeat with as much dignity as frustration and anguish will permit. We do learn more of her, but nothing that diminishes or develops her one passional commitment. We are kept aware of two things: she will never relax her self-imposed discipline as pursuer of Amerigo and she cannot win.

If we were not alert to James's careful provisions for establishing the latter fact by the end of Part First, it must certainly have been established beyond doubt by the end of Part Second. Throughout Part Third, where we see her in several scenes — triumphant at the Embassy Ball, defiant of the Assinghams, seeking and embracing Amerigo and fully in command at Matcham of the plans to consummate her passion with him at Gloucester — James's scenario quietly insists on her doom, until, at the end of this part, Fanny's account of Maggie's new state of alertness implies that doom unequivocally. In Part Fourth, Charlotte, shown indirectly now, in the middle distance, is seen as correspondingly alert, joining with Amerigo in "treating" Maggie. In Part Fifth, Maggie's "caged beast" escapes and we see her, at first aggressively defensive with Maggie on the terrace at Fawns, later "haltered" and in anguish in the gallery, then, as in the terrace scene, in "close-up" again, this time with

Maggie in the garden rotunda where both play roles to conceal their real feelings and to feign others, Charlotte playing the injured wife. The part ends by again presenting her anguish with an extreme of indirection through the images of Maggie's hypothetical account of her and in Part Sixth she is one of the effigies in the final tableau, trying to salvage dignity from the complete defeat that her implied suffering insists she cannot even now accept.

Yet no matter how close or far James places her during all six parts of her passionate battle, he preserves with absolute constancy the *kind* of "interest" in her that I have tried to define. Never for a moment, amid the countless opportunities for such a deflection, does he give us any warrant for changing moral consciousness into moral judgment. Never are we encouraged to ponder her on her own; always the scenario forces us to ponder her in the company of her complicating companions and thus we are kept busy sharing with James his implied consciousness of the multivalence of motive and of consequence in the general spectacle of human gesture and response. Only if we thus accept the discipline James's final art imposes on his subject and demands of his reader will we see a coherent Charlotte and understand her function in the novel. We will "take" the "meaning" only when we thus keep ourselves immune from the potentially distracting "appearance" she is from point to point "given".

My argument may be borne out as I resume closer analysis of the last four parts, sparse though the direct rendering of her is in them after Part Fourth. We do, as I said above, see her at the beginning of Part Third, triumphant at the formal Embassy function; "at no moment yet had she been so justified of her faith . . .". Only when she sees Bob Assingham quietly regarding her is she aware of "an arrest of vibration, a more muffled thump", but she summons "an easy command" to meet the crisis of this her first appearance with Amerigo alone. The exultation she feels in her social success is subordinate to what her personal repossession of her lover inspires in her: "it was when he reached her and she could, taking his arm, show herself as placed in her relation, that she felt supremely justified". The last four words reach back, to our first sight of her in Fanny's drawing room, recalling by the way our scenes with her in Green Park and in Bloomsbury, in Brighton and in Paris. We recognize what has driven her this distance. James spares no emphasis. "The Prince was at present for instance, though he had quitted her but ten minutes before, still more than then the person it pleased her to be left with." Nor, of course, does James omit her consciousness of Bob Assingham: "she was aware that, ***in spite of*** hovering and warning inward voices, ***she even enjoyed*** the testimony rendered by his lonely vigil to the lustre she reflected" (I, 245, 246, 248, 249).

I have dealt in the introduction to this section with the point James seems to be making about her defiance during the subsequent scene with Fanny. The interest of it, I repeat, is in *why* she so deliberately chooses and plays such a role and the way it increasingly appears doomed to failure, despite the brilliant consistency of her playing. Though she makes undeniable truths her chief evidence during the dialectic of this confrontation, it is this other undeniable truth that James keeps before us. We would certainly be the last to deny that, as she tells her accuser, she remains alone with Amerigo now because that is one of her husband's preferences, all of which she accepts " 'absolutely, as a fixed rule' "; that his feeling for his daughter is " 'the greatest affection of which he's capable' "; that she, Charlotte, has done all she could to " 'make him capable of a greater' "; that she had of course been " 'duly warned' " by him as to why he married her; and that " 'Maggie thinks more on the whole of fathers than of husbands' ". We have already watched and listened to all those facts; and we have Fanny's own earlier testimony as to the truth of Charlotte's reminder that she and the Prince have " 'shown together' " before, during, of course, their Roman adventure (I, 257, 262, 257).

The other truth is just as continually attested and by the girl herself. She has reached this line of action and committed herself to this "process" solely by her own decision: "no one, not even Amerigo — ***Amerigo least of all, who would have nothing to do with it*** — had given her aid." Here, as in those earlier scenes and, I believe I can demonstrate, in ensuing ones, James reminds us of how unfounded is her confidence in how far she can rely on her lover. Much more potent evidence than that parenthetical comment is the tenor of her reply when Fanny asks whether the Prince arranges to come and see her. "She shook her head, but it was beautifully gentle. 'He never comes' ". As she goes on candidly to declare as to its being " 'too absurd' " that they " 'shouldn't meet' ", we are shown the determined impatience that should be replaced by the requisite insight. All the initiatives are too clearly hers for the limits of his commitment not to be significantly obvious, or for her actual solitariness not to be written legibly enough on the wall of the reader's interested attention (I, 250, 255, 260).

One such initiative is her joining him in Portland Place at the tea hour, during which her rationalizations that precede their passionate embrace remain on the periphery of that attention. We know well enough that they have not "done everything to avoid" their "relation of mutual close contact", and so does Amerigo. James signals this — and the distance from which we may best contemplate it — by the tense of the subtly reported scene. "***She was to remember*** not a little meanwhile the particular prolonged silent look with which the Prince had met her allusion to these primary efforts at escape. ***She was inwardly to dwell*** on the element of the unuttered that her tone had caused to play up into his irresistible eyes; and this because she ***considered*** with pride and joy that she ***had*** on the spot ***disposed*** of the doubt, the question, the challenge, or whatever else ***might have been***, that such a look ***could*** convey." Those things which she was to remember are things of which we are made immediately conscious; the element of the unuttered that plays up for our eyes to see is not disposed of on the spot, for it clearly might, and indeed, can, convey to us certainties that make movingly ironic her present pride and joy (I, 289).

It is now, too, that James chooses we should learn the precise form of Amerigo's telegram to her. Couched firmly within the pragmatic terms of war ("'*A la guerre comme à la guerre then*'"), it makes a careful use of the plural ("'*We must lead our lives as we see them*'"), that is lost on her, for though it "had remained ambiguous", she limits her readings to those that could commit him to cooperation with her: her marriage "would compel him to live still more under arms" or, whatever the dangers of it, "she was to think of him as prepared in advance, as reasonably seasoned and secure". Its caution is for us the self-precaution of the lover who will cooperate only as far as is compatible with his "safety". This is the context in which she now persistently refers to their unity and he as persistently disclaims it. Her not having a child, she says, "'leaves us . . . more alone'". He seemed to wonder. 'It leaves *you* more alone'". But she chooses not to admit this discrimination and instead emphasizes their oneness. "It's as strange as you like, but we're immensely alone.'" Again he refuses the begged reaction. "He kept vaguely moving . . ." and when he does confront her, "with an awkward ease", he finds that "these last words" of hers "had the effect of making him for the little throw back his head and, as thinking something out, stare up at the ceiling". It is thus amid our lucid awareness of who in this scene is most "alone" that we are told how Adam's wife and Maggie's husband "passionately sealed their pledge" (I, 290, 291, 307, 308, 312).

Throughout the remainder of Part Third, Charlotte's increase in confidence correlates positively with James's reminders of how unwarranted it is, especially during her time with Amerigo at Matcham where her notion of their being " '*safe*' " contrasts so illuminatingly with his own notion of " 'safety' ". There, on the morning of their Gloucester visit, she smiles down at him from the window, while he reflects on the " 'rightness' " of their " 'union' " and the prose formulates for us the view we may take of it all. "What in fact most often happened was that her rightness went, as who should say, even further than his own" — a strangely detached rumination for the lover to whom she flings the white rosebud. "As who should say" summons as witness the *ghost* of a spectator, which we cannot help being (I, 343, 356).

James continues to extend this invitation in the formula his language provides during their ensuing discussion because the images and diction refer, with such reach, far back and far forward. For the Prince, the day is "a great gold cup" and when she reminds him of the " 'gilded crystal bowl' " he refused to accept from her, *that* is for him still " 'the treacherous cracked thing' " and when she confesses with bravura her willingness to "risk the cracks' ", his reply shows *us*, at least, he has not budged an inch from the position he confessed long before in Bloomsbury. " 'Risk them as much as you like for yourself, but don't risk them for me.' " Their history foreshadows their future but her pride and her joy still prevent her reading either (I, 359, 360).

Her passion is never attested in any scene more potently or possessively than in the moment that follows and, given the context which, image and dialogue remind us, is no less than the entire antecedent narrative, that passion has never yet been seen as so utterly isolating her. He says he goes by his superstitions. "Resting on the parapet toward the great view she was silent a little, and he saw the next moment that her eyes were closed. 'I go but by one thing . . . . I go by *you*,' she said. 'I go by you.' " Her eyes are soon to be opened, refuse to see though she still may, and the prose remains so redolent of her doom that even their later casual reference to the tomb they will visit can reverberate ominously. Her own last words in this part contain her fatal premise. How will he ever keep anything from her? " 'Ah for things I mayn't want to know I promise you shall find me stupid' " (I, 360, 363).

It is some time before we see Charlotte again at such close quarters. Throughout Part Fourth she is glimpsed in Maggie's recollections of her and we see her once in the middle distance with "her" Prince, not this time on their private parapet but on the balcony of his Portland Place home, amid the keener tensions created by Maggie's and Adam's new consciousness of them. In Part Fifth, where James emphasizes the suffering she endures as she recognizes yet still refuses to accept her doom, the intensity of our impression is in direct ratio to the indirection of the rendering. Our impression includes Maggie's and, insofar as hers explicates what we have earlier seen dramatized for us, it is acceptable. Thus, "the spacious but suspended cage" imagined by Maggie as protecting her from Charlotte and containing such "baffled consciousness" as Amerigo's silence now creates, is, as Maggie explicitly tells us, "the deluded condition" but it has "bars richly gilt" and it is therefore also the one Charlotte has built around herself and fastened firm with Adam's gold. Thus, too, Maggie images our thought as well as her own when she sees her as "off in some darkness of space that would steep her in solitude and harass her with care". We may therefore continue to "feel" with the one without ceasing to "feel" with the other, and we are never given, the while, any warrant for forgetting the relation of both to Amerigo and to Adam (II, 229, 230, 250).

What James does in the next three chapters, the two closing this part and the one opening the next, is to bring to bear on this penultimate account of Charlotte those resources of his major art which, apparently, may best ensure that she will be even more fully present to us in the two final chapters of the novel than she is to the characters who there discuss her. A trio of his most sophisticated devices is employed. She is presented in highly graphic scenes; she is presented figuratively with the greatest potency; and she is presented dramatically, not only through her actual but also through her hypothetical utterances. The visual, the figurative and the dramatic — as the later James can reflect them in Maggie's crowded mind — serve the more ample as well as the more intense rendering for, addicted as he is "to seeing 'through' — one thing through another, accordingly, and still more things through *that*"[7] he manages also to let us see how Fanny, Amerigo and Adam see her. He would thus seem concerned to give her "case" with as much fullness as is compatible with his giving us too the "cases" of all those who are such integral parts of her own.

The examples of scenic vividness enhanced by what I may now be permitted to call the long-reaching context are of course her encounters with Maggie, at Fawns on the terrace at night and in the garden in mid-afternoon. In the first we learn of her "high elegance", her "noble erectness", and these appearances are now informed by a conscious defiance that James is at pains to point up by revision. In the earlier version Maggie receives from her "this effect, unmistakably, of [her] timing" Maggie's "indecision" and "fear";[8] in the final version the adverb becomes "flagrantly". Later still, she is bereft of her characteristic social persona, of her confident command. We see her face "ruefully" addressed to the prospect of returning to an America she loathes. Maggie can "watch for its turning pale" as Charlotte contemplates the " 'doomed' " state and the eyes are now "grave". During the rotunda duologue we learn that "she bristled with the signs of her extremity" that her now tattered mantle of pride can no longer conceal. It is a Charlotte to whom has been revealed the gulf that we have long known to be there. In the duologues Maggie imagines between the now sundered lovers, we recognize the voice of a Prince we have known and that Charlotte has refused to acknowledge (II, 243, 242, 283, 312).

The resumptive qualities in the imagery enable it to embrace and reproduce much that has gone before and the notorious "silken halter" simile serves this function by reminding us how the "freedom" that Charlotte has celebrated or protested or embodied is now nullified. For the Prince, as he so knowledgeably beholds her again at Fanny's that afternoon before his marriage, she had had "a reference in all her person . . . to winds and waves and custom-houses, to far countries and long journeys . . .". In Bloomsbury she had told him she would marry, she thought, to have something from him "in all freedom" and she had from the beginning of their intrigue recognized how they "might enjoy together extraordinary freedom". When she came to him in Portland Place at the tea hour, despite the inclement weather and without her own carriage, she had first explained, " 'It makes me feel as I used to — when I could do as I liked' ", and she had then detailed her freely-roving tour of the London "sights". That move in itself was a direct result of her decision, taken during her first frankly sharp encounter with Fanny, that determined the direction of their future dealings: "The direction was that of her greater freedom — which was all in the world she had in mind." Even during the rotunda scene Maggie reads her "proud" posture of dissimulation as "a denial of any loss of her freedom" (II, 287, I, 45, 121, 288, 299, 255, II, 312).

We have seen her escape from the cage, just as we have seen her escape from the house to the garden, but from her relation to her alerted husband she can never escape. Both images stress that she is self-entrapped: the halter is silken, as the bars were golden and she wittingly accepted these alluring accompaniments of renewed proximity with Amerigo which now mean the loss of all meaningful liberty. The loop she placed around her own neck, the loop that Adam does not ever "twitch", testifies to her own former illusions about freedom, rather than to others having deprived her of it (II, 287).

The idea of retribution, though, is eclipsed by the sense of compassion, keen in Maggie and Adam, expressed by a whole series of images of her as a haunted figure, as a figure seeking a hiding-place for her lover's rebuke, as an exiled *émigré* salvaging a "last saved object of price" and, overwhelmingly, as a figure vainly tapping on an imprisoning glass "by way of supreme irrepressible entreaty". For Maggie had already seen their lives together at Fawns as enacted in "a great overrarched and overglazed rotunda" and the hotel court in Paris where she received Amerigo's telegram was also "overarched and glazed, muffled against loud sounds". All these images affirm with pity that she herself has been the architect of any glassed-in prison now confining her and isolating her in such unremitting solitariness (II, 284, 330, 329, II, 288, I, 233).

All her words, those uttered by her and those attributed to her, express her passion for Amerigo and the bitterness and pain of its frustration. Practically all of those she delivers with such vindictive force in the garden-rotunda scene, though ostensibly about her repossession of her husband, are just as pertinent to this real loss. Hence we have the effectively controlled ambivalence, during her "passionate parade", of her grim " 'Oh . . . I know my difficulty!' " and her " 'How I see . . . that you've worked against me!' " The words that fill the gallery where she conducts guests to distract herself from distraction come to us as "a high coerced quaver"; they are "like the shriek of a soul in pain" and "of a creature in anguish"; they form the "strange wail" from which Amerigo flees to London. They at one point express with the bitterest irony her account of him as a Verver possession. " 'The largest of the three pieces has the rare peculiarity that the garlands looped round it, which as you see are the finest possible *vieux Saxe*, aren't of the same origin or period, or even, wonderful as they are, of a taste quite so perfect.' " He, the Latin, is in truth of an origin, and the heir of a period, different from the American-Saxon who can embellish him with loops that restrain him just as surely as would a silken halter. " 'They've been put on at a later time by a process known through very few examples, and through none so important as this, which is really quite unique — so that though the whole thing is a little *baroque* its value as a specimen is I believe almost inestimable.' " In every sense for her, here, an object of high value, the Prince is not this time the Palladian church he was to Adam, but an object much closer to the golden bowl, made of " 'a lost art' " in " 'a lost time' ", that she once wanted to give him, the bowl gilded not gold, cracked not perfect, that one Verver eventually bought for another and that proved right the Prince's superstitious dread of it (II, 317, 315, 317, 294, 292, 295, 291, I, 114).

Those of her words which Maggie divines, the last we ever "hear" from her, reveal James, while clinging to his characteristic indirection as a novelist, bringing together the poet's imagery and the dramatist's rhetoric. In this, the third great appeal Charlotte makes during the whole narrative, there is added to the passion she confessed to the Prince in Green Park and to the frustration she declared to Adam in their Paris hotel, the desolation of her final state. Here she directs her bitterness and contempt and fury at the figure she insists on seeing as the cause of her loss. Her silent *tirade* draws eloquence from all that gold, that cups and that flames have connoted throughout the novel.

The reach is as far as the poignancy is deep. " 'Ours was everything a relation could be, filled to the brim with the wine of consciousness' ", she cries, still denying the one-sidedness we from the first could see evident in it, " 'and if it was to have no meaning, no better meaning than that a creature such as you could breathe upon it, at your hour, for blight, why was I myself dealt with all for deception? why condemned after a couple of short years to find the golden flame — oh the golden flame! — a mere handful of black ashes?' " This is the unanswerable question that she will ask herself for the rest of her years. James makes sure it will resound throughout the rest of the tale by the emphasis he here contrives for it from among the most sophisticated of his resources as a literary artist (II, 329-30).

It is because it does so resound that all the subsequent discussions of her by those around her fall into the kind of perspective more suitable to the interest James is cultivating. We are unlikely to share the vindictive view of her that the still badly frightened Fanny expresses to Maggie. " 'She'll be — yes — what she'll *have* to be. And it will be — won't it? — for ever and ever.' She spoke as if abounding in her friend's sense, but it made Maggie still only look at her." The relish of Fanny's relief is as irrelevant as Amerigo's guilty flight, which Maggie also reads aright. "Charlotte was in pain, Charlotte was in torment, but he himself had given her reason enough for that." Adam also realizes that inevitably he has given her reason enough for fear (" '. . . I lead her to her doom . . .' ") but these words that his daughter imagines for us and that I must discuss at greater length when considering Adam, do not applaud her nemesis but grimly confirm its inevitability. Maggie's own compassion is genuine but complex and we are warned how to read it. "There was honestly an awful mixture in things, and it wasn't closed to her aftersense of such passages — we have already indeed in other cases seen it open — that the deepest depth of all, in a perceived penalty, was that you couldn't be sure some of your compunctions and contortions wouldn't show for ridiculous" (II, 304, 345, 287, 292).

All these responses, rendered by Fanny, Amerigo, Adam and Maggie, as to Charlotte's position, are those of figures who in varying ways contribute to it and are in a sense victims of it as well as being witnesses of it. Heard against the constant *obbligato* of Charlotte's own silent rhetoric, their variety affords James his desired "high refinement" of control. Apparently we are to make of her position something other than Fanny does; something additional to Amerigo's view; something encompassing Adam's ampler one that already embraces "the shame, the pity, the better knowledge, the smothered protest, the divined anguish even"; and something including Maggie's "compunctions" but also an awareness of their "contortions". A "penalty" is clearly enough "perceived" by these other figures, by James and by us, but we have to attend longer, closer and to more still before we can know whether we all agree as to what it is and how she pays it. This much is clear, however: though she alone is not the only one to pay, she pays hers entirely alone and while never accepting it. As Maggie perceives, and tells Amerigo, Charlotte " 'does not believe us' " (II, 292, 349).

James pursues his fineness of control and advertises that the language of his fiction can take him only so far. Those extravagant epithets applied to her in their continued discussion, the " 'wonderful' ", the " 'incomparable' ", the " 'great' ", the " 'beautiful' " and now particularly the " 'splendid' ", all echo hollowly, their function clearly dramatic rather than definitive. They are counters the others pass among themselves, talismans, even prayer beads, but, as words, their connotations remain as inadequate as the "heroines" and "villainesses" of the earlier critical commentators. The subject of these exercises remains contingent as her " 'unhappiness' " is discussed. The Prince does not deny it; he merely cuts through to the motives for Maggie's mentioning it and Maggie herself quickly enough confesses her chief one is her inability to discuss Adam. Charlotte's final position is discussed because it cannot be avoided, and this negative operation is preparatory to and only one part of the final view of her. " 'She's making her life' " Amerigo tells Maggie. " 'She'll make it.' " Maggie considers how the other couple must set about "learning to 'live into' their queer future". James now shows us how

Charlotte proceeds to do so (II, 346, 363, 364, 365, 368, 346, 349, 346).

We are treated, at the leave-taking, to "Charlotte's affirmed presence — as Charlotte affirmed it". She and her husband come as man and wife. "Mr and Mrs Verver were making the occasion easy. They were ***somehow*** conjoined in it, ***conjoined for a present effect*** as Maggie had absolutely never yet seen them." The apparent is stressed but the real is not neglected as Charlotte Verver, nee Stant, plays a dictated role which for any reader with a memory as long as the novel must evoke the ghost of her earlier attitudes — "so resplendent a show of serenity she succeeded in making. The shade of the ***official***, in her beauty and security, never for a moment dropped; it was a cool high ***refuge***, the deep arched recess of some coloured and ***gilded image***, in which she sat and smiled and ***waited***, drank her tea, ***referred*** to her husband and ***remembered*** her mission." The static and the ostensibly obedient have replaced the dynamic and the instinctively defiant; the golden has become the gilded; the "something intently made for exhibition, for a prize", as Amerigo once put it, has become an idol in a recess. Ironically, she is herself now in the position of one of " 'the holy images set up on the wall' " to which, with Fanny in a very different time, she had so extravagently likened her own grateful dedication to Adam (II, 356, 357, I, 47, 318).

When the lover, pursuit of whom has placed her there and with whom the giving and accepting of gifts were so complicated, proffers "a plate of *petits fours*", we are told she "cleared her acceptance, cleared her impersonal smile, of any betrayal, any slightest value, of consciousness". They do have together the moment alone, the offer of which by Maggie so mystified him, but they too are almost entirely beyond where words can reach. Maggie, watching from the balcony with Adam, agrees with him: " 'Ah don't they look well?' Their companions, at the sound of this, gave them, in ***a spacious intermission of slow talk***, an attention, all of ***gravity***, that was like an ampler ***submission*** to the general ***duty*** of magnificence; sitting as ***still***, to be thus appraised, as a pair of effigies of the contemporary great on one of the platforms of Madame Tussaud." Only wax is the medium adequate to express Charlotte's essential appearance at this moment. A moment later James returns to the scenario of his silent moving-film for the last glimpse he gives us of her, when, Miss Bogle introducing the Principino into the room, "Charlotte and the Prince got up — seemingly with an impressiveness that had caused Miss Bogle not to give further effect to her own entrance". This is the last we see of the lover of Amerigo, the rival of Maggie, the partner of Adam in the great mission to American City. James has refined his presentation of her in the interests of a quietness of contemplation that, he need hardly further remind us, has nothing to do with the utterances that accompany it — with Maggie's " 'incomparable' " and " 'great' ", with Adam's repeated " 'beautiful' ", with Amerigo's automatic, almost dismissive, " 'splendid' " or with Maggie's and Adam's exchanges about who "knows" Charlotte "best" (II, 358, 359, 360-61, 366, 364).

I have called her the most intense of the values with which James conjures and suggested that her motive remains as simple as the single passion informing it. The consequences for her, as for those about her, are not simple, certainly not as simple as many critics have formulated and labelled them. Those who are merely "for" or "against" her resemble theatre critics who have not even read all the script, much less patiently watched a performance directed by the scenarist. None of the readily-available evidence denies that she displays the hardness Krook sees, nor that she chooses to be Dupee's opportunist, Owen's exploiter or Maves's figure of pride; but it supports also that she is no more merely these aspects than she is merely Hartsock's adulteress or Kimball's notion of a heroine.[9] She is, rather, a much richer characterization fully responsive to the kind of attentive interest James evokes for it. As with his presentation of the Prince, the final appeal to the incalculable remains finely controlled and we may approach closer yet to the final view of her we may more safety entertain, only after we have devoted equivalent attention to Adam, to the Assinghams and to Maggie and have appreciated what they contribute to the final "handsome wholeness of effect".[10]

NOTES

1. R.W. Short, "The Sentence Structure of Henry James", *American Literature* 18 (May 1946): 71-88, (hereafter *Sentence Structure*), Krook, *Ordeal* and Maves, *Sensuous Pessimism.*
2. Elizabeth Owen, "The Given Appearance of Charlotte Verver", *Essays in Criticism* 13 (October 1963): 364-74. Hereafter *Given Appearance.*
3. Ellen D. Leyburn, *Strange Alloy: The Relation of Comedy to Tragedy in the Fiction of Henry James*, fwd. by William T. Stafford (Chapel Hill: U. of North Carolina P., 1968), p. 171. Hereafter *Alloy.*
4. Owen, *Given Appearance*, p. 368.
5. Maves, *Sensuous Pessimism*, p. 131.
6. James, *GB* (Methuen), p. 39.
7. James, *Prefaces*, pp. 153-54.
8. James, *GB* (Methuen), p. 458.
9. Krook, *Ordeal*, pp. 302, 303, 304; *Dupee HJ*, p. 264; Owen, *Given Appearance*, p. 368; Maves, *Sensuous Pessimism*, p. 131; Hartsock, *Unintentional Fallacy*, pp. 283, 278; and Kimball, *Last Portrait*, pp. 449-68.
10. Edel adduces from Miss Weld's *Diaries* (James Family Papers, Houghton Library, Harvard) that " 'Charlotte' was the first tentative title of the novel". (*Master*, p. 574). The testimony of this amanuensis to whom it was dictated supports, rather, my argument about James's provisions for indirection and for ostensible and real subjects at each point in his scenario. "Charlotte" would simply be the logical name for him to append to the first page of the first batch of typescript, where he begins reporting her impact on all the other characters and theirs on her.

C. Adam and authorial curiosity

It is understandable that Adam Verver should be demanding more and more critical attention. In this most difficult book he is the most difficult characterization. He appears to have a function quite central to the drama and in the special Jamesian sense to be continuously relevant to it, yet he is revealed directly to us only once, takes part in scenes that are crucial but relatively few and is more frequently "off" and behind, functioning almost as does, for Strether, the "general high-pitched essence"[1] of Mrs Newsome. Readers have usually been unsure how much he "knows" and any attempts to find out usually founder because so much of the evidence is filtered indirectly through partisan consciousnesses. Then there has risen alongside the provocative ambiguity of this character's impact the charge of faulty characterization, incredibility and of things having generally gone wrong for James here.

Certainly there have been among the interpretations not only greater extremes but also diversity. For Nuhn[2] he is a fiat character, for Alexander Welsh[3] he has no presence; for Wegelin[4] he is a villain, for Gordon[5] he is a national hero. For Bowden[6] he is insensitive; for Tanner[7] he sees all. For Crews[8] he is a supreme power; for Krook,[9] an exposed Philistine. For Mulqueen[10] he is a consummate strategist; for Maves,[11] an immature manipulator. For Matthiessen,[12] James takes Adam at his own estimate; for Bayley,[13] James accidentally lets him appear as a monster. For Holland[14] there are two Adams; for Girling,[15] one enigma. For Firebaugh[16] he is the object of James's most biting irony; for

Hartsock[17] he is the character who suffers most. For Sears[18] and Mull[19] he undergoes an important spiritual transformation; for Jefferson[20] and Pearson[21] there is no doubt as to where James stands in relation to him and for Short[22] the answer to this can be found through the closest attention to the imagery. One could well have predicted these kinds of reaction to the most ambitiously conceived of those "values" James uses in his most ambitious novel.

These critics have been concerned with four issues in this characterization: its credibility, its nature, its function and James's relation to it. It is the last of these that is most interesting and requires the closest reading of the text and several of these critics have looked for a conveniently explicating James in the infamous "silken-halter" passage. Pearson said "we read such a passage as James's own narrative. James does not blush to show us the father intimating wordless complicities in victory to his daughter over their fallen foe".[23] James does not blush to show us many things, but his judgment of them is a nicer question. Chernaik, at any rate, saw here a different James, one "presenting us with the image of a catastrophe — and yet this possibility is distinctly qualified by Adam Verver's assurances to Maggie that Charlotte will not be 'wasted' ".[24] At such moments of paradox, Holland always talks — and more cogently — not of "James" but of "the novel", as when he struggled with the text to explain Adam's nature: "the novel probes unsuccessfully for the link in Adam's case between so 'insolent' a concentration in business matters and so sociable a temperment in all other affairs".[25] Precisely: a probe, unlike calipers, investigates rather than retrieves. But J.A. Ward, in his latest attempt on the novel, talked about "mystification for its own sake", of our being teased with Adam in Volume One and denied him in Volume Two, while all the other characters are tormented with doubt as to what he knows, and concluded: "Surely this is an ambiguity that does not originate in the author's bafflement in the face of human behaviour. James knows Adam; *he* knows what

Adam knows. Why doesn't he give us a glimpse into that consciousness?" Is he, asked Ward, dramatizing ignorance? Is he perhaps trying to be complex merely to avoid being simple?[26]

Ward's rhetorical questions have interesting implications. The long-known answer to why we are not given a glimpse is of course that James is simulating the kind of gradual revelation that we know in life. Yet has he always the choice? In what sense can this author be said to know any of the characters in this book? Can we really say he knows what Adam knows? We may feel he is interested in trying to know Adam and the others in a more comprehensive manner than Jane Austen knows Knightley and therefore he cannot know him as confidently as she knows all her people. We may feel he is trying to to more with what he does know than, say, Trollope is trying to do with Plantaganet. But in this novel that is almost totally *about* knowing — the piecemeal, illusory and ambiguous nature of it, whether in knowing others or ourselves — it may not be surprising that James is operating not with a god-like omniscience but with a human percipience.

He sees much and understands a considerable amount of what he sees, but the few occasions when he does permit himself explicit authorial utterance are ones when we are perplexedly reaching for knowledge and he says, as he says of Adam at the moment of that characterization's most extreme density: "The greatest of wonders moreover was exactly in this, that so interrupted a man should ever have got, as the phrase was, should above all have got so early, to where he was". A page later when the "mysterious" in Adam in still being frankly acknowledged: "A dim explanation of phenomena once vivid must at all events for the moment suffice us; it being obviously no account of the matter to throw on our friend's amiability alone the weight of the demonstration of his economic history". This is the authorial stance more characteristic, significantly, of the James of this book and we see it repeatedly: "Nothing perhaps might affect us as queerer, had we time to look into it, than this application of the same measure of value to such different pieces of property as old Persian carpets, say, and new human acquisitions; all the more indeed that the amiable man was not without an inkling on his own side that he was, as a taster of life, economically constructed". This is not an author bouncing us into acceptance of apparent incompatibilities but one asking us to share his own sense of their queerness. There is no promise here that "had we time to look into it" we would understand it any better, but simply that "nothing might affect us as queerer" even then (I, 127, 128, 196).

Ward might be answered thus: we are given a glimpse but only a glimpse because that is the best James can do with his idea, his own limited impression, of this kind of character at this stage in this novel. Surely then this *is* ambiguity which *does* originate in the author's bafflement in the face of human behaviour. I hope to show that this bafflement remains relative and never disappears, not even after the development he suggests has taken place in Adam; James does not intrude to make decisions but to join our silent debate. Though he operates so much more subtly, through the total structure as well as more recognizably through the style, he is not making even intermediate decisions for us with any kind of editorial infallibility. Jefferson, who did see the authorial mobility within the style, did not however really help when he said: "Through this style the novelist himself is present as interpreter, sometimes near to his character, seeing the situation virtually in the latter's terms, and at other times further removed, allowing his poetic imagination, his humour, or his rhetoric scope to shape the situation more freely, but always with consideration for the character's central position and point of view"[27]. Jefferson's lack of specific reference is here crucial and even if they were supplied, this novelist may well prove to come through to us less as interpreter than as guide (and of course never at all as a bouncer!).

Far more than Forster's famous term can be challenged in discussion of *The Golden Bowl.* What of his assertion that "we know each other approximately, by external signs . . .. But people in a novel can be understood completely by the reader, if the novelist wishes; their inner as well as their outer life can be exposed. And this is why they often seem more definite than characters in history, or even our own friends; we have been told all about them that can be told; even if they are imperfect or unreal they do not contain any secrets, whereas our friends do and must, mutual secrecy being one of the conditions of life upon this globe."[28] Does this distinction between *homo sapiens* and *homo fictus* hold with the same force for this novel? Perhaps the full extent of James's radicalism as an artist may best be appreciated when we recognize his attempt to reduce the gap between them. Adam has appeared to many imperfect and unreal largely because James has candidly acknowledged that this character has secrets to which he as author is not privy in this novel, which is apparently dramatizing the fact that mutual secrecy is one of the conditions of life upon this globe. Even as guide, James is leading us through his own speculations about the glimpsed evidence rather than on an informed tour of the mind of Adam Verver. He is fully coherent and consistent about about as much of that mind as he knows. Adam's credibility as tycoon and connoisseur; his credibility as a figure in which simplicity of one kind looks like innocence of another kind and can embrace a growth from power to wisdom; and the efficacy of his function in the fictional world through which he passes, may be better appreciated if we challenge those gently confident asides Forster makes in a discourse on aspects of the novel that have pervaded critical discussion for half a century with the force of a natural law.

I must now try with care to assess the impact of the knowledge James does gradually share with us as he shares too the appeal of Adam's incalculability.

• • •

There is nothing obscure or hesitant in James's rendering of the habits of calculation and of appropriation that are features of Adam and of his earlier and later ways of life; nor is there difficulty of any kind in the given view of the father of Maggie, the father-in-law of Amerigo, the husband of Charlotte or friend of the Assinghams. The two big challenges, however, the one for James and the other for the reader, derive from the strategy that would seem to become obligatory for the presentation of this whole figure and from the range and sophistication of any such dramatic account within the major phase.

The first challenge strains to the utmost James's strategic ingenuities. If he is to abide by his plan to have the first half of the novel shown to us through the Prince and the second half through the Princess and a great deal of attention necessarily paid to Charlotte in each, then the fourth of the principals will generally be known to us be extreme indirection, and the nature and placement of all details relating to him must be designed for maximum effect. It becomes a matter of the distilling and disposing of an operative essence. The second strains the reader's capacity for accompanying James as the latter swiftly alters his dramatic focus to provide us with a sense of complete immersion in the mind and manners of yet another totally different character.

The manner of discourse remains the constant it always is but the values completely change from those we remained conscious of while we were borrowing the Prince's eyes or Charlotte's viewpoint and everything else changes, too: motives, preferences, temper, tempo and prevailing ideas. The revolution is swift and we are in another world altogether. Nearly every assertion made now is embodying the assumptions of Adam Verver, for whom glowing testimonials have been earlier supplied by the inhabitants of near or distant but certainly of other worlds, but about whom James himself is almost never explicit. James has made another jump and the reader will not be aware that the authorial vantage point is still nevertheless exactly where it has always been — that James is as distanced from his character as from all the others — unless he remains alert to all the signals in the language and all the artfulness of its context. James really is, as he says, down there in the arena, rubbing shoulders with the participants; the majesty of authorship is indeed muffled. The "simplicity" of Adam, that has such interesting consequences for the drama of which he is such an essential part, is transmitted under difficult conditions and by subtly elaborate means.

Maximum effect is provided for by the emphasis in, and the timing of, the information we receive about him. The bulk of this comes in Part Second and is thus given the ironic context of all the Prince and Charlotte are doing throughout Part First. With Part Fourth, information with an entirely different emphasis is conveyed. A brief but significant detail of it, coming in chapter xxvii, has for context the intrusion of the pagoda image into his daughter's consciousness, an image that informs their subsequent duologue in Regent's Park. Their later and even more determinant duologue occupying chapter xxxvii, in the middle of Part Fifth, resounds within all that the novel to that point can provide for it, but enjoys also the immediate context provided by the preceding chapter's depiction of that night encounter on the Fawns terrace between his daughter and Charlotte, to the remarkable conclusion of which he is one of the witnesses.

We are thus given the opportunity of "reading" the Adam of the farewell afternoon-tea in the light of these two different emphases within information given, respectively, first in a manner quintessentially summative and then very sparsely indeed. James, it would seem, realized that the dictates of the art of this novel as a whole could be made serve the kind of development this character undergoes. Adam comes to fuller knowledge in a manner markedly different from that of each of the other characters. I have suggested that the Prince's acceptance of it correlates with the course of events; Charlotte fights it to the end; the Assinghams are forced to deal with it as and when they can; Maggie, as I hope to show, examines and assimilates in the same interval a remarkable amount of it; and by various means we are actually shown all these people grappling with it. But the transformation it brings about in Adam's attitude takes place off stage and we are shown the effects of the later one just as we have been shown the effects of the earlier. The Adam of Book Second is perfectly consistent with that of Book First. His character, development and function — his impact on events and their impact on him — are all rendered by provisions enlisting the art of foreshortening, the art of so placing sparse text that it gains high intensity from the total context. Though there is far less commentary and dialogue devoted to him than to any other character (with the exception of the Principino and his Miss Bogle!) he bulks as large in the reader's consciousness as do each of the other three principal figures and his fate at the end is as moving as theirs.

Introduced by the conflicting scepticism and ardour of the Prince and Maggie in the early pages of the novel, the "mystery" of Adam besets the reader from the first. He is " 'a *real* galantuomo' " says the Prince, implying distinctness from his own kind (otherwise James could have had him emphasize the noun), admiring Adam's " 'form' " and " 'where it has brought him out' ". Maggie demurs naively, insisting on " 'his goodness' " but her suitor will not accept this as the solution to his benefactor's enviable success. His " 'way' ", she insists, is " 'the American way' ", which therefore, he sardonically rejoins, " 'must be good for something' ". But her Italian remains unconvinced by this version of "the romantic disposition" that enjoys "pleasures without penalties". We therefore scrutinize the fervent testimony of the daughter as to the beauty of this romantic relation to " 'the collection, the Museum' " which is " 'the work of his life and the motive of everything he does' ". They travel with their smaller best " 'pieces' " but he is

" 'willing to run his risks' " because, as she says, " 'we've had extraordinary luck . . . we've never lost anything yet' ". The Prince is obviously not convinced, but we are still free to defer commitment one way or the other (I, 6, 7, 11, 12, 13, 14).

The issue is not resolved and scrutiny keeps us busy when we come much closer to the subject himself, particularly in the first two of the seven chapters comprising Part Second, where there is further arresting tension between dramatic embodiment and implied authorial comment. Significantly, he is shown alone in the Fawns billiard-room, fleeing a petitioning humanity that has taken the form of the pursuing Mrs Rance. He is characteristically enjoying, as he puts it, "the sense . . . of one's having the world to one's self". Adam, "surrounded" by and "committed" to people, had never been able "to make out where the many-coloured human appeal, represented by gradations of tint, diminishing concentric zones of intensity, of importunity, really faded to the impersonal whiteness for which his vision sometimes ached". His principle is ever a reductive one; thus, his human feeling is reserved for the paternal, and so the above yearning for escape from relationships is qualified by the one her preserves with Maggie. He is "conscious of but a single near tie, one affection, one duty deepest-rooted in his life" (I, 125, 126).

A similar capacity for reduction, we learn, may help explain the problem that existed for the Prince, though not for Maggie, as to how "so interrupted a man should ever have got . . . so early, to where hs was". He has been capable of self-discipline that has negative as well as positive consequences. "It argued a special genius; he was clearly a case of that"; one that "had made of the chamber of his brain a strange workshop of fortune". To James, as to the other characters, as also to us, the centre of activity is "mysterious and almost anonymous"; the resultant "glow" of "miraculous white-heat" is, James proposes, just as inexplicable to Adam himself: "the receipt for producing which it was practically felt that the master of the forge couldn't have communicated even with the best intentions". The glow and the heat are nevertheless "facts" and we are invited to accept them with the utmost in candid authorial qualification; "they had constituted the kind of acquisitive power engendered and applied, the necessary triumph of all operations". And it is then that he asserts that "a dim explanation of phenomena once vivid must at all events for the moment suffice us . . ." (I, 127, 128).

One consequence evidently needs the even more careful emphasis it is given. "Variety of imagination — what is that but fatal in the world of affairs unless so disciplined as not to be distinguished from monotony? Mr Verver then, for a fresh full period, a period betraying, extraordinarily, no wasted year, had been inscrutably monotonous behind an iridescent cloud." It is a cloud that warrants careful examination: it has no "amplitude of folds" but has "a quality unmistakable for sensitive feelers". The monotony and the narrowness and the limitation of the man are thus not allowed to escape our attention, even though — as in the acknowledgment of sensibility — they are couched in terms that will allay alienation. James, whose own sensibility is not incompatible with an amplitude of folds, apparently desires that we know all that is knowable but by means that keep our interest pure, free of easy acceptances as of easy rejections (I, 128).

James now, as follow-up, demonstrates the implications for the other humans in Adam's life. They are seen in relation to the power they attribute to his money, much to his annoyance. "Every one had need of one's power, whereas one's own need, at the best, would have seemed to be but some trick for not communicating it." We see the menacing form it might take if Maggie's happiness were in any way imperilled; if, that is, the one emotional tie he indulges were ever to be at risk: his grounds for approving of the Prince are revealing. His son-in-law has "filled the scene and blocked the future", but "***not at all inconveniently or***

in ways not to have been desired'. Nothing about the younger man is "disconcerting" and he had, ***"for his father-in-law***, while remaining solidly a feature, ***ceased to be at all ominously, a block".*** The father-in-law, with an extraordinary degree of accommodation, makes a " 'round' " Amerigo out of the " 'angularity' " of the Palladian church he likens him to. " 'Oh if he *had* been angular! — who could say what might *then* have happened?' He spoke . . . as if he grasped the facts, without exception, for which angularity stood." This is instructive. The romantic imagination with which Adam Verver from the first denies Amerigo's reality thus betrays a steely self-indulgence and a ruthless protection of Verver interests (I, 131, 134, 135, 136, 137).

Most revealing of all is the ironic detail Adam all unconsciously includes in his patronizing tribute and the way it leaves us free to interpret his confidence as a connoisseur. We hear him, too, use what could be regarded as the crucial metaphor of the preceding part, that of " 'a pure and perfect crystal' ", then we hear Amerigo mention the possibilities of " 'cracks and flaws' ". James thereupon directly reinforces the apparent fallibility of Adam as judge and with an unusual explicitness, generalizes from it.

> It is the latter's [Adam's] relation to such aspects, however, that now most concerns us, and the bearing of his pleased view of this absence of friction upon Amerigo's character as a representative precious object. Representative precious objects, great ancient pictures and other works of art, fine eminent "pieces" in gold, in silver, in enamel, majolica, ivory, bronze, had for a number of years so multiplied themselves round him and, as a general challenge to acquisition and appreciation, so engaged all the faculties of his mind, that the instinct, the particular sharpened appetite of the collector, had fairly served as a basis for his acceptance of the Prince's suit (I, 138, 139, 140).

In what immediately follows the key metaphor and this frank authorial help, James invites us, by implication, to make our own deduction about Adam's alleged powers of discrimination as collector of art: "the aspirant to his daughter's hand showed ***somehow*** the great marks and signs, stood before him with the high authenticities, he had learned to look for in pieces of the first order". The next sentence, though its opening clause may at first sound like a reversion to the authorial, must, I suggest, be related to the "his" and "him" in the immediately preceding sentence, as a continuation of James's dramatic embodiment of Adam's consciousness. "Adam Verver knew by this time, knew thoroughly; no man in Europe or America, ***he privately believed***, was for such estimates less capable, of vulgar mistakes." As the revelation proceeds, what Adam ofers us on the subject of his supreme confidence continues to be undercut by his own supplementary comments. "He had never spoken of himself as infallible — ***it wasn't his way***; but apart from the natural affections he had acquainted himself with no greater joy of the intimately personal type than joy of his originally coming to feel, ***and all so unexpectedly***, that he had in him the spirit of the connoisseur" (I, 140).

Again and again the adverbials stress, and beg questions about, the rapidity with which these alleged powers were bestowed. "His 'peak in Darien' was ***the sudden hour*** that had transformed his life; . . . To rifle the Golden Isles had become ***on the spot*** the business of his future"; and his

> thought was that of the affinity of Genius, or at least of Taste, with ***something*** in himself — with the dormant intelligence of which he had thus ***almost violently*** become aware and that affected him as ***changing by a mere revolution of the screw*** his whole intellectual plane. He was equal ***somehow*** with the great seers, the invokers and encouragers of beauty — and he didn't after all ***perhaps*** dangle so far below the great producers and creators. ***He had been nothing of that kind before — too decidedly, too dreadfully not***; but now he saw *why* he had been what he had, *why* he had failed and fallen short even in huge success; ***now he read into his career, in one single magnificent night***, the immense meaning it had waited for.

A vague "something" has "somehow" with suspicious speed brought about a miracle and the doubtful and the negative in all this filtered monologue are amplified by James evoking, indirectly, that historic conqueror who with a similar confident belief in himself as chosen redeemer of barbarians, laid waste all about him while rifling treasures (I, 141, 141-142).

Ironically, again, Adam "could wince" as he recalls, condescendingly, the limitations of his first wife in such matters; she "hadn't so much failed of faith as of the right application of it" and there is relief evident in his musing that her death has been salutary for his alleged ascendancy to what he has coyly refused to call infallibility. He asks himself if she would have led him "into the wilderness of mere mistakes". At all events he now has "the supreme idea", his notion of the Museum and of the kind of Instant Culture it is supposed to bestow. "It hadn't merely, his plan, all the sanctions of civilization; it was positively civilization condensed, concrete, consummate, set down by his hands as a house on a rock . . . ." The euphoria generated by his self-conviction and self-congratulation mounts and mounts: his Museum will be " — a house from whose open doors and windows, open to grateful, to thirsty millions, the higher, the highest knowledge would shine out to bless the land". There is further yet to go: the Museum will be "a monument to the religion he wished to propagate, the exemplary passion, the passion for perfection at any price". Then again he punctures, unconsciously, his own rhetoric with his own afterthoughts. "A couple of years of Europe again, of renewed nearness to changes and chances, refreshed sensibility to the currents of the market, would fall in with the consistency of wisdom, the particular shade of enlightened conviction, that he wished to observe." "A couple" is casual enough; "enlightened" is sufficiently shown up by it. A shade more emphasis in the rendering of this illusion would have made it an inconveniently alienating one (I, 142, 143, 144, 145, 146).

Monotony has become monomania and there is a drop, pathetic in its irony, in the solemn avowal amid these fervent, personal flights of fancy: "He cared that a work of art of price should 'look like' the master to whom it might perhaps be deceitfully attributed; but he had ceased on the whole to know any matter of the rest of life by its looks." James meanwhile stands off, until after Adam's further ruminations on his "facility", his "immense development" and his superiority, as a Patron, to Julius II and Leo X, then contributes the bland comment that reminds us how such manic missionary zeal is rarely confined to the single issue that may have inspired it. "Going to our friend's head, moreover, some of the results of such comparisons may doubtless be described as having stayed there. His freedom to see — of which the comparisons were part — what could it do but steadily grow and grow? It came perhaps even too much to stand to him for *all* freedom . . .". The editorial comment can afford such mildness after such relentless dramatization. Adam Verver as patron of arts is indeed "a demigod of his own creation"[29] (I, 146-147, 149, 150).

Adam has already been able to declare with freedom from all doubt that Maggie's "immersion in the fact of being married" strikes him as representing, "exquisitely, divinely, the maximum". In virtually taking possession of the son of that marriage, he as freely enjoys "his own serenity". We are in fact shown this notion of freedom becoming absolute and obsessive as it unites Adam with Maggie. "What was now clear at all events for the father and the daughter was their simply knowing they wanted, for the time, to be together — at any cost, as it were" and they escape from their guests to their sequestered bench. The former single-minded tycoon, now dedicated to his single purpose as patron of the arts, freely takes this moment with the single affectional tie in his life, to enjoy their state of grace. It is a moment of hush in which James reminds us that "it involved, this serenity, innumerable complete assumptions" and while the pair enjoy "a kind of helplessness in their felicity", he asks his own question more unequivocally than anywhere else in their connection.

> Their rightness, the justification of everything — something they so felt the pulse of — sat there with them; but they might have been asking themselves a little blankly to what further use they could put anything so perfect. They had created and nursed and established it; they had housed it here in dignity and crowned it with comfort; but mightn't the moment possibly count for them — or count at least for us while we watch them with their fate all before them — as the dawn of the discovery that it doesn't always meet *all* contingencies to be right?

Fawns is even now a museum in which Adam has housed his illusion of possession (I, 148, 157, 158, 166, 167).

For the novel's account of Adam it is a moment of pause after which the potential dangers in his attitudes, demonstrated already by instances of his imperceptiveness and proven mistakes, are shown as threatening to become even more embarrassing actualities. Whereas, before, the flow of information about him was careful to balance a positive with a negative, now it is a case of the unflattering being encountered first. Thus, during the section devoted to the marrying of him to Charlotte, we learn of his appearance, of his "being a small spare slightly stale person, deprived of the general prerogative of presence. It wasn't by mass or weight or vulgar immediate quantity that he would in future, any more than he had done in the past, insist or resist or prevail" — a passage foreshadowing the nature of his future participation in the drama. Again, we learn of "his neat colourless face" but also that "there was something in Adam Verver's eyes that both admitted the morning and the evening in unusual quantities and gave the modest area the outward extension of a view that was 'big' even when restricted to the stars" — another foreshadowing of how much he is to see and know of ensuing developments. He rapidly becomes alert to Maggie's intention in interesting him in Charlotte as a partner in marriage and "that terrible issue" encourages the shrewd financier to prevail over the indulgent, worshipping father. He probes for the reasons behind his daughter's superlatives. He will not " 'give credit without knowing the facts' " and even after he has been called " 'Angel' " by Maggie as she delights in her success with him, we learn that "he was an angel with a human curiosity" and he continues to cross-question her in a manner quite free of the levity attending his response, later, to Mrs Assingham's similar overtures on Charlotte's behalf (I, 169, 170, 133, 184, 189).

James's rendering is thus unsparingly candid about the former financier and the sudden new connoisseur but invites our further exploring the man with him. It is a sharing of the wonderment assumed present in any reader confronted with such anomaly, such confidence linked with such fallibility, such serenity grounded on such a solipsistic "reality". That session with Fanny, another of the deluded, is followed by Adam's reflecting upon the nature of his realities in ways that make unmistakable his limitations as husband, father and patron and the continuity of them.

> It not only remained with them and hung about them, it positively developed and deepened, after this talk [with Fanny] that the luxurious side of his personal existence was now again furnished, socially speaking, with the thing classed and stamped as "real" — just as ***he had been able to think of it*** as not otherwise enriched in consequence of his daughter's marriage. The note of reality, in so much projected light, ***continued to have for him*** the charm and the importance of which the maximum had occasionally been reached in his great "finds"; it ***continued, beyond any other, to keep him attentive and gratified*** (I, 196).

My underlinings are hardly needed to emphasize further the precise kind of authorial distance James sustains in the confession of shared bewilderment that immediately follows. "Nothing perhaps might affect us as queerer, had we time to look into it, than this application of the same measure of value to such different pieces of property as old Persian carpets, say, and new human acquisitions; all the more indeed that the amiable man was not without an inkling on his own side that he was, as a taster of life, economically constructed." This subdued exclamation makes its comment by implying the existence of a reality that may not be so readily contained or so easily controlled and, while the irony in the preceding passage is frank enough, that of the subsequent one invites a more compassionate view of this man who can so challenge credulity by putting "into his one little glass everything he raised to his lips" (I, 196).

In the context of the whole book to this point, we do have "time to look into it", time to consider the innocence and the monomania that can apply "the same measure of value" to an Amerigo and a Luini, a Charlotte and a set of oriental tiles, before James draws together all he has been able to glean in proffered explanation — as distinct from judgment — of Adam Verver. "It was all at bottom in him, the aesthetic principle, planted where it could burn with a cold still flame; where it fed almost wholly on the material directly involved, on the idea (followed by appropriation) of plastic beauty, of the thing visibly perfect in its kind; where, in short, despite the general tendency of the 'devouring element' to spread, the rest of his spiritual furniture, modest scattered and tended with unconscious care, escaped the consumption that in so many cases proceeds from the undue keeping up of profane altar-fires" (I, 197).

Such a formulation honestly includes the monotonous stillness as well as the unattractive coldness of the flame but it dwells on the pathetic limitedness of it. The consistency and self-sufficiency are acknowledged but the barrenness and impoverishment consequent upon it are stressed. "Adam Verver had in other words learnt the lesson of the senses, to the end of his own little book, without having for a day raised the smallest scandal in his economy at large . . ." and when James then so deliberately likens him to a licentious bachelor discreet enough not to discompose a vigilant housekeeper, he further emphasises the queerness and strangeness of the case by adding, not without gentle banter: "That figure has however a freedom for us that the occasion doubtless scarce demands, though we may retain it for its rough negative value". The editorial ushering of what I shall call the "Adam value" in the scheme of the novel's values is discreet but unmistakably places it where we may best see at least all that James can see. James gives us a non-reductive account of this man's reductive attitude and of its consequences (I, 197).

The scenes that follow drive home the disastrous inadequacy of such an "economy", revealing just how far Adam himself is at the mercy of these simplicities that are fatal simplifications. Alone on the Fawns terrace after Charlotte has retired for the night, he rapidly resolves his brief "agitations" by deciding that what Charlotte "could contribute *to*" is the business of "putting his child at peace". At Brighton with this enlisted contributor, who, as I have had little difficulty in earlier indicating, is presented by James as deeply riven, Adam is conscious of "acting . . . with the deliberation of a plan, a plan that might be a thing of less joy than a passion, but that probably would, in compensation for that loss, be found to have the essential property, to wear even the decent dignity, of reaching further and of providing for more contingencies". In Paris, he continues to substitute disciplined decorum for imaginative insight when conscious that "there were strange appearances in the air, and before you knew it you might be unmistakably matching them" and he is certain, he wished "to match no appearance but that of a gentleman playing with perfect fairness any game in life he might be called to . . .". That his pathetic myopia allows so little for incalculables that may yet prove determinant and that would then include him among their victims is obvious enough as we read the page, but as we recall all antecedent pages an even more embracing irony is manifest. Though he and Charlotte are so evidently such light-years apart, they are depicted also as sharing the same doom for the same kind of reason, for we are never permitted to forget her myopia in regard to the

Prince, nor that her obsession with him is the clear equivalent of Adam's for his daughter's "peace". Both believe in and treasure "freedom". The actions of both are dominated by their respective singleness of motive, just as the pain foreshadowed for each is the result of limitations cultivated and imposed by them in their respective pursuits of their objectives. The reductive that has brought them to this point will be responsible for consequences at some future point. On Charlotte, and on Adam's relation to her here, I have already commented; Adam himself, presented now at the end of Part Second and not to be known in close terms at all throughout Part Third, enjoys the illusion that the resources of his "economy at large" remain perfectly adequate for any demands that life might make upon them. Our final glimpse of him at this point is in fact of him rejoicing over his impression of the Prince's telegram and its immediate consequences. The Adam who re-emerges in Part Fourth, to be first glimpsed again in chapter xxvii of Book Second, has clearly become conscious of "contingencies" hitherto undreamed of in his philosophy; that he remains a figure consistent with, and indeed explained by, the earlier one is an achievement taxing to the limit all of James's major art (I, 208, 211, 228-229, 229).

In the interests of consistency, I must stress once more the degree to which we are dependent on Maggie's view of Adam and indeed of everything else throughout Book Second and the uses that can be made of her testimony. One reason for the increasing intensity of *The Golden Bowl* is that James uses her as an immediate referent far more rigorously than has been the case with the Prince in the first half. I therefore propose in my interpretation of the "given appearance" of Adam in the rest of the narrative to distinguish between Maggie's impression of, even empathy with, him and her value judgments of him. The reliability of the one explains the unreliability of the other. That she and her father have always shared such remarkable empathy and have wished to continue to do so is clearly one of the chief causes of the whole dilemma. But James has also demonstrated implicitly that this closeness makes impossible their really seeing each other and I will show that he continues to dramatize the fallibility of the moral estimates each makes of the other as they continue their mutual adoration. Despite all we have been shown of what Charlotte calls Maggie's thinking, " 'more on the whole of fathers than of husbands' ", Adam idealizes her as expressing the "divine maximum" of the wedded state. Despite all we have been shown of Adam's unhesitating relegation of the interests of everyone else to those of her own and despite the tunnel-vision he manifests regarding his cultural enterprises, Maggie's idealization of him increases to the point of rhapsody (I, 257).

Thus, Maggie's insights into her father's attitudes are generally less suspect than are the grounds for her approval of them. She can reflect his sensibilities more reliably than she can evaluate his motives. Yet even this statement requires further careful qualification, for her father is now for the first time shown as persistently concealing and disguising his feelings from her, even more than he usually does with everyone, just as she tries to disguise and conceal hers from him in the interest of their common salvation. There is thus a very subtle process involved here and James has much on his hands to keep it clear to us. We have no trouble seeing his provisions for rendering in an immediate dramatic manner Maggie's scrutiny of Adam but we need attend with patience to James's scrutiny of him if we are to learn how much he, Adam, knows as well as just when he comes to know it and exactly when he is willing to let his daughter become aware that he knows it. At all events, Maggie's perception of the full reach of her father's consciousness at any given point, complicated as her perception is by her fears and her wishes, is even more difficult for her than is the perception of it that James affords the cooperative reader. Though Maggie's moral estimate of Adam never achieves that detachment with which James is constantly equipping us, her understanding of her father's degree of knowledge does gradually catch up with ours. Our task has been to see *through* her (in two senses) and *into* James's rendering of what her father is evidently trying to do.

The first opportunity we have of hearing Adam's words in this context that makes them so richly interesting in the later-Jamesian sense of that term is when he does, as she reports it, "exactly what she had been waiting for and despairing of" by suddenly cancelling, after the dinner at Eaton Square for the Matcham set, their long-cherished plan for a trip together to Spain. The impact of this is as "prodigious" for her as it apparently is for Charlotte and the Prince and, though anticipated by her, it teases rather than tells. For the reader, it is a clear signal in a new code, a code to be learnt if this new and sudden attitude is to be understood. Understanding is accelerated during the time they later spend in Regent's Park, ostensibly in search of the Principino and Miss Bogle, when the code is spelled out sign by sign with less and less reserve and when Adam achieves a startling new eloquence that in itself clamours for investigation (II, 53).

The sense of urgency and purpose detectable within the apparent casualness of his discourse as they stroll is one of her chief impressions and one of our increasing convictions, for it is thus that we read that "he struck her as giving, unexpectedly, the go-by to any serious search for the Principino" by "his dropping with her into the first pair of sequestered chairs they came across and waiting a little, after they were placed, as if now at last she might bring out, as between them, something more specific". Thus, too, we learn and make conclusions about her "impression from him of his holding off to see what she would do", of his "only pretending to talk" of the projected Fawns visit as an alternative to Spain. What they are really talking about of course is her wish to separate Charlotte and the Prince by having the latter accompany Adam somewhere for a trip, a wish that, as Maggie divines, Charlotte has foiled by presenting it to her own husband in a manner that has provoked his seeking this interview with her. That "he markedly stood off from the risk involved in trying to draw out her reason" is further evidence that "he had taken everything on himself" (II, 84, 85, 86, 89).

It is tacit between them "that each would fight to the last for the protection, for the perversion, of any real anxiety" — this we learn from her and duly recognize as true; and it is manifest to both Maggie and the reader that Adam has taken on a programme of reassuring her that all is well between him and Charlotte: "he had grinned back, paternally, through his rather shielding glasses, in easy emphasis of this". She is as yet shielded at least from complete awareness of what he is about with his wife, for, she notes, "he had played then either all consciously or all unconsciously into Charlotte's hands" and James's phrasing keeps clear that Maggie is uncertain — as we cannot be — of the extent of the personal resources he has marshalled and applied: "it was ***for our young woman herself***, still more prodigiously, ***as if*** her father had been capable of calculations to match, of judging it important that he shouldn't be brought to demand of what was the matter with her". The shrewd Adam, already proven as so capable of concentrated calculation behind an ambiguously calm demeanour, now devoting these skills entirely to the service of the one deep emotional tie of which he is conscious in his life, is perfectly explicable in terms of our earlier knowledge of him as he here rallies to meet a crisis in, for him, a totally uncalculated quarter (II, 87, 89, 90).

Adam's plight and tactics exact fascinating attention as he thus proceeds to compensate for earlier myopia. The notable difference in him from now on is his painful consciousness of the unreality of all their former relationships and the insufficiency of the assumptions that supported them. Maggie has "the sense that he had begun to *imitate* — oh as never yet! — the ancient tone of gold", a detail aptly enough contrasting the gilded with the golden, and making inescapable our seeing this whole encounter in the context of "the summer evening in the park at Fawns, when, side by side under the trees just as now, they had let their happy confidence lull them with its most golden tone". Adam apparently has sought this meeting not only to inquire and to placate but also to repudiate. The pragmatic capitalist is immediately investing any new knowledge he has gained and the disquisition, remarkably sustained for one usually so verbally restrained, he here gives on their former state shows him seeking immediate dividends. He repudiates specifically the Olympian detachment, their " 'lying like gods together, all careless of mankind' ", their not having enough "the sense of difficulty" that, he implies, is inevitable in the conditions of mankind, and the selfishness and immorality of their dangerous, mutual absorption (II, 86, 85, 91).

When the attention of his partner in such illicit indulgences now condemned is totally claimed, he rattles on with a relentless relevance that defines his new insight: " '. . . I won't pretend that I know exactly at whose particular personal expense you and I for instance are happy' ". It is one declared instance which glaringly implies another: would he pretend to know at whose particular personal expense Amerigo and Charlotte are happy? The question is left begging as he exchanges the Olympian image, which after all connotes only privileges seemingly god-given, for an image much more condemnatory, one connoting self-chosen avoidance of reality in preference for the illusory, the image of their " 'smoking opium and seeing visions' " in a den into which the police must break (II, 92).

Both figures serve his explanations and his warnings, but he reserves his most sustained rhetoric for the emphatic finale wherein he continues his programme of reassuring the human being closest to him that his relationship with Charlotte is entirely successful. " 'It's a good deal for me,' he had wound up, 'to have made Charlotte so happy — to have so perfectly contented her.' " He risks protesting at least that much and even reasserting — in a manner that, significantly, should have been needless — his confidence in the marital bliss that he earlier celebrated Maggie and her husband as enjoying: " '*You*, from a good way back, were a matter of course — I mean your being all right; so that I needn't mind your knowing that my great interest since then has rather inevitably been in making sure of the same success, very much to your advantage as well, for Charlotte' " (II, 92).

He pursues his programme strenuously and it is embarrassing for him to be betrayed by old facts just as he is trying to command newly-perceived situations and he is forced in the succeeding moments to recognize how little he knows his wife, his predicament belying his earlier and later protestations. Maggie suddenly reveals she knows that she herself was his reason for remarrying; the exchanges must be quoted in full, to appreciate the lies and evasions to which he is willing to resort in protection of her.

> He had hesitated, but only a moment. "I never told you so."
> "Well, Charlotte herself soon enough told me."
> "But I never told *her*," her father had answered.
> "Are you very sure?" she had presently asked.
> "Well, I like to think how thoroughly I was taken with her, and how right I was, and how fortunate, to have that for my basis. I told her all the good I thought of her."

Maggie rescues him, but "she saw she had made his colour rise" and that not only was he hearing of this passage of hers with Charlotte for the first time but was significantly abstaining from questioning her further about it. They escape from these surprises and intensities in their encounter "with a certain effect of oddity in their more or less successful ease". She is well aware that "he had, from his chair, been noting her look" and she "had read meanings" into the tone in which he welcomes the presence at Fawns of the Assinghams. "It amounted to an intimation, off his guard, that he should be thankful for someone to turn to" and she decides that "he had now in short quite given himself away" (II, 93, 94, 95, 97, 98).

She does not know how much he knows; she knows only that he is alert, active, conscious. She knows mainly the father she loves and wishes to protect. *We* know an Adam Verver much developed, interestingly vulnerable now to the life which he had once taken "higher up the stream" — an Adam Verver using the only weapons at his disposal, the ones that had brought him this far and which now, beleaguered, he must rapidly adapt to new forms, defensive and offensive. Maggie's coming to fuller consciousness, the moral responsibility of which Adam has here been so belatedly asserting, is rendered by James in passages of sustained reflection featuring recurring memories of crucial scenes and dominated by the appropriate strangeness and foreignness of the attenuated image of the pagoda. Adam's new consciousness, glimpsed a moment at a time, implied as much as dramatized, is brought more gradually to the foreground and is accompanied by a revelation of character that is deeply moving as much for its covert as for its overt responses. If maturation is a process of continuous disillusionment, and if value resides in what we salvage from it, his ordeal is arrestingly profitable. The history of it is surely documented as fully as are the confrontations with reality experienced by each of the other principals. It commits him to a solitariness as stark as each of theirs (I, 147).

We plumb this ordeal in the other bench conference that father and daughter have at Fawns after the averted crisis of her terrace scene with Charlotte. It is a moment for facing bitter decisions. It recalls even more deliberately the conference of their sublime and serene golden time — this is after all exactly the same bench — and the perspective it gives them moves them more than they dare directly express; "they were avoiding the serious, standing off anxiously from the real, and they fell again and again, as if to disguise their precaution itself, into the tone of the time that came back to them from their other talk, when they had shared together this same refuge". James records Maggie's description of that earlier talk as "the then purblind discussion" of her father's possibly marrying and Adam himself now shares her relief in talking "of all the people they weren't really thinking of and didn't really care about", such as the Lutches and Mrs Rance. It is a refuge more than physical, for they briefly foster the fantasy of having temporarily ceased to be, respectively, a husband and a wife and of being instead once again "father and daughter". The regression is as painfully significant as the nostalgia is obvious (II, 257, 253, 254, 255).

The perspective available to the reader, reaching further in length and in breadth, and always peopled by four figures rather than two, subsumes this regression and nostalgia into the much fuller interest given these two in the total context of the novel to this point. As with all the scenes of James's major manner, this one resembles a transparent sheet where the carefully-selected details contained on it take on their full outline only when superimposed on other sheets containing other details. The effect is quite the opposite of a palimpsest — where stronger calligraphy appears on another, dimmer and quite different one — for there are here many more than one, each as vivid as the others and, because all are complementary, they contribute progressively to meaningfulness. Thus, in their chosen substitute chatter, ostensibly about what Maggie calls " 'the feelings we used to have' ", their words take on a particular pregnancy: " 'Oh yes,' he responded philosophically — 'I remember the feelings we used to have.' " Some lines of dialogue become directly pertinent in ways of which the speakers have obviously an acute awareness. It is their respective *sposi* and not, certainly, "Kitty and Dotty" who are present when Maggie volunteers: " 'One must always, whether or no, have some imagination of the states of others — of what they may feel deprived of.' " Other lines are known, by speaker, by listener and by reader, as direct and sad contradictions of the true state of affairs at this point; as when Adam says of their visitors, " 'And now they see still more that we can have got everything and kept everything and yet not be proud.' " Again and again a line will achieve this extra reach. We learn, as they refer to their having gone in for a grander more populous life, that Adam "nodded his head amusedly", and also that he "kept nervously shaking his foot" as he concludes his rejoinder thus: " 'I remember,' he said again: 'that was the way it *all* happened.' " (II, 257, 258, 259).

Thus far the authorial signals of deep change in Adam have been confined to quiet "as if's", to persistent use of "seem". When she reminds him that he confessed their old life " 'did seem to be beautiful' "; he agrees: " 'for so it did seem to me.' " Now, as Maggie launches into her declaration of the immunity her capacity for love gives her, a declaration echoing the profession to Fanny that refused to distinguish between love of husband, love of father and love itself, James dwells in a manner unmistakably emphatic on the poignant awareness Adam has at this moment of his own passional limitations.

> The mere fine pulse of passion in it, the suggestion as of a creature consciously floating and shining in a warm summer sea, some element of dazzling sapphire and silver, a creature *cradled upon depths, buoyant among dangers, in which fear or folly or sinking otherwise than in play was impossible* — something of all this *might have been making once more present to him*, with his discreet, his half-shy assent to it, *her probable enjoyment of a rapture that he in his day had presumably convinced no great number of persons either of his giving or of his receiving.* He sat a while as if he knew himself *hushed, almost admonished, and not for the first time . . ..*

My underlinings point up even further the notes of the

wistful, of the chastened, in this painful consciousness which he rapidly rationalizes away: "yet it was an effect that might have brought before him rather what she had gained than what he had missed. Besides, who but himself really knew what *he*, after all, hadn't, or even had, gained?" (II, 257, 260, 261, 263).

Thus it is a lonely moment for him, one for which his creator momentarily alters the narrative mode away from a report of Maggie's consciousness and onto more direct speculation about Adam's own and gives it a rhetorical intensity equalling any of those three passionate outbursts of Charlotte's. He opts for the substitute of a vicarious passion: "though his personal dips were over", he can settle "for breathing the bliss, in a communicated irresistible way — for tasting the balm"; and he resorts, in a sentence clearly revealing the rhythm and pulse of his emotion, to his more habitual source of comfort, his consciousness of his power. "It could pass, further, for knowing — for knowing that without him nothing might have been: which would have been missing least of all (II, 263, 263-264).

Then James has him utter a line that operates like a thrown pebble that sets up ripples in the pool of the reader's memory of the narrative thus far. " 'I guess I've never been jealous,' he finally remarked." As an admission it is historic in his personal development and it is tantamount also to an admission of never having known any deep love other than the paternal. But the ripples reach not only his immediate witness, but also her husband and, especially, his wife, whose passional range has clearly not suffered from the delimiting effects of his own narrow and monotonous economy. The victim of self-discipline and the victims of a lack of it are all encompassed by the same ever-widening circles as the pebble sinks. "And it said more to [Maggie], he had occasion next to perceive, than he was intending; for it made her, as by the pressure of a spring, give him a look that seemed to tell of things she couldn't speak." It says in short almost too much for his present programme, which he thenceforth pursues with greater circumspection, and it adds a dimension to the interest being generated (II, 264).

From this moment on, an *obbligato* of sombreness prevails in the rendering of Adam; despite the sustained apparent "sociability of their easy communion", despite his smiles being even "intenser" and more "fixed" than hers; and despite his having "settled", for safety, "on the merely obvious" — " 'Well then we make a pair. We're all right.' " — a phrase repeated by his accomplice-in-evasion. When we return to indirect perception of his demeanour, the abiding note is that "he, as at the best the more battered vessel, perhaps just vaguely drooped". Of Maggie's responses here as they both go through the motions of discussing who could be the victims of their alleged selfishness and both studiously avoid mentioning their marriage partners; of her awareness that he is offering himself as sacrifice; and of her eventual overwhelming conviction that his decision to " 'ship' " with Charlotte reveals his having all the while shared Maggie's knowledge, I shall have more to suggest when later commenting on James's presentation of her. Her paean of praise for her father is also obviously of an interest more dramatic than definitive; indeed, "he positively, under the impression, seemed to loom larger than life for her . . ." (II, 264, 269-270, 264, 265, 271, 273).

For us he is none the less interesting for his remaining life-size, as James does not permit the daughter's emotion to obscure the father's more sober, even grim, response to what she calls " 'their predicament' ", and to those decisions that he has just announced and that have provoked her effusive tribute to his quality. "His very quietness was part of it now, as always part of everything, of his success, his originality, his modesty, his exquisite public perversity, his inscrutable incalculable energy; and this quality perhaps it might be — ***all the more too as the result, for the present occasion, of an admirable traceable effort*** — that placed him in her eyes as no precious work of art probably had ever been placed in his own." Adam does not hear her adjectives but we do and they ring ironically at this point in the steadier vision of his plight that our author has preserved for us; for each epithet, whether applied to his energetic pursuit of millions, of art, of people, of his daughter's happiness or of his own personal fulfilment as he has envisaged it, describes a quality that has in fact conspired to bring him to this present strange pass. They are " 'all right' " only as a pair and now they must be sundered and paired off, in fact now as well as in form, with their marriage partners. Adam's energy is not at all inscrutable to us as he applies every ounce of it now to the task of salvage, to sustaining her belief in him, a belief, as he explains to her, which should negate her notion that she has sacrificed him. Her silent reactions to this explanation we have already noted; her voiced ones need closer scrutiny, as do his.

> "I believe in you more than anyone."
> "Than any one at all?"
> She hesitated for all it might mean; but there was — oh a thousand times! — no doubt of it. "Than anyone at all." She kept nothing of it back now, met his eyes over it, let him have the whole of it; after which she went on: "And that's the way, I think, you believe in me."
> He looked at her a minute longer, but his tone at last was right. "About the way — yes."
> "Well then —?" She spoke as for the end and for other matters — for anything, everything else there might be. They would never return to it.
> "Well then —!" His hands came out, and while her own took them he drew her to his breast and held her. He held her hard and kept her long, and she let herself go; but it was an embrace that, august and almost stern, produced for all its intimacy no revulsion and broke into no inconsequence of tears (II, 274, 273, 275).

Their words and actions now amply illustrate the precise sense in which they are a pair. Each of them hesitates long enough to be fully conscious of what the words imply before each deliberately utters them. The ghosts of

Amerigo and Charlotte attend these avowals by two people whose embrace is "august and almost stern" and who face dry-eyed the farewell it commits them to as well as the mutual dependency it declares. Their scene is enacted amid our keen awareness of "anything, everything, else there might be", of all that comes between them now and that makes each in fact so isolated. When he must use words at all, Adam manages to keep his tone "right" but only "at last", after more of the effort that constitutes this particular ordeal of having to keep up appearances for her sake when acutely conscious of his degree of responsibility for all of the consequences, as he now sees them, of his celebrated power. His "manner" which was that of having no manner at all, no longer conceals euphoric confidence: too much has turned to ashes — his whole basis for action has been challenged and he is left with pitifully little.

Just how little remains for him is demonstrated in the final scene, but before taking up this next occasion of our being brought into direct relation with his words, his silences, his gestures and his stillness, I must attend to Maggie's impressions of "the little meditative man in the straw hat . . . with his indescribable air of weaving his spell" as they together witness Charlotte's suffering. Maggie is not lauding here, she is divining and the reliability of her testimony is further enhanced when we see how it reinforces the view of Adam's attitudes at this point, which James has been independently developing for us — especially of the salvage operation Adam has undertaken. The spectacle of him in assertive action recalls his conviction, declared much earlier, that "it wasn't by mass or weight or vulgar immediate quantity that he would in the future, any more than he had done in the past, insist or resist or prevail"; and now we learn that Maggie has been "receiving from him the hint that he measured the impression he produced". She grows alert to "the greater depth of his small perpetual hum of contemplation"; the effect of which is of course not lost upon the now fearful Charlotte when she joins him in "making their daily round" of his possessions (II, 284, I, 169, II, 285, 286, 287).

They strike Maggie as being "so together yet at the same time so separate" and it is this relationship, so expressive at once of her father's new consciousness and of his wife's belated realizations, that inspires in his daughter — and not in himself — the image of the silken halter. James's care in introducing this figure must be heeded if we are to read Adam aright, for it is accompanied by one of his rare introductions of the authorial "I":

> and those betrayals [originally "indications"] that I have described the Princess as finding irresistible [originally "extraordinary"][30] in him were two or three mute facial intimations which his wife's presence didn't prevent his addressing his daughter — nor prevent his daughter, as she passed, it was doubtless to be added, from flushing a little at the receipt of. They amounted perhaps only to a wordless, wordless smile, but the smile was the soft shake of the twisted silken rope, and Maggie's translation of it, held in her breast till she got well away, came out only, as if it might have been overheard, when some door was closed behind her (II, 287).

The translation could not belong more clearly to Maggie, for though she communicates acceptably the *idea* of her father's now asserting his influence where he believes it to be in the best interests of all, the *language* is unmistakably that which she can permit her mental tongue as she appreciates what that idea implies for Charlotte. The facts of the text simply do not suggest he is relishing his power. What they do suggest in a passage immediately subsequent to this one where they are so moved by Charlotte's voice in the gallery is an attitude deeply compassionate, the overt signs of which, duly indicated, entirely accord with the *ideas* his daughter attributes to him. "Then it was that, across half the gallery — for ***he hadn't moved from where she had first seen him*** — he struck her as confessing, ***with***

strange tears in his own eyes, to sharp identity of emotion. 'Poor thing, poor thing' — it reached straight — '*isn't* she, for one's credit, on the swagger?' After which, as held thus together they had still another strained minute, the shame, the pity, the better knowledge, the smothered protest, the divined anguish even, so overcame him that, ***blushing to his eyes***, he ***turned short away***" (II, 292).

If we are to attend to Adam in exactly the terms that James apparently wishes, we must realize the full reach that each of the items in the last sentence attains in the context given them by his discourse. The authorial phrasing ensures that the shame, pity, better knowledge, smothered protest and divined anguish are read as applicable to, and experienced by, all of the three human beings involved in them. All five terms surely read as true of Charlotte's state at the that moment as they do of Adam's, Maggie's and, indeed, of Amerigo's. It is the moment in the whole narrative when all that Maggie believes that Adam apprehends approaches closest to some of what James apparently does and it is because the distance traversed to bring Adam to this less confident, less narrow, view has been so immense that he becomes such an "interesting" value in the final scene.

During James' final account of the quartet of characters in which all of the above five emotions are still so electrically present, it is Adam whose initiatives are operative. Mr and Mrs Verver, who have " 'cut' " the Assinghams down " 'to luncheon' ", have cut the Portland Place couple down to tea and the silken rope is implied in these decisions. "It was the strangest, once more, of all impressions; but what [Maggie] most felt, for the half-hour, was that Mr and Mrs Verver was ***making*** the occasion easy. They were ***somehow conjoined*** in it, conjoined ***for a present effect*** as Maggie had absolutely never yet seen them;" and the look she immediately exchanges with Amerigo gives new bearings to their recently concluded discussion as to "the amount of correction to which Charlotte had laid herself open". Charlotte plays her adopted role while her husband directs the whole scene. "Adam Verver profited indeed at this time even with his daughter by his so marked peculiarity of seeming on no occasion to *have* an attitude; and so long as they were in the room together she felt him still simply weave his web and play out his long fine cord, knew herself in the presence of this tacit process very much as she had known herself at Fawns." His way of "moving about the room, noiselessly, to see what it might contain; and his manner of now resorting to this habit, acquainted as he already was with the objects in view, expressed with a certain sharpness the intention of leaving his wife to her devices", and these actions signified for Maggie that he took "almost a special view of these devices . . . which scarcely required the accompaniment of his faint contemplative hum". This power, which is all he has left, now serves the negative function of ensuring an orderly retreat; the prose insists on this new form of expressing it (II, 341, 356-57, 358).

One of those objects in view with which he is already well acquainted, he most pointedly ignores. At this moment of long farewell he has nothing to say to his son-in-law: "the harmony wasn't less sustained for being superficial, and the only approach to a break in it was while Amerigo remained standing long enough for his father-in-law, vaguely wondering, to appeal to him, invite or address him, and then in default of any such word selected for presentation to the other visitor a plate of *petits fours*". It is the older man's most monumental moment of stillness and silence. Significantly, the only other approach to a break is when, on his asking about the Principino, she exclaims " 'Trust him, me dear, not to fail you!' " and her father's reply, "uttered in so explicitly jocose a relation to the possibilities of failure" becomes another eloquent reference to his son-in-law. " 'Oh I don't want *him* to fail me!' " (II, 358, 361).

Adam's relationship with Amerigo is clear enough and he chooses to deal with it by omission, but the *appearance* of his relationship with Charlotte — whatever it may in *fact* be — commits him to contriving yet another form of the explicit, for if she is obliged to make clear her acceptance of *her* doom, he is obliged, for the reassurance of his daughter, to make clear that Charlotte is in no way *his* doom. Certainly we can safely conclude, in the light of their declarations to each other at Fawns, that father and daughter enjoy together an emotion which in kind and in degree is, for each, paramount and that this would relegate his feelings for his wife to a secondary order of emotion, even if not only because his range has been confessed as so limited.

On the balcony with Maggie, out of sight of the other pair, Maggie, who cannot trust herself to "speak" of Adam, deliberately declines further use of Fawns on the grounds that Charlotte will not be there and gives her reason specific utterance: " 'Because Charlotte, dear, you know,' she said, 'is incomparable.' " This helps him, too, it would seem, and as he gains time with the business of taking out a cigarette, we learn from Maggie's impressions that "nothing he could try, she immediately saw, was to keep his eyes from lighting". This appearance, unlike his involuntary blushes and tears during their mute gallery exchanges, can be contrived, and when she further exclaims " 'Father, father — Charlotte's great!' " we learn that "It was not till after he had begun to smoke that he looked at her", and that he then replies, " 'Charlotte's great.' " The scenic, under James's "major" control, records the way these actions eloquently express Adam's strain in the pause as he works for Maggie's ease of mind (II, 363, 364).

James's immediate formulation of their response to this is crucial: "They could close upon it — ***such a basis as they might immediately feel it make***, and so they stood together over it ***quite gratefully***, each recording to the other's eyes that it was firm under their feet. They had even thus a renewed wait ***as for proof of it;*** much ***as if he were letting her see***, while the minutes lapsed for their concealed companions, that this was finally just why — but just *why*!"

In their ensuing duologue, he is obviously exploiting every opportunity to reassure her of his motive in marrying, their Fawns discussion of which had caught him unprepared (II, 364).

This dialogue between them about how " 'the risk' " has proved justified and how he " 'knows' " Charlotte best, places him firmly in control of appearances. For Maggie, "the vision of all he might mean" evidently reassures her. "The sense of it in her rose higher, rose with each moment that ***he invited her thus to see him linger.***" James, whose art is never called upon to deal with matters spun more finely than at this juncture, underlines a shade more directly the effectiveness of Adam's reassurances. "If Maggie had desired at so late a hour some last conclusive comfortable category to place him in for dismissal, she might have found it here in its all coming back to his ability to rest upon high values", chief of which is the "greatness" of Charlotte who "wasn't to be wasted". She is successfully convinced — as her consciousness duly reports to us: "To let his daughter know it he had sought this brief privacy". Her convictions are clearly those that her father has adroitly manipulated. She can read his feelings — this we have seen demonstrated on many other occasions — but never when he chooses that she should not, and he can here easily enough edge her into accepting what he knows she desires to believe. At the one stroke he allays her known compunctions about Charlotte's enforced exile and her anxieties about his own (II, 364, 365, 366).

The ultimate commander of appearance and reality here being James, we are meanwhile given relentlessly not only Adam's relation with his son-in-law, wife, daughter and grandson, but also his private relation with himself. The prevailing tone of this is one of grim disenchantment and this is implied by the context given this scene in the novel as a whole. My analogy of the superimposed transparent sheets again applies. In place of his sense of a freedom that he formerly felt was unlimited, there is now this enforced separation. Surely now there is for him in abundance the "sense of difficulty" that he had become conscious of lacking. The collector who had had "such extraordinary luck" and had "never lost anything yet", has had to reappraise two notable acquisitions and to relinquish not only the most cherished of his possessions but also his closer enjoyment of the most recent one he had monopolized, her son. As they stand together enjoying another of them, a painting "he had given her on her marriage", he comments on it in the same phrase that they both used so equivocally to draw to a close their final Fawns discussion: " 'It's ***all right***, eh?' " Its reference is generalized and the limits of its truth are realized when their gaze thereupon ranges over all "the 'important' pieces" in the room and includes the other couple seated there among them. Immediately after an authorial reminder that "complete and admirable" as these "two noble persons" are, "to a lingering view, a view more penetrating than the occasion really demanded, they also might have figured as concrete attestations of a rare power of purchase", Adam's pregnant comment is carefully introduced: "There was much indeed in the tone in which Adam Verver spoke again, and who shall say where his thought stopped? '*Le compte y est.* You've got some good things' " (II, 91, I, 14, II, 359, 360).

The adjective " 'some' " is invidious enough and James has recourse in fact to two other singularly subtle and appropriate choices here to help us see exactly where Adam now finds himself and where we see him. In choosing from the French a phrase that is so apt an echo from his past as a financier, he has many alternatives. Equally idiomatic and more or less as relevant would be "*le compte est juste*", "*c'est le compte*" and, among still others, "*le compte c'est cela*". But the first of these connotes "correctness" or "rightness", the second is too non-committal and the third implies too narrowly particular a referent. "*Le compte y est*", on the other hand, avoids the complacency and approval suggested by the first while suggesting also an appropriate inclusivesness:

"The account is here". It is here in this place, at this time, certainly, for this (to paraphrase again) is where they must "account" for everything.[31]

"*Le compte y est*" is therefore the variant that most logically precedes the qualification entrenched in the following line. What Adam has seen, in what Maggie calls his " 'last look' " (after her exclamation, " 'Ah don't they look well?' ") is a couple who, James tells us, resemble "a pair of effigies of the contemporary great", a couple who in their static and imitative qualities adequately explain his linguistic choices and why these militate so strongly against those pieces of "human furniture" which must be included in the columns of the total account. They are a couple who attest the "power of purchase" by having "fairly 'placed' themselves" in the position of the purchased. Their American purchaser, seeking a phrase that placates his daughter while also expressing his own assessment, borrows from one of the private languages the lovers have used, the one Amerigo told Maggie he speaks " 'worse' " than English. (II, 360, I, 6).

The other detail rewarding our inspection is the "early Florentine sacred subject" which we know from a much earlier passage in the novel to be a Luini. It is more likely to be one of this painter's numerous Madonnas than, say, his "Jerome", or his "Susannah", and my own guess would be his "Madonna of the Rose Garden", but speculation as to one particular painting becomes irrelevant as soon as we recall James's inveterate eschewing of particularity in preference for the suggestiveness of a general idea. What the idea of Bernadino Luini's treatment of an early Florentine sacred subject generally invokes is prettiness and sentimentality. He "was one of the most popular Milanese painters in the early 16th century, principally because he succeeded in vulgarizing the style of Leonardo (as indeed all his Milanese followers tried to do)"[32]. The point is well supported by even cursory comparison of his copy of the "Virgin of the Rocks" with either or both of Leonardo's treatments of the same subject in the Louvre and the National Gallery in London. It is supported even more strongly when the last-named picture by the Master is compared with his imitator's "Madonna of the Marguerite" in the Wallace Collection, where the over-sweetness is most manifest[33] (II, 359, I, 197).

Thus the "Luini" idea in James's text is made to serve irony and poignancy. Adam Verver, whose powers as a connoisseur have been demonstrated as so limited, is given his moment in front of it. "He might have been in silence taking his last leave of it; it was a work for which [Maggie] knew, he entertained an ***unqualified*** esteem"; and her elaboration of her own response implies the essence of the above "idea". We learn that "the beauty of his sentiment looked out at her always, from the beauty of the rest, as if the frame made positively a window for his spiritual face". It is poignantly ironic that at this moment in his history, when he is in one way or another bereft of supporting human relations, he should receive aesthetic and spiritual sustenance from such a secondary artist and that Maggie should see such a work as expressing the spirit of the father she romantically idealizes (II, 359).

Adam is conscious enough of second best and general compromise elsewhere during this hasty leave-taking in the "stale" time of the "September hush . . . at the end of the dull day", in this room of which "a couple of the long windows stood open to the balcony that overhung the desolation" in "the desert of Portland Place". This is the immediate context for the final words we hear him exchange with his daughter as his grandson enters. Responding to the positive impressions he has deftly induced in her to soften their imminent farewells, Maggie pronounces, " 'It's success, father.' " To which he replies in a form that meets her need without ignoring the further reaches of his own consciousness: " 'It's success. And even *this*,' he added, as the Principino, appearing alone, deep within, piped across an instant greeting — 'even this isn't altogether failure!' " (II, 354, 321, 354-55, 366).

My account of how Adam is presented throughout the novel thus suggests a much richer "value" than has been acknowledged in even the most patient of the recent critical responses. As the coherence of this unique characterization emerges there would seem to be fewer grounds for charges of authorial mismanagement. Adam fatally simplifies, just as Amerigo and Charlotte are shown to, but James does not. The more quietly he delineates him, the more we learn about him. He keeps paramount the interesting development by which Adam becomes conscious of his own simplifications and of their general consequences. This is what he knows about the man and he shows only as much as he knows, which, I suggest, is ample for credibility and thus for effective function among the other "values". James has been adroit. He has admitted the strange and anomalous within his knowledge and then without faking or blinking has made the total presentation transcend the unattractive and potentially alienating within it. The James whose phantom spectator in the Fawns billiard-room could suggest that our attention might be "tender indeed almost to compassion" continues to eschew the explicit, while the art of *The Golden Bowl* manifests the justice of our finally granting that compassion. Like Amerigo and Charlotte, in their respective isolated states, Adam Verver goes out of sight into an essential solitariness on which the only suitable commentary is a reflective silence as inevitable as James's own (I, 125).

Once again I must submit that the final effect of this art of implication by imaginative omission and of deft, low-keyed inclusions can be appreciated in full only after it is seen in relation to the remaining principal figure, Maggie. But first I must consider how James evidently wishes us to see two figures who abound in explication — the Assinghams.

NOTES

1. James, *Notebooks*, p. 391.
2. Nuhn, *Wind*, p. 130.

3. Alexander Welsh, "Allegory of Truth in English Fiction", *Victorian Studies* 8:3 (September 1965), p. 26.
4. Wegelin, *Internationalism*, p. 162.
5. Caroline Gordon, "Mr Verver, Our National Hero", *Sewanee Review* 63 (Winter 1955), pp. 29-47. Hereafter *National Hero.*
6. Bowden, *Themes*, p. 104.
7. *Tanner GB*, p. 39.
8. Crews, *Tragedy*, pp. 107-8.
9. Krook, *Ordeal*, p. 252.
10. James E. Mulqueen, "Perfection of a Pattern: The Structure of *The Ambassadors, The Wings of the Dove*, and *The Golden Bowl*", *Arizona Quarterly* 27:2 (1971): 142.
11. Maves, *Sensuous Pessimism*, p. 128.
12. Matthiessen, *Major Phase*, p. 89.
13. Bayley, *Characters of Love*, p. 249.
14. Holland, *Expense*, pp. 354-55.
15. Girling, *Slang*, p. 134.
16. Firebaugh, *Ververs*, p. 403.
17. Hartsock, *Unintentional Fallacy*, p. 285.
18. Sears, *Negative Imagination*, pp. 161-62, 203.
19. Donald L. Mull, *Henry James's "Sublime Economy": Money as Symbolic Center in the Fiction* (Middletown, Connecticut: Wesleyan Univ. P., 1973), p. 159.
20. *Jefferson HJ*, p. 111.
21. Pearson, *Novel to End Novels*, p. 338.
22. Short, *Images*, p. 951.
23. Pearson, *Novel to End Novels*, p. 328.
24. Chernaik, *Moralist*, p. 119.
25. Holland, *Expense*, p. 354.
26. J.A. Ward, "The Ambiguities of Henry James", *Sewanee Review* 83:1 (January-March 1975): 58, 59.
27. *Jefferson HJ*, pp. 94-95.
28. Forster, *Aspects*, pp. 46-47.
29. John Carlos Rowe, "The Deceptive Symmetry of Art in *The Golden Bowl*", in his *Henry Adams and Henry James* (Ithaca, N.Y.: Cornell U.P., 1976), p. 207.
30. James, *GB* (Methuen), p. 492.
31. Emile Littré, *Dictionnaire de la Langue Française*, Tome 2 (Paris: Jean-Jacques Pauvert, 1956), p. 578. *Harrap's Standard French and English Dictionary*, ed. J.E. Mansion (London: Harrap, 1960), p. 177.
32. Peter and Linda Murray, *Dictionary of Art and Artists* (London: Thames and Hudson, 1965), p. 122.
33. For further confirmation of this view, see Austen Henry Layard, *The Italian Schools of Painting: Based on the Handbook of Kugler*, Part 2 (London: Murry, 1907), p. 420. "[Luini's] heads of women, children and angels present every grade from calm serenity, sweet cheerfulness, and innocent happiness, to ecstatic rapture".

D. The Assinghams and explication

The Assinghams have irritated or mystified half a century of critics more frequently than they have invited scrutiny from them. As Ora Segal notes, it is surprising that except for Sister Sharp's account their "exceedingly complex role"[1] has received such inadequate treatment. The most sophisticated of James's three major efforts might well call for commensurately sophisticated *ficelles*. Bayley was the first to demonstrate their full stature as characterizations and the great deal of subtly-pointed information carefully included in them; especially that James depicts in Fanny an "anarchic interior life" as well as depicting through her "a most discerning portrait of a certain kind of society average"[2]. Sister M. Corona Sharp, extending much further those appositions Bayley saw Fanny enjoying with the Prince and Charlotte, showed how, in wealthy English society, she and Bob are in an anomalous position, but hers "is even more ambivalent than her husband's because of her American birth, European 'discipline' and Oriental features"[3]. If we add her English husband, we find she has national affinities with every other character, major and minor, in the novel and is thus, in every sense, of the world in which it is unequivocally anchored.

Criticism would thus appear to have begun to do justice to her multiple functions. Though her role in the action is a subordinate one, her influence is continuous and her impact becomes a major part of the final effect. It was left to Mildred E. Hartstock in 1976 to notice James's obviously relevant comment in the *Prefaces* about "the fools who minister, at the particular crisis, to the intensity of the free spirit engaged with them"[4]. When we see how this "fool" so appropriately named Assingham is caught up in the chain reaction that she herself initiates, the term takes on almost Shakespearian connotations, especially as she and her fellow-fool become profoundly conscious of sharing its pertinence with all of those allegedly free apirits.

But my following account of how James's text presents the Assinghams should disallow Ruth Yeazell's more recent sophistication of this reading where she argues that in Fanny he is parodying his own style, that in Bob he is parodying literal-minded critics such as his own brother William and that Fanny "comes closest to sharing in [his own] . . . vision"[5]. I shall argue that he keeps his distance from both before dropping them completely in the final scene which reveals this vision; and that through them both he implies something about the uses of all language, whether the users be supersubtle or literal, in any attempt to express such a vision.

I discuss the Assinghams at this point, directly after my attempt to establish the nature and extent of Adam's knowledge, because the character and role of each, changing as they do during the course of the action, are apparently designed to contribute very directly to this central notion of "knowing". As the possibilities in the two marriages ramify and speculation begins as to motives and consequences, James ensures that this busy couple will dispose of the more obvious ones so that we may the sooner attend to the penumbra of those more challenging to discourse. The process of constant disillusionment that forms their education during the tale, forms a large part of ours too, up to the point where, by their given natures, they reach their limit. We learn how to assess their reactions and the results of their ruminations. On background facts about each of the principals they are reliable enough: we can accept their testimony of Maggie and Charlotte at school, of Adam as devoted to Maggie, of Amerigo's and of Charlotte's individual histories and of the outlines of their Roman relationship. But their guesses about motive and consequence are usually wrong, or, if right, right for the wrong reasons. They are shown as incapable of keeping pace with the fuller developments that James suggests and so are excluded from the finale.

We learn to qualify their commentary on events and effects by our knowledge of their natures as James clearly delineates them. Fanny is one of James's most effective statements on the effrontery of the marriage-maker. She is fictive cousin both of Aunt Maud, that single minded "Britannia of the Market Place"[6] and of the Susan Stringham so given to romantic views. The Prince tells us: "She had *made* his marriage, quite as truly as his papal ancestor had made his family — though he could scarce see what she had made it for unless because she too was perversely romantic." James uses words in describing her that cannot be blinked: she could easily look like a "*revendeuse*" and we do see her transact for the Ververs two human partners by no means virginal. Though she takes a more ironic view of them, her person and house are as cluttered with possessions as is the one at Lancaster Gate. "She was covered and surrounded with 'things', which were frankly toys and shams, a part of the amusement with which she rejoiced to supply her friends. . . . With her false indolence, in short, her false leisure, her false pearls and palms and courts and fountains, she was a person for whom life was multitudinous detail, detail that left her, as it at any moment found her, unappalled and unwearied." James remains as unequivocal when he tells us she thus fills the gaps in her life made by her childlessness and lack of wealth. Confident that her "cleverness" is superior to her husband's and that she does not fear but really likes complications, she throughout collects far more bits and pieces than she can ever make into a meaningful pattern. Her complications, which she gradually does come to fear, remain irrelevant to those James keeps central. Hers lag behind his, providing for his an *obbligato*, off-key and only contingently contributory (I, 21, 34, 35, 36).

Her husband is her complement but his limited reliability is well advertised. If Fanny sees too much, Bob sees too little. Both are products of the worldly. He had "left the army, which had clearly by that time done its laudable all for the enrichment of his personal experience". While Fanny plays supersubtle verbal games in her solipsistic realm, Bob indulges in "extravagant language", in "violence of speech" and the use that each makes of words is signally different from the demands made on them by James in service of the same subject. Bob's premises are declared: he is the "simplest, the sanest, the most obliging of men"; but we are also told of attitudes with which these attributes are not incompatible: "He knew everything that could be known about life, which he regarded as, for far the greater part, a matter of pecuniary arrangement." In the earlier stages of the imbroglio that he witnesses, he does not really care; he disengages. When Fanny accuses him "of a want alike of moral and intellectual reaction, or rather indeed of a complete incapacity for either", he is clear as to his degree of detachment: "he could be in spite of the limitation a perfectly social creature". It is a sentence containing the simulacrum of all James's long years of observation in society, in country houses over long weekends and, especially, in Clubland, "the world that was least of a mystery" — predictably enough — to the retired Robert Assingham, who "could deal with things, perfectly, for all his needs, without getting near them". While Fanny endlessly embroiders, he peremptorily edits, life. As she is clearly too close to the imbroglio and he is clearly too far from it, neither — James implies — attains the distance he recommends to us (I, 35, 64, 67).

They do approach it, though, and this in itself makes for

interest and suspense as the principals move into territory beyond the common social reach. The tenor of their regarding the spectacle alters. As Fanny's febrile gossiping with herself in Bob's company is eventually stilled, Bob's own ribald grunts and sardonic interjections are silenced and the reader is inevitably impressed by this conversion of the cynics. Though not fully understanding the knowledge revealed they are awed by the revelation.

They are in short made aware of the fundamental incalculability of human conduct. Fanny's premises begin to know challenge from the moment the Prince first visits her, betraying uneasiness, and when she sees his response to the returned Charlotte they are distinctly shaken. Later with the Colonel she rationalizes her way to a truce with herself and then abounds with confident estimations that are immediately perceived by the reader to be crassly incorrect. Charlotte, Fanny tells Bob, has come back to see Maggie through, because she knows the Prince and Maggie does not; Charlotte is going to be sublime; Charlotte is cured. If the preliminary signals along the way have not already thrown the first syllable of her surname into relief, this exchange must surely do so. By the time she is recommending Charlotte to Adam at Fawns, oblivious of his patient amusement, she is again in full career as a passionately sincere manipulator of people for their own good and her chatter echoes portentously in the authorial silence. She receives her first real fright at the Foreign Office ball after Bob has reported to her the Prince's and Charlotte's first appearance alone and when Charlotte takes her uncompromising stance with her. She suffers first "a sort of anxiety of intelligence", then becomes "conscious above all that she was in the presence of still deeper things than she had yet dared to fear" (I, 256, 262).

With the Prince, too, "she was embarrassed by the difference between what she took in and what she could say, what she felt and what she could show" and he too moves her into realms, indeed, where there is for the first time a difference between what he might mean and what she can measure. Though she determines to analyze both these quantities in "the snug laboratory of her afterthought", we learn that "there were moments positively, . . . when something as yet unnameable came out for her in his look . . .". Even her glib social patter breaks down. This startles Fanny out of her complacency. "Discussion had of itself, to her sense, become danger — such light, as from open crevices, it let in . . .". Later, in the brougham with Bob, she clutches desperately her notion that Charlotte's " 'moral delicacy' " will ensure she will leave Amerigo alone. Bob in fact has only a moment before this likened her "game" to one of "three guesses — like forfeits on Christmas Eve" and their whole exchange is immediately followed by the scene in which the lovers so passionately seal their "sacred" pledge, a scene that brings out the irony of his thrice telling Fanny that " 'They'll manage in in their own way' ". This, we are told, "represented the limited vibration of which his confirmed old toughness had been capable" (I, 267, 271, 273, 283, 281, 285).

Fanny, who has several more mistakes to realize before she appreciates the full superficiality of her calculations, meanwhile shows herself in the pathetically ludicrous light of trying to sound Amerigo out as to whether he will go to Matcham with Charlotte without their *sposi* and of her getting herself invited so that she may the better watch the latter's interests. There, Charlotte sees her as irrelevant; Amerigo speaks of " 'Poor, poor Fanny' ". She totally underestimates the passional level on which the lovers are then existing and which drives them to those scenes we witness on the parapet, after her departure with Bob. Fanny, for whom the forms are a full two-thirds of conduct, utterly miscalculates how operative the remaining third can be. Fanny, for whom morality is nothing but high intelligence and who can impute to Charlotte moral delicacies at this point, must abandon one more position and characteristically rebound to yet another incorrect one.

Her being at the mercy of the Matcham milieu and her being powerless in the face of the lovers' absorption in each other is of less interest to the reader than are those limitations of perception and of understanding that produce her gymnastics. These, each time she indulges in them, become for her less amusing: she could easily enough quell her uneasiness after Charlotte's return from America; she could even with an effort allay her fears after the Foreign Office ball; but now after Matcham her plight is compounded by a "strangeness" and "a mixture of things" defying far more than her anxious agilities and her husband's terse summaries (I, 343, 390, 88).

Their midnight colloquy, summing up the latest (incorrect) position they have reached, is their lengthiest and their last. It closes Book First and provides a splendid ironic context for Book Second. It is marked by a different relationship between the Assinghams, a different tenor in their questing discourse. Though they can never keep pace with the true nature of the events, they bring to them at successive points a degree of increased caution, even — relative to their earlier forays — a marked degree of humility. "They had in general in these days longer pauses and more abrupt transitions." They defer a little more to each other's opinions and wait on each other's words. "There was in these minor manoeuvres and conscious patiences something of a suspension of their old custom of divergent discussion, that intercourse by misunderstanding which had grown so clumsy now; . . . no trouble was at present to be vulgarly recognized as clear." He as well as she can now confess "a consciousness of deep waters" and as they discuss the " 'rum' " arrangements of Maggie and her father and the " 'extraordinary' " in Charlotte, "he must be something more than a plain man now". Fanny continues to produce for him her "ideas" in a "dim procession" and "he could but watch its immensity", but she eventually breaks down into tears at the prospect of " 'God knows what!' " She earnestly pursues her business of "seeing", "knowing" and "understanding", aided now by a generally sympathetic Colonel, but the names she now gives herself for her earlier imperceptiveness — " 'idiot' ", " 'meddlesome fool' ", " 'wretch' ", and " 'double dyed donkey' " — apply even now with as general a force (I, 364, 365, 366, 375, 368, 377, 387, 388, 392).

James indeed reinforces the fact with all the skill by which his later mode can enable the objects within a scene to take on a quality of suggestion that makes them a bridge between literal and figurative description. They hold this discussion amid the physical glooms and gleams of their night-shrouded home. As they share together "the region of the understood" they are brought "still more nearly face to face. They remained for some minutes looking at it though the dim window which opened upon the world of human trouble in general and which let the vague light play here and there upon gilt and crystal and colour. . . ." The provenly unwise Fanny is likened to a Sphinx; the deep waters become a "mystic lake" into which they both eventually sink together, "hand in hand". The most completely definitive of the figures used to describe this much-travelled couple is the one that sees them as "a pair of specious worldly adventurers driven for relief, under sudden stress, to some grim midnight reckoning in an odd corner" (I, 378, 371).

Towards the close of this passage, the figurative and the literal combine in the one vivid, economical, implied authorial comment on them, just as she has triumphantly offered him her latest summary.

> Whereupon, breaking short off to ascend to her room, she presented her highly-decorated back — in which, in odd places, controlling the complications of its aspect, the ruby or the garnet, the turquoise and the topaz, gleamed like faint symbols of *the wit that pinned together the satin patches of her argument.*

> He watched her *as if* she left him positively under the impression of her mastery of her subject; yes, *as if* the real upshot of the drama before them was but that he had, when it came to the tight places of life — as life had shrunk for him now — the most ***luminous*** of wives. He turned off, in this view of her majestic retreat, ***the comparatively faint little electric lamp that had presided over their talk***; then he went up as immediately behind her as the billows of her amber train allowed, making out ***how all the clearness they had conquered was even for herself a relief*** — how at last *the sense of the amplitude of her exposition* sustained and floated her.

They are to lie, she says, to all, and particularly to Maggie their saviour and it is under the prevailing influence of the sensitive ironies in the above sustained passage of dramatic poetry that we listen to a more massive one. " 'We know nothing on earth —!' " James has them make such solemn declarations while they remain unconscious of the farther reaches of the validity in them. Fanny wears the coat of the pied fool, in a scene where the real light is faint, where she convinces not even her Colonel who recognizes that her moral decisions, the product of the ample wit she would call high intelligence, are still supported only by her own shiny patchwork of illusions (I, 399, 400).

These, anyway, are the last she is to entertain with even a show of such confidence. Book Second reveals her soon realizing that Maggie sees through her lie and makes use of it as she in fact determinedly makes use of her in her own forms of lying. Fanny looks to her — just as Bob looks *at* her — for guidance and with wonderment, and the nature of their spectatorship changes.

In Fanny's five remaining appearances there is increasing emphasis on her making the kind of efforts that the reader is making to keep up with developments and to accept squarely the inevitable discomforts of facing the incalculable. Fanny is shown desperately fencing with Maggie's now startlingly explicit fears; she is shown with Bob abdicating her extravagant guesses for quieter forms of prediction. When Maggie confronts her with explicit evidence as to the true nature of things, the older woman is shown deserting her wit altogether for the futile, melodramatic gesture of smashing the bowl; at Fawns she is the helped, rather than the confident helper; in London, finally, she tries to understand the complications without further contributing to them.

James spells out these five remaining stages with an appeal to variety that keeps the Assingham "value" a richly contributory one to the novel's total effect. Confronted with Maggie's passionate demand for facts — " 'What do you believe, what do you *know*?' " — she turns pale for general as well as special fears, bereft now of "the high pitch of her cheer". Fanny is acutely conscious that Maggie is, perversely, "treating her, without insistence, rather with caressing confidence, as there to see and to know, to advise and to assist". But she sees and knows little. She does find time, though, amid her adroit fencing, for what we can recognize as one honest confession to her interrogator: " 'I'm bound to confess I've never been so awfully sure of what I may call knowing you.' " James makes us conscious of another confession in her somewhat frantic response " 'as a woman of imagination' ". But her limit is soon enough reached now, as Maggie learns to her despair at the "failure of responsive wit in her friend". It is, however, a failure distinctly relative in a novel apparently designed to show that knowledge, imagination and wit never take anyone far enough (II, 107, 104, 102, 110, 114, 119).

Fanny's response to Maggie's discovery of the golden bowl is characteristic: what she cannot rationalize out of existence she will smash. She at first is fearful even of touching it and as she hears Maggie tell her that " 'it makes today too much to explain. I mean to explain away' ", she recognizes Nemesis. " 'There are many things . . . that we shall never know' " is all she can make words do for her now.

Meanwhile the bowl remains, not explained away, and when Fanny discovers it is flawed, she seizes on the chance to reject facts now so unpredictably but incontrovertibly present. " 'Then your whole idea has a crack' ", she illogically argues and, nimbly shifting to ground less damning for herself, she insists: " There's only one knowledge that concerns us. . . .' " This of course is the belief she chooses to embrace that Amerigo " 'has never been half so interested in [Maggie] as now' ", but Maggie shakes her head "as against all easy glosses" and so Fanny is driven to a final effort to erase meanings (II, 168, 175, 178).

When the bowl lies shattered she indulges in the empty theatricality of " 'whatever you meant by it — and I don't want to know *now* — has ceased to exist' ". It is patently a pious effort at simplification, a reversion, under pressure, to old discredited means of dealing with newly ramifying difficulties. It is also her attempt to serve her new idol while not ceasing to serve the Prince, whose eyes she now holds "in a manner" suggesting "a redemption of pledges" exchanged long before. Maggie remains in every sense beyond her reach and nothing is sadder here than Fanny's subsequent self-congratulatory air of having thus materially affected matters. It is of course Maggie, who is "looking too — and was moreover looking at them both", who will be left to deal with the Prince's question about meanings and who will in so doing eschew those negative gestures in which the departed woman has evidently such a high degree of misplaced trust (II, 179, 179-180, 180).

Henceforth Fanny is depicted as enjoying her illusion of helpfulness in addition to her consciousness of the need to be ever "fairly gaping with good will". Maggie, reflecting on her own task, decides: "There was no one to help her with it — not even Fanny Assingham now; this good friend's presence having been doomed to become, with that climax of their last interview in Portland Place, a severely simplified function." That good friend, with her "bruised philosophy", is sufficiently aware of the difficulty of keeping up with it all. When a notion is put to her, "Fanny followed as she could" or "did what she might to embrace it". Her relationship with Maggie is completely reversed and she cries, " 'Oh if you knew how you help me!' " We learn that "Maggie had liked her to understand so far as this was possible, but hadn't been slow to see afterwards how the possibility was limited, when one came to think, by mysteries she was not to sound". The farther Maggie moves among these mysteries, the more adrift, of course, both Assinghams appear. We learn, in the final section devoted to them, after their following Maggie and the Prince back to London from Fawns, where Charlotte has been supervising the packing, that they "swam back into her ken besprinkled with sawdust and looking as pale as if they had seen Samson pull down the temple. They had seen at least what she wasn't seeing, rich dim things under the impression of which they retired" (II, 213, 208, 211, 216, 218, 324).

At best now, Fanny can help her "by not wholly failing to guess her thought" but generally in her duologues she blunders in, or, more rarely, avoids in the nick of time so doing. The woman who at one point had concluded: "Old arithmetic had perhaps been fallacious, but the new settled the question" is shown in her final scene with Maggie as not even knowing the problems, much less the right questions to ask. Their subject is still their "knowledge" but no arithmetic, either new or old, or even the most terrible algebra, can calculate the state of mind of Amerigo, of Adam, of Charlotte or of Maggie herself. That these are manifestly incalculable would appear to be the point and it is an eloquent comment on Fanny that she remains to the last merely "inquisitive" still (II, 327, I, 76, II, 325).

Fanny retains throughout, despite a degree of inevitable maturation, a coarseness of sensibility: it is important for her to be able to snub in Eaton Square those who have snubbed her at Matcham. To the end she is trapped by her false position. While seeking knowledge about present developments, she must still pretend to ignorance about past ones, as when she traps herself during their discussion of "how far" Charlotte and the Prince went. "Fanny had appeared to make sure, but there was something she remembered — remembered in time and even with a smile. 'I've told you before that I know absolutely nothing.' " This is her lie — just as her inability to understand how the Prince is now in relation to Maggie will ever be her limitation. Her importance for James is that she remains so demonstrably amateur. As a highly complex *ficelle*, ever organic to his discourse, she serves its irony in ways radically more thorough than those which current criticism has acknowledged. Her discussion is either stupid or melodramatic or obvious or grossly wrong and reveals an inflated notion of her means and of her powers for using them. We do feel, as James obviously wished, that she contributes her forms of knowledge "all too officiously"[7]. Her mind (to paraphrase Eliot) is continually violated by neat theories. She is always attempting what Conrad would call the impossible. She provides story-telling at the level of chattering humanity. She is, to paraphrase yet another poet, always quacking[8] beside us in the wood, the wood (as well as the individual trees of which) James so quietly leads us to behold from his vantage point — silently (II, 335).

NOTES

1. Ora Segal, *The Lucid Reflector: The Observer in Henry James's Fiction* (New Haven: Yale U. P., 1969), p. 207.
2. Bayley, *Characters of Love*, pp. 242, 243.
3. Sister M. Corona Sharp, *The Confidante in Henry James: Evolution and Moral Value of a Fictive Character* (Indiana: U. of Notre Dame P., 1963), p. 282.
4. Mildred E. Hartsock, "Time for Comedy: The Late Novels of Henry James", *English Studies* 56 (April 1975), p. 122 quoting *Prefaces*, p. 129; see also *Prefaces*, p. 67.
5. Ruth Yeazell, "The New 'Arithmetic' of Henry James", *Criticism* 16 (Spring 1974): 116.
6. James, *The Wings of the Dove*, I, 30.
7. James, *Prefaces*, p. 330.

8. Rupert Brooke, "You came and quacked beside me in the wood", "The Voice", *The Complete Poems of Rupert Brooke* (London: Sidgwick Jackson, 1936), pp. 79-80.

E. Maggie Verver and the Princess, the dialectic of imagery, the authorial comment, the scaled epithets, her resulting view of love, pity and dread, and the function of the gilt cup

The critics who have neglected the Prince, sentimentalized or maligned Charlotte, been baffled by Adam and irritated by the Assinghams have usually devoted most of their attention to Maggie. This is predictable enough if she is seen in relation to Isabel, Maisie, Nanda and Milly instead of to the art of this novel in which she has one of the principal roles, but most have gone further and seen her as the point of the novel, its chief moral agent. Those who admit some kind of process or development going on within her, still see her as finishing up very close to James, and the Maggie most popular in critical circles is the innocent who, after a fright, keeps her head and grows up, to the benefit of all around her. I do not believe the text supports these views of her nature and function.

Her alleged virtue needed defining in terms more adequate than Gordon's — "*caritas*, Christian charity"[1]. Bayley tackled the task: "She *is* good, but her goodness is subject to the author's deliberate 'appeal to incalculability'; like that of the observed person in life it remains both incomplete and open to question." His emphasis on James's attention to "the muffled incalculability of living" and on how "mystery — as James sees and presents it — is the very stuff of life", cut straight through to what I believe is the heart of this major chronicle: mystery, not obfuscation, not muddle, not perversity; mystery not created but recognized and explored. With "goodness", as a moral imperative, out of the way, Bayley perceived the formal consequences, for as he continued, Maggie is rescued from appearing priggish "when we have grasped the fantastic richness and humour of James's mode of appeal"[2].

Krook[3] itemized credibly and exhaustively the traits of which the girl's moods are an expression and she took account of many more of James's provisions for a character much fuller than that which others, except for Bayley, had realized might be there, even though the final sum Krook reached might be queried in the total equation. Generally, however, Maggie has become the chief casualty of a general critical failure to appreciate the radical sophistication of the mode of the novel. She is seen as James's moral delegate, the novel's alter-authorial. Ruth Todasco continued the trend. Maggie is "the novelist's conception of a 'sound humanity'. . . the proper measure of her companions' variations"[4] — the critic here applying to James's final work the notion that the James of 1865 had applied to *Our Mutual Friend.* Holland, in a chapter headed "The Redemptive Process", argued thus: "The process is redeemed, and its risks and the cost in suffering are measured, through Maggie's assumption of responsibility for it as she becomes James's mediating centre of consciousness and the heroine of the drama being built around her."[5] But the drama can be built around her without her being the heroine of it and, though she does assume responsibility, we are witness to her mediating for James much that she misconstrues while he continues to mediate by other means our view of her.

Pearson sophisticated his notion of "identification" and "association". He believed that at the climax of each of the late novels, "one of the characters' consciousness . . . fuses, as it were, with James's own: this gives James's consciousness a kind of social endorsement and extension, suggesting . . . some spiritual community . . ."[6]. He cited the Adam-Maggie and the Assingham duologues as examples, but he did not examine them or their relation to the entire scenario, nor did he mention any of the other numerous provisions for irony in particular or distancing in general, which make the notion untenable. Bayley did do some of this necessary work, detecting the fuller reach of the "divine principle", and drawing attention to James's interest, in the *Prefaces*, in "the sounded note" and in the "*soundless* meaning". Here, wrote Bayley, "Maggie sees herself as groping noiselessly among her problems"; and we do indeed watch her mind as we attend to her portentous silences, just as, on other occasions, we "listen" to those hypothetical utterances of hers that offer a bridge to her actual pause-ridden ones.[7] Crews, arguing that Maggie "never reaches a point of intellectual and moral delicacy that we might properly call James's own", maintained that James had in this novel "so refined his approach that he feels free to remain completely outside of his drama"[8]. Yet Wayne Booth,[9] rightly, would dispute the possibility of any writer doing this and I believe James would dispute the value of such absence — even if it were achievable — just as unequivocally as he disputed obtrusive presence, especially the elaborate form Conrad's took in *Chance*.[10]

The critic who has done much of the necessary work on this crucial issue is Bryan Reddick. His article took up the whole question of "involvement, intimacy, immediacy" and some of the ways in which the retrospective "narrative shifts", and "overlapping" scenes, the dialogue, syntax and diction all contribute to distancing. He saw how "Maggie's own point of view becomes *less* limited"; and he saw how "the reader does become intimately involved, though not with the story so much as the narration of it"; and how "the most general way the reader is kept at a distance from any one character in *The Golden Bowl* and is yet drawn into the created universe of the novel is the formal control he is made to feel in every passage"[11]. The provisions are even more thorough and their combined operation contributes a much more subtle and comprehensive control than even he suggests, as I hope to show. This certainly is the territory in which "meaning", and Maggie's component in it, may be most profitably explored, especially if we take with us Bayley's reminders about the "soundless" and Yeazell's more recent suggestions about the use of speech in these major enterprises and if we never underestimate how the imagery is forever working.

James's fictive simulation of a *Comédie* performance takes him so far and then, it may be shown, the imagery operates in the contrived silence. This art enables us to "see" Maggie, notably in Book Second, not as James *endorses* her but as he *shows* her. Yeazell came close to what I believe the novel does for us in James's firm control. "Maggie", she said, "constructs a saving interpretation of her world — an interpretation we may be inclined, especially if we are fond of Maggie, to take as truth. But we have no way of verifying our theories: denied access to the minds of Charlotte, Adam, and even the Prince, we are confined in the second half of *The Golden Bowl* to the chambers of Maggie's consciousness and, briefly, of the Assingham's drawing room."[12] That Maggie is seen to be rationalizing is important, but we are, in fact, given access to the minds of all those others by authorial manipulation of their appearance and words in relation to the context provided by the antecedent narrative and by our long and sustained distanced-intimacy with them that is concurrent with our distanced-intimacy with Maggie.

Yeazell was certainly closer to the mark than was Schneider, who took her to task for suggesting that the morality of this novel " 'remains irreducibly ambiguous' "[13] and who claimed he could "verify" a moral judgment through its "image patterns"[14]. Yeazell replied properly I believe, that "ritualistically to evoke 'images' in this fashion is to overlook the obvious fact that the meaning of a novel is the function of all its language, whether overtly figurative or not" and that to say that Maggie " 'rises above' desire . . . seems . . . to guide us through *The Golden Bowl* by an alien map: James's last novel is not *The Wings of the Dove*"[15]. She could, I also believe, have made, for James's account of each of the other principals, the case she made for his account of Maggie and could thus have posited a "meaning" which, while being neither "irreducibly ambiguous" nor over-simply judgmental, accounted for more of the whole radically original work, to which I now once again turn.

Maggie Verver and the Princess

Coming to consider the full extent of the attention James gives to each of the other characters, especially the other three principals, may in itself render unnecessary any further protest about her not being the protagonist of the novel. But James's provisions for extreme mobility and subtle modulation in authorial control of her function compel me to discuss these before examining her nature and her relation to love. It is logical to consider her last. In trying to show how the structure and the characterization keep us alert all the time to all the figures of the drama, I have yet inevitably had to follow the sequence of emphasis the narrative gives us. Thus we start with the Prince and his relationship with Charlotte leads us to dwell on her, just as hers with Adam makes us then dwell on him. Maggie is continually very much the concern of all three, as well as of the Assinghams, and the evolution is such that even if her consciousness were not chosen for the reflection of events throughout the latter half of the novel and even if she were not to assume the responsibility of trying to determine them, she would still incur much direct attention at the end because everyone else is very busily relating to her.

I have already dealt with those historic reasons in James's development that make her kind of character the appropriate choice when James wants a *tabula rasa* in which to reflect all that he is to spin so fine, but I must now indicate the distance which he himself sustains from her and the way he, right to the last, depicts her romanticism in the most realistic of lights. If, as I have said, Amerigo is the characterization most frequently underestimated by critics; if Charlotte, whom I call the most intense one, is granted by them more attention than the novel justifies; and if Adam's difficult subtleties most often defeat them; then Maggie is surely the one most often oversimplified by them. In the first three, James is characterizing in his major manner people who are to indulge their preoccupations: Amerigo wants wealth and will indulge his pleasures; Charlotte wants him; Adam wants to establish Maggie's happiness and his great collection. But Maggie, at first by nature the simplest of all, finds herself impelled to understand and accommodate them all and she is the character who from the first to the last page of the novel travels the greatest distance in the tortuous journey from innocence through experience to a new level of consciousness.

The context in which we enter her uneasy mind at the beginning of Book Second warrants the closest attention. It is informed by her Prince's account of her in Part First, her father's in Part Second, her rival's in Part Third and the Assinghams in all three parts. Its immediate antecedent is Fanny's fevered protestation to the Colonel that an enlightened Maggie will somehow find the resources within herself to see them all through. Fanny's words, though, of which there always seem too many, must be set against those passionate ones impelling Charlottte and the Prince on the parapet at Matcham. But, for us, this context is itself informed by the even richer one of our long acquaintance with her on all those other occasions when James ensures that the view given of her is clearly relative to other realities. He is from the first relentless here.

We meet her, on the eve of her marriage, after having adjusted our vision to the quite different kind of experience involved in meeting her fiance, of whom she is patently ignorant. The conversation he recollects as an effort to reduce his own ignorance is for her "the mere play of her joy" as, " 'not afraid of history' ", she tells him about " 'the beautiful world' " and how American romanticism " 'makes everything that's nice' " in it. Her impact is that of a person excusably euphoric and inexcusably immature.

She may well be for us, as for Colonel Assingham three chapters later on, merely " 'the young woman who has a million a year' ". James appropriately lets Charlotte, in that even later devious stroll with Amerigo, articulate those natural misgivings that anyone less " 'decent' " might have about someone who is " 'not selfish enough' " and who invites exploitation in a manner so " 'terrible' ". James's attention to her here in Part First, as manifested in the texture of the narrative, may arouse a rather generalized pity, as well as an implied intermittent incredulity; certainly, liking for her vivacity and generosity of spirit may easily be subordinated to curiosity as to what explains her and as to where it will lead her (I, 8, 9, 11, 77, 102, 101, 102).

Part Second begins an explanation. She is very much Adam Verver's daughter and we learn not only of "their decent little old-time union", but also of how they have preserved a form of it: the hour after lunch always finds them privately engrossed with her child just as he, in a sense equally as evident, remains engrossed with his. Leaving her still bewildered husband to her friend Fanny ("She was there to keep him quiet — it was Amerigo's own description of her influence") is her way of continuing undisturbed her habitual handling of knowledge. "It wasn't that the Princess could be indebted to another person, even to so clever a one as this friend, for *seeing* anything in her husband that she mightn't see unaided; but she had ever, hitherto, been of a nature to accept with modest gratitude any better description of a felt truth than her little limits — terribly marked, she knew, in the direction of saying the right things — enabled her to make" (I, 135, 161, 163).

Insulated and indulged by her father, she appreciates how pleasant everything is for her but has no confidence in herself and though knowing she, like her father, is " 'free as air' ", she operates personally within a very narrow compass, obeying her own set of "rules — full as she was of ***little*** rules, considerations, provisions". Comparing herself to her brilliant friend Charlotte Stant, she realizes that that girl is

" '*interesting* — which plenty of other people with plenty of other merits never are a bit.' In which fine flicker of vision the truth widened to the Princess's view. 'I myself of course don't take liberties, but then I do always by nature tremble for my life. That's the way I live.' " When her father vaguely demurs, she continues: " 'Yes, I live in terror,' . . . 'I'm a small creeping thing.' " Though she expresses this idea of herself with her habitual romantic exaggeration, it squares with our observation of her: her delegation to Fanny of the husband whom she knows is dependent on her in the milieu new to him, her reluctance to assume her available social role and her detachment from realities (I, 176, 166, 181).

James does not spare us her fatuities. Discussing her former school-friend with her father, she pronounces solemnly that she expects to see in her " 'more than I've ever seen' ", because " 'I've lived more myself, I'm older, and one judges better' ". It even takes the form of an arch complacency in the privileges of ignorance. When she disclaims detailed knowledge of Charlotte's having loved and lost, and he answers her question, about the common practice of "telling," with another one — " 'How do I know, my dear, what young men do?' " — she so quickly flashes back her prim " 'Then how do *I* know, father, what vulgar girls do?' " that he loses no time in placating her. " 'I see — I see,' he quickly returned." Primness in her is never less attractive than when Adam plays with the word in her connection while playing too with the notion of her as nymph and as nun. He reflects that "Maggie had been described, even in her prettiness as 'prim' — Mrs Rance herself had enthusiastically used the word for her". That lady no doubt would, but it is Maggie's and Adam's responses to this figurative play that gives the reader pause: "when once she had been told before him familiarly that she resembled a nun she had replied that she was delighted to hear it and would certainly try to" (I, 182, 186, 188).

For him, whose product she is, she resembles

> some slight slim draped "antique" of Vatican or Capitoline halls, . . . keeping still the quality, the ***perfect*** felicity, of the statue; the ***blurred absent*** eyes, the smoothed elegant ***nameless*** head, ***the impersonal flit of a creature lost in an alien age*** and passing as an image in worn relief round and round a precious vase. She had always had odd moments of striking him, daughter of his very own though she was, ***as a figure thus simplified***, "generalised" in its grace, a figure with which his human connexion was fairly interrupted by some vague analogy of turn and attitude, something shyly mythological and nymph-like.

I have already discussed the implications for his character of his thus "caring for precious vases only less than for precious daughters", but we must note too the implications, for the victim, of a father who so complacently entertains as perfect her suggestion of the blind, the anonymous, the impersonal and of one so lost and alien in a modern setting. All too dangerously simplified and generalized, the human connection is clearly too interrupted. When she asks him if he realizes that she has " 'never had the least blow' ", his serenity is undisturbed. "He gave her a long quiet look. 'Who *should* realise if I don't?' " Here, indeed, the response recalls and is classified with Mrs Assingham's inane comment to the Colonel earlier that the girl " 'wasn't born to know evil. She must never know it.' " Adam's premises are advertised as being as inconsistent as his images. "Nymphs and nuns were certainly separate types, but Mr Verver, when he really amused himself, let consistency go." James demonstrates carefully enough how her disconnection from realities has been contrived and sustained (I, 188-89, 188, 186, 78, 188).

He demonstrates too how her attempts to "connect" show either too much or too little imagination. Her reported rhetorical question about what may happen to the Principino during her absence in Italy with her husband is one example. "Her question had fairly resounded, but it had afterwards, like many of her questions, dropped still more effectively than it had risen." As Charlotte tells Fanny, " 'she worries easily . . .' ". When, in Part Third, we see Charlotte busily exploiting the opportunities this kind of person offers her, we see Maggie unconsciously but inexcusably exploiting every situation that she herself, as Charlotte puts it, " 'likes to arrange' ", and that " 'suits her' ". Charlotte must travel about London in a cab because Maggie, after being ensconced with her father and her baby, has " 'gone out — taking the carriage for something he had been intending, but that she offered to do instead' " (I, 199-200, 253, 259, 304).

Nor is Charlotte the mistress of her own house. "Maggie, with a proper spirit, held that her father ought from time to time to give a really considered dinner, and Mr Verver, who had as little idea as ever of not meeting expectation, was of the harmonious opinion that his wife ought." At these dinners, where Amerigo's impressions of her were always of a "rather neutral and negative propriety", she automatically usurps the role of hostess, for "the party was her father's party" and "she bristled with filial reference, with little filial recalls of expression, movement, tone". Though her intention is clearly otherwise, the exhibition inevitably attests that her union with her father has been undisturbed by his marriage to the brilliant woman present: "the princess — *il n'y avait pas à dire* — might sit where she liked: she would still always in that house be irremediably Maggie Verver" (I, 320, 322, 323).

When Fanny at the end of Book First takes up with Bob the appalling consequences of Maggie's " 'little scruples and her little lucidities, which were really so divinely blind' " she is taking up the refrain that James has already established in Maggie's "little old-time union", "her little limits", and her "little rules, considerations, appearances". It is in this context that her Roman husband, evoking the daughter of Scipio Africanus, sees her as "a Cornelia in miniature". Sincere, candid, direct and utterly guileless, she is displayed aboard her father's boat in a social sea where these necessary qualities are sadly insufficient whether one rows with or against its tide. As she continues always doing the wrong thing always for the right reasons, James continues to keep our interest free of distractions. Her ignorances are not allowed to irritate. Her naively romantic response to her affianced Prince is never childish, always childlike. Her idealizing of her father and her continued concern for him are never even remotely pathological and are always rendered as spontaneous wishes to share her freshly discovered good fortune. Her commandeering of his new wife's house, patently never a matter of calculation, is patently ever a matter of impulse and reflex (I, 396, 135, 163, 166, 322).

Any impatience we might find growing is tempered by our view of her relationships with people, none of whom are of the least help to her in the developing situation of which she remains so poignantly unconscious. The Prince simply does not understand her at all and merely falls back on his general assurance of his own good fortune. Adam takes her and everyone and everything for granted, thus tacitly encouraging her confidence in an eternally " 'nice' " security. Charlotte is too concerned with Amerigo to employ on her behalf anything more than clever tact and convenient discretion. Fanny wallows in her own guilty anxiety. Society is quietly amused, coolly curious — as indifferent as the sea itself. I have argued that each of the four principals in this novel is rendered as isolated and I stress now that this image of Maggie has the longest history. When in that midnight session with Bob, Fanny, having sensed Maggie's dawning awareness of her solitude, says " 'She's always so different from any one else in the world that it's hard to say when she's different from herself' ", she accidentally hits on the essence of that interest that James has evidently been from the first so delicately nurturing. When the simple is so alarmingly different, any interest in it is itself arresting, promising, possibly incalculable (I, 11, 373).

Book Second is certainly concerned to a large extent with

showing the interest deriving from her attempts to realize and transcend her littleness, but the evidence of the authorial stance, of the scenario principle and of the functions of the language in this half of James's elaborate chronicle suggests that his conception of a further interest makes his task here infinitely more difficult. It is not merely a matter of his keeping us aware of the other figures in order to imply what her relations with them mean for her and how they complicate her idea of preserving the general "equilibrium". His modulation of mode here as he enters Part Fourth, though in every way congruous with the whole, is distinctly not an attempt to put us on more intimate terms with the consciousness of a single character. Just as that was only ostensibly the case even in the first three parts, where we successively became thus acquainted with the other three principals while actually learning much about all four simultaneously, it is now not even ostensibly so (II, 39).

Nor was it formerly necessary. We have already been introduced to as much of Maggie as there is to know up to this point, just as we have been introduced to a similar relative knowledge of each of the others. With introductions over, James can now concentrate on showing with "a high refinement" the remaining developments *in* each of the four and *among* their relationships. The radical originality of his attempt, however, is that he evidently wishes to approach as close as the temporal art of narrative can to showing all of them all at once. Deprived of music's chords he of course cannot achieve the instant simultaneity by which concerted instruments can orchestrate for us many implications of an idea at once. Conrad's James, never attempting the impossible, knowing his inevitable commitment to the consecutive, is content to simulate very strenuously the concurrent by three agencies: an extreme mobility of authorial vantage point in which imagery is the most potent idiom; a reliance on the power of the scenario principle to serve at once the drama as well as the narrative and thus constantly to remind us to see one thing "through" another; and an emphatic positioning of recurrent words, the connotations of which continue to proliferate and to insist that our attention remains comprehensive. The result, I shall argue, is an aesthetic distancing that encourages a richly interested contemplation involving our continued awareness of all the figures and not only the one most immediately rendered. The mobility of Maggie's mind is an exquisitely interesting part of his subject; the mobility of James's mode ensures that we entertain the rest of it.

The Maggie we do see in the remaining three parts is much more worthy of the more immediate rendering than the one we have so far known. We are after all seeing her learn not only what we either knew already or learned much more quickly but also what we are learning along with her. Earlier almost monotonously predictable, she now becomes part of the "appeal to variety", for, to paraphrase Fanny, James remains unremittingly faithful in his account of the lion-like reactions of this aroused lamb. To consider a mere outline of the "discriminated occasions" that the scenario subsequently provides is to see in fact many different Maggies.

In the first of them we see what her "brooding fancy" makes of the moments, "*watchable* still", when her husband rewards her long wait for his return from Matcham. We thus see her plagued by an indefinable unease that becomes, when she realizes how he and Charlotte are "*treating*" her, a very definable loneliness. We see her first historic resistance, in the carriage, after the Verver dinner for the Castledeans, to her husband's sexual overtures. We see her " 'going' ", with unaccustomed commitment in the social scene. Before even Part Fourth ends, we see her fearful, exploratory fencing with her father in Regent's Park; her distraught outburst to Fanny after their private Sunday luncheon; her euphoric regaining of momentary confidence from her visit to Amerigo's archives; her grim sharing with Fanny of the antiquarian's revelations and her icy implacability with her husband after she has confronted him with the fragments of her golden bowl (II, 9, 11, 41, 69).

In Part Fifth we watch her perform her deliberately selected roles: the trusting friend who, on the terrace of Fawns that night, so publicly kisses her rival; the contented daughter who on their familiar Fawns bench encourages her father to "ship" with his wife for American City; the silent witness, in the gallery, of Charlotte's anguish; and the possessive daughter, jealous of her father's remarriage, accepting defeat, relinquishing him to his new wife in their garden confrontation. In the appropriately brief final part we are shown what relinquishment of him means for her, what forms her compassion for them all takes, how she can now be capable of such majestic imperatives as the " 'Come!' " and the " 'Go!' " she issues to the husband whose wife she now believes herself ready to become and, before we leave her, we are shown where she at last finds herself to be and something of what she may glimpse from there. There is, in her characterization, sufficient "quantity of truth" to ensure the apparently desired quality of interest in her (II, 271, 356, 350).

The dialectic of imagery

But my above account conveys little of either quantity or quality — and not so much because it is sketchy outline as because it inevitably underlines her ongoing actions, whereas James's provisions all subordinate our sense of these and keep us busy with her reactions, with their history and with how everyone has been affected by them. I shall therefore now consider the ample evidence of how James insists on this kind of perspective through various forms of distancing. The first is of course his authorial participation, the nature, frequency and timing of which are crucial to his manifest goals.

It is the play between his own images and those he attributes to Maggie that is immediately arresting in his advertised authorial relationship with her. When, in those densely figured pages opening Book Second, we enter her consciousness, we find it dominated by the pagoda-Mosque simile by which she represents to herself her new awareness. That her figure for it is foreign, even exotic, is itself ironic for us who have been watching her throughout Book First make the situation inevitable; the irony is deepened when these sacred edifices are shown to house the couple who have just consummated at least one part of their "sacred" pledge. But it is essentially dramatic. This, he reports, is how it is "to her considering mind" and after asking "if this image . . . may represent our young woman's consciousness of a recent change in her life", he develops it as hers: "The pagoda in her blooming garden figured the arrangement — how otherwise was it to be named? — by which, so strikingly, she had been able to marry without breaking, as she liked to put it, with her past" (II, 4, 4-5).

The welter of images that follows hard upon this is, on the other hand, clearly authorial. She is likened to a "silken-coated spaniel who has scrambled out of a pond and who rattles water from his ears" by James, who continues: "might I so far multiply my metaphors, I should compare her to the frightened but clinging young mother of an unlawful child". He then multiplies them further to describe her resolve to participate more directly in their common lives by dancing again, going to balls. "She would have been easily to be figured for us at this occupation; dipping, at off moments and quiet hours, in snatched visits and by draughty candle-light, into her rich collections and seeing her jewels again a little shyly but unmistakably glow. That in fact my pass as the very picture of her semi-smothered agitation . . .". He keeps it up till we have learnt "that she was no longer playing with blunt and idle tools, with weapons that didn't cut. There passed across her vision ten times a day the gleam of a bare blade . . ." and "her little crouching posture" as she awaited Amerigo's return from Matcham is "that of a timid tigress". There is nothing remote or foreign about James's cluster of images: they are all playful, domestic and familiarly, even popularly, romantic. A domestic pet scrambling from the pond; an unmarried girl wanting to keep her baby; a young woman of former social glories who discreetly visits her jewels, candle in hand — these are all conventionally romantic almost to the point of the sentimental. Though the blade now gleams bare it is still part of the game played with blunt tools, and the tigress is a timid one (II, 6-7, 7, 8, 9, 10).

I suggest that what we have, then, is an opening passage of prose which successfully tackles the challenging task of giving an unromantic account of the romantic mind of Adam's daughter as she begins to realize she is not Amerigo's wife. This chronicle about the necessity of the imaginative life is hereafter to be in even richer imaginative terms but we are evidently to distinguish from the first between those of the character and those of her creator. The former dramatize her awakening; the latter keep us aware that it has only begun. The newly-quickened mobility of her mind, such an essential part of his subject, is given to us with a new nimbleness and mobility in the authorial mode which is, it would seem, an essential part of his treating it. His images, consonant as they are with her nature, her background, her sympathies and her predictable instinct and idiom, nevertheless tumble into our attention like a pile of toys, a pile we behold in the shadow of the "tall tower of ivory", the "outlandish pagoda" and the "Mahometan mosque". When Maggie gives herself away, James ensures we remember it, but not by any intervention that would alienate us from either her or himself. Down there in the arena with this character, he rubs shoulders without even rudely elbowing or jostling. The obfuscatingly romantic must be shown as a weed in the whole field of the imagination we depend on to produce our healthier nourishment (II, 3, 3, 4).

Precisely the same tension between a dramatic and a

definitive use of allied images is sustained in the following chapter of this Part Fourth. It is Maggie who likens Charlotte's entry into their lives to the fourth wheel of the family coach and who consciously develops the fancy of Charlotte and Amerigo pulling the vehicle while she and her father ride with the Principino. Any elaboration of this fancy is, we are carefully told, "for the completeness of her image" and we are told too its significant impact on her: "she might have been fixing with intensity her projected vision, have been conscious even of its taking an absurd, a fantastic shape". "Maggie found in this image a repeated challenge." Then in rapid succession appear the accompanying authorial similes in which her awareness of being "treated" in a precautionary manner by an Amerigo and a Charlotte who are distinctly in "harmony" is likened to her fingering of a precious locket containing matched miniatures; to their hanging over her a "canopy of state"; to her having to play cards with new care; to her being "noiselessly ferried" in a boat; and to her being immersed in a "bath of benevolence" (II, 23, 24, 42, 38, 41, 44).

Her efforts to work it all out are shown in another vivid domestic image that recalls the earlier series: "she might have been picking small shining diamonds out of the sweepings of her ordered house. She bent, in this pursuit, over her dust-bin; she challenged to the last grain the refuse of her innocent economy". This time she becomes the domestic pet: "She had flapped her little wings as a symbol of desired flight, not merely as a plea for a more gilded cage and an extra allowance of lumps of sugar." Again the cluster does not patronize; it merely keeps her at the distance needed if we are to watch a process without missing any stages in it. The pathetically inadequate imaginings of the belatedly awakened innocent are given the context of the appropriate but subtly critical imaginings the author shares with us. Again there is distancing without alienation. The interest is keenly intimate yet always informed by perspective. Equally important for this kind of interest, the pathos is never indulged. The "victim" of the adulteress is seen as also the victim of herself, of her father, of her opportunities and of one of those chance arrangements of life that all of the parties to it have exploited. Any conventional reactions to Maggie as merely wronged wife or abused friend are discouraged by the omission of everything conducive to such a stereotype and by the "foregrounding" of this dialectic of vivid figurative language (II, 42, 44).

When, on ensuing "occasions", James does let her indulge her imaginings without his authorial counterpoint taking figurative form, her similes and metaphors save him the trouble. Her choice of figures and her development of them inevitably recall the significant distinctions demonstrated when we first entered her mind in Book Second. One such figure ideally serving the need for distance as well as the needs of drama is chosen from that other reality, offered by the theatre and implying inevitably the relation of the one to the many in a manner most apposite. This figure, sustained throughout the rest of the novel, likens her to an actress, for, from this point on, her conduct does become conscious performance.

The morning after the lovers return from Matcham, Maggie, visiting her father and an obviously awaiting Charlotte, "reminded herself of an actress who had been studying a part and rehearsing it, but who suddenly, on the stage, before the footlights, had begun to improvise, to speak lines not in the text". By Part Fifth, at Fawns, acutely aware of her situation, "she felt . . . suddenly promoted to leading lady and expected to appear in every act of the five". Watching the card players from her sofa before the ordeal of the terrace scene with Charlotte, she is "much in the mood of a tired actress who has the good fortune to be 'off,' while her mates are on . . .". But the figure, developped in reach though it has, ceases to signify the extent of her responsibilities and so as she looks through the terrace window at the players, we learn how they actually struck her: "they might have been figures rehearsing some play of which she herself was the author" and by the end of this part, the social gymnastics demanded of her are so great that Fanny is for her "like the kind lady who, . . . at the circus . . ., falls in with the overworked little trapezist girl — the acrobatic support presumably of embarrassed and exacting parents". The self-consciousnes of her figure and what she does with it adds to the intensity of her plight without subtracting from the ample general reference (II, 33, 208, 231, 235, 302).

If true of this sustained image, it is true also of those she suddenly multiplies at the moment when the strains on her are so great that she is tempted to rebel and break out of her carefully-preserved role during the others' game of bridge. She still sees her situation in extravagent terms but she is no longer so entirely at the mercy of their romantic connotation and the emphasis is now relational. It is all on the others, who "thus tacitly put it upon her to be disposed of, the whole complexity of their peril . . .; to charge herself with it as the scapegoat of old, of whom she had once seen a terrible picture, had been charged with the sins of the people and gone forth into the desert to sink under his burden and die". She can look at this picture now more steadily and when she figures temptation in terms similarly exotic and even more luridly coloured and animated, it is as steadily to reject it by insistently remembering those other relationships for which she has accepted responsibility (II, 234).

Her yearning at that moment for "the protests of passion", which she lists, constitutes "a range of feelings which for many women would have meant so much, but which for *her* husband's wife, for *her* father's daughter, figured nothing nearer to experience than a wild eastern caravan, looming into view with crude colours in the sun, fierce pipes in the air, high spears against the sky, all a thrill, a natural joy to mingle with, but turning off short before it reached her and plunging into other defiles". With striking new maturity she takes up James's earlier domestic images and turns their cosy little house into one for adults where she too can learn to live. After she has confessed to the horror of finding the real behind the apparent and to having assimilated the shock, she again shows her new command and control. "It was the first sharp falsity she had known in her life, to touch at all or be touched by; it had met her like some bad-faced stranger surprised in one of the thick-carpeted corridors of a house of quiet on a Sunday afternoon; and yet, yes, amazingly, she had been able to look at terror and disgust only to know that she must put away from her the bitter-sweet of their freshness" (II, 236, 236-7, 237).

Similarly, the domestic pets, some of them caged, and the timid tigress, give way to fully grown-up dangers: "The splendid shining supple creature was out of the cage, was at large." Again, the blunt tools and bare blades of former play are now transformed into "a doom impossibly sharp and hard, but to which, after looking at it with her eyes wide open, she had none the less bowed her head". Her fears, no longer petty nor childishly indulgent, are for the immediate reality of Charlotte's closing the distance between them on the dark terrace. "Oh the 'advantage,' it was perfectly enough, in truth, with Mrs Verver; for what was Maggie's own sense but that of having been thrown over on her back with her neck from the first half-broken and her helpless face staring up?" The most violent image in the whole novel, depicted here in the ordeal of Maggie's consciousness, is characteristically and appropriately selected by her from the history and literature of the French "Terror", a detail of which now informs her imaginative appreciation of realities instantly present to her. She is thus committed to acting in the kind of drama she had merely playfully imagined, in an earlier phase we are not permitted to forget, and we can thus measure her distance from it (II, 239, 242).

James, ever consistent here, shows her developing, without changing her into a different or implausible character, by his careful reminder that though she can now reject the romantic imagination she has to keep doing so. It provides her with her terms and reference still, even when, continuing to develop her command of all her realities, she conjectures about the deeper levels of the lovers' adulterous relation and when, after fearing and resenting them, she can achieve a compassionate view of them. She uses her imaginative fancy with fuller consciousness but she still uses it, and James makes a rare direct appearance to comment on it.

> There had been, through life, as we know, few quarters in which the Princess's fancy could let itself loose; but it shook off restraint when it plunged into the figured void of the detail of that relation. This was a realm it could people with images — again and again with fresh ones; they swarmed there like the strange combinations that lurked in the woods at twilight; they loomed into the definite and faded into the vague, their main present sign for her being however that they were always, that they were duskily, agitated (II, 280).

James's account of how her fancy works carefully recalls her own "blissful" moment shared with her father at Fawns on their " 'sequestered' bench" in "one of the quietest places" and among "the grandest trees" — the moment which she now recalls "as the 'first beginning' of their present situation". She can now check, even control, her habitual idiom. "Her earlier vision of a state of bliss made insecure by the very intensity of the bliss — this had dropped from her; she had ceased to see, as she lost herself, the pair of operatic, of high Wagnerian lovers (she found deep within her these comparisons) interlocked in their wood of enchantment, a green glade as romantic as one's dream of an old German forest." Her final comment on these instinctive but rejected ways of looking at the world echoes eloquently among all we have so far learned about both couples. "The picture was veiled on the contrary with the dimness of trouble; behind which she felt indistinguishable the procession of forms that had lost all so pitifully their precious confidence." It is a lament reaching far beyond sentiment or even self-pity and out to a common condition all four share (I, 166, II, 253, 280).

From this point onward, James's account of how Maggie continues to use self-consciously the romantic idiom enables him to show at once the fuller reach of her maturing consciousness and the situation that is developing for these four. Maggie's discovery of the real, of what humans "cannot possibly *not* know, sooner or later, in one way or another", is displayed in terms of "the things that can reach us only through the beautiful circuit and subterfuge of our thought and our desire" by which alone those humans can, in James's well-known distinction, entertain the romantic.[16] Only the image of her solitary moments is permitted to be a privately personal one. "There were hours enough, lonely hours, in which she let dignity go; then there were others when, clinging with her winged concentration to some deep cell in her heart, she stored away her hived tenderness for [Amerigo] as if she had gathered it all from flowers." All the accompanying images figure the subtlety and complexity of her relations with other characters. The present impossiblity of frankness in her contact with Amerigo is "a privation that had left on his lips perhaps a little of the same thirst with which she fairly felt her own distorted, the torment of the lost pilgrim who listens in the desert sands for the possible, the impossible plash of water". She can no longer envisage herself as the scapegoat cast out alone in that desert. Her acquired degree of compassionate imagination equips her for seeing "with Charlotte's grave eyes" (II, 281, 283).

The house of quiet where she met the bad-faced stranger is now one where "she had guardedly tracked her stepmother, in the great house, from room to room and from window to window, only to see her, here and there and everywhere, *try* her uneasy outlook, question her issue and her fate". The unmarried mother with unlawful child and the visitor of jewels by draughty candle-light, metaphors formerly applied by Maggie to herself, now give way to a view of a Charlotte confronted with a "new complication and . . . a new anxiety — things these that she carried about with her done up in the napkin of her lover's accepted rebuke while she vainly hunted for some corner where she might put them safely down". The "Terror" over for Maggie, she feels the need "of pleading for some benefit that might be carried away [by Charlotte] into exile like the last saved object of price of the *émigré*, the jewel wrapped in a piece of old silk and negotiable some day in the market of misery" (II, 284, 330).

Then, the figurative moving steadily towards the more and more inclusive, we are shown Maggie's perception of the new relation that Charlotte has adopted with Adam, shown it in terms of the halter simile. Nothing could be less gratuitous or malicious than this perception which, James repeats twice, Maggie felt "forced upon her" by Charlotte's studied commitment to her husband's aesthetic interests and accumulated trophies: "so together yet at the same time so separate, they were making their daily round. Charlotte hung behind with emphasised attention; she stopped when her husband stopped, but at the distance of a case or two, or of whatever other succession of objects; and the likeness of their connection wouldn't have been wrongly figured if he had been thought of as holding in one of his pocketed hands the end of a long silken halter looped around her beautiful neck. He didn't twitch it, yet it was there; he didn't drag it, but she came . . ." (II, 287).

This is the symbolic tableau imprinted on her mind as, in the gallery, she ponders their relationships, and it is an easy step to the image immediately following, which becomes even more inclusive in its rendering of their present situation and in its inevitable recall of that glass-roofed hotel court in Paris where Charlotte wove the first thread of her own halter. Thus the violated house of quiet and the house of corridors and windows come now to stand for "the perfunctory" in which they all, without exception, live: "it took on finally the likeness of some spacious central chamber in a haunted house, a great overarched and overglazed rotunda where gaiety might reign, but the doors of which opened into sinister circular passages". The figure is developed with almost Gothic detail but the long and wide reach of the context insures the novel against any of its Gothic licence, as does the circus reference and all it connotes in relation to Maggie. "Here they turned up for each other, as they said, with the blank faces that denied any uneasiness felt in the approach; here they closed numerous doors carefully behind them — all save the door that connected the place, as by a straight tented corridor, with the outer world, and, encouraging thus the irruption of society, imitated the aperture through which the bedizened performers of the circus are poured into the ring" (II, 288, 289).

The image which most economically serves the functions of showing the residual Maggie Verver within the Princess, and both among the other people around her, is the golden-flame-turned-to-black-ashes that features so strikingly in her imagining of how the lover of her husband must now see her. Gold is of course well established as the chief metal in the novel's figurative currency and while the speech is dramatically faithful to the Charlotte we know, it is inevitably translated by Maggie into a rhetoric essentially romantic and so is eloquently dramatic also for her.

Images of restraint and entrapment have recurred only slightly less frequently than have those of the golden and gilded. James adheres to them right through to Part Sixth where, after seeing the cages, the halter and the enclosing glass behind which Charlotte frantically taps, Maggie sees Amerigo as voluntarily remaining in a cage and herself as only just escaping a bird-trap. "This imagined service to the woman who could no longer help herself was one of the traps set for Maggie's spirit at every turn of the road; the click of which, catching and holding the divine faculty fast, was followed inevitably by a flutter, by a struggle of wings and even, as we may say, by a scattering of fine feathers."

To recognize the class of figure to which this one belongs in this novel concerned with "the great trap of life" is to recall the characters to whom similar figures have been applied and is to note one more of the many characters who are forever eluding traps of their own making (II, 330, 227).

Even the general class of the romantic itself is recognized and its significance realized when James persists in selecting from it to ensure that our reception of Maggie is the one he obviously desires. She is never more deviously pragmatic than when she lies to Charlotte during their final duologue in the garden of Fawns and that is precisely when James has her "remind herself really of people she had read about in stories of the wild west, people who threw up their hands on certain occasions for a sign they weren't carrying revolvers". The primitiveness of the analogy underlines the real instinctive simplicity within her apparent charade (II, 310-11).

Again, the basic and primitive are evoked on her behalf in the same interest when she tries to imagine Amerigo's sense of his position while he waits with her in London. For her, he is

> ... as fixed in his place as some statue of one of his forefathers ... while [her] own [place] had come to show simply as that improvised "post" — a post of the kind spoken of as advanced — with which she was to have found herself connected in the fashion of a settler or a trader in a new country; in the likeness even of some Indian squaw with a papoose on her back and barbarous beadwork to sell. Maggie's own, in short, would have been sought in vain in the most rudimentary map of the social relations as such. The only geography marking it would be doubtless that of the fundamental passions (II, 323-24).

The Maggie whose desperate commitment to the fundamental passions makes vivid for her that she is instrumental in turning her rival's golden flame to black ash is sufficiently sophisticated in them to be able to fly their traps but they remain, still, in their undeniable simplicities, her first referent when the pressures on her are greatest. Thus we may read as more tentative than celebratory her likening of the Prince's final protestations of good faith to "some handful of gold-dust thrown into the air" and certainly she has misgivings as she waits for her Prince finally to join her. "Here it was then, the moment, the golden fruit that had shone from afar; only what *were* these things in the fact, for the hand and for the lips, when tested, when tasted — what were they as a reward?" They are part merely, it appears, of the reality one cannot possibly *not* know. They are harbingers of the reality from which she is to hide her eyes only moments later, the bitter fruit of her imaginatively golden endeavours (II, 350, 367).

The authorial comment

I have suggested that imagery becomes the most potent means by which James maintains an extreme authorial mobility as he moves "towards the point of view that, within the compass, will give [him] most instead of least to answer for"[17], but it is not the only one and we must consider now the context which he assiduously provides for it with his explicit authorial comments. Minimal and subdued as these are they are still significantly timed and become an extra insurance against loss of the right distance from Maggie at moments in the narrative crucial to a sustaining of the desired interest in this dangerous agent. We do not need to hear any kind of editorial voice during any of the Assinghams' sessions but we do hear one in that second chapter of Book Second (xxvi) when infinite care is needed to transmit the way Maggie's awakening begins and it is inevitable that we hear it during the narrative of Maggie's visit to Mr Crichton at the British Museum and the consequent dealings with the antiquarian. But generally the function of this delicately modulated intervention is to allow James to disclaim authority, to deny omniscience, to demonstrate that though he does apparently rub shoulders with her in the arena he really keeps her at arm's length and that he is just as curious about and interested in her as he evidently hopes we are.

Whenever James briefly advertises the difficulty of authenticating her quite extraordinary situation, his sudden self-consciousness as writer acts astringently against any conventional reactions which we may be inconveniently harbouring. Thus when she decides on a more active participation in the life around her, the decision is ushered to us by a personal James. "She would go to balls again — that seemed, freely, even crudely, stated, the remedy . . ."; and the figure of her visiting her jewels by draughty candle-light comes with three more distancing comments. "She would have been easily to be figured for us at this occupation", he says. "That in fact my pass as the very picture of her semi-smothered agitation . . ." he tells us. "It must be added, however, that she would have been at a loss to determine — and certainly at first — to which order, that of self-control or that of large expression, the step she had taken the afternoon of her husband's return from Matcham with his companion properly belonged", he carefully contributes. We therefore have no warrant for attributing to him the responsibility for the romantic association of that "picture" (II, 8, 9).

Sometimes he reminds us that he is frankly speculating ("she might have been fixing with intensity her projected vision"); sometimes he is clearly reporting ("Sharp to her above all was the renewed attestation of her father's comprehensive acceptances . . ."). More frequently — as her consciousness complicates — he makes a brief appearance as the writer occupied in the business of communicating to us his view of her. Thus, when she becomes aware of being specially "treated" by the lovers, James steps in: "and I must add moreover that she at last found herself rather oddly wondering what else, as a consciousness, could have been quite so overwhelming". For this crucial link in Maggie's new chain connecting her with realities, the care must be even more explicit and elaborate. "Maggie was to have retained, for that matter, more than one aftertaste, and if I have spoken of the impressions fixed in her as soon as she had so insidiously taken the field, a definite note must be made of her perception, during those moments, of Charlotte's prompt uncertainty." The emphasis is made by ostentatious intrusion reminding us that we are not in a theatre, freely empathizing with a heroine, but in a lecture hall where vivid slides are from time to time projected. To retain the interest in them that he desires, the lecturer may interpolate merely a rhetorical question, as when the usual affection in Charlotte's attention to her is recorded as "all enhanced furthermore — enhanced or qualified, who should say which? — by a new note of diplomacy . . ." (II, 23, 31, 35, 37).

More frequently he addresses us, turning a more simple response, as between Maggie and us, into a triangular one including his own interest. Maggie receives her new impression "and it may interest us", James interjects, "on the ground of its having prompted in Maggie a final reflexion, a reflexion out of the heart of which a light flashed for her like a great flower grown in a night". The graphic is there surely enough but so is the provision for scrutiny of it. Sometimes, as with her perception of the impact of her new show of social confidence on Lady Castledean, the details remain beyond explication but we are shown how that impact nevertheless reaches the three other principals. "The intensity of the taste of these registered phenomena was in fact that somehow, by a process and through a connexion not again to be traced, she so practised at the same time on Amerigo and Charlotte — with only the drawback, her constant check and second-thought, that she concomitantly practised perhaps still more on her father" (II, 41, 72).

The authorial concern is persistently for the proliferating implications of what is happening to everyone and, therefore, "Maggie" is again and again cut back by James to "our young woman" or to "our young confidante" — to exactly the same form of possessive reference applied authorially to *all* the other principals at some stage. She is never allowed to exploit the simple, calculable interest, if only because that could so easily be the cheap one and James obviously has other plans for her. His interest in, curiosity about, and "case" for her must not be mistaken for his identification with her and whenever the appeal of her plight intensifies — as in her Regent's Park avoidance of the "specific" — he makes the necessary safeguards. "It would come out, the specific, where the dog would come out; would run to earth somehow the truth — for she was believing herself in relation to the truth! — at which she mustn't so much as directly point. Such at any rate was the fashion in which her passionate prudence played over possibilities of danger,. . ." We learn of this passionate prudence in the cool, lightly ironic tones of the James who ever watches it at our side, refusing answers about her, provoking questions about all (II, 4, 84).

Though our distance from her never changes, the nature of the comment upon her does, keeping pace with the ideas proliferating within the interest. Towards the end of Part Fourth James applies to her the first of several apparently evaluative words but they commit him to little. Her frank "*using* [of] her friend" Fanny, the guilt-conscious one whom she avoids embarrassing, and her candid plan to "interweave" her "as plausibly as possible with the parts and parcels of their surface", wins an authorial superlative that is clearly exclamatory rather than definitive. "More and more magnificent now in her blameless egoism, Maggie asked no questions of her, and thus only signified the greatness of the opportunity she gave her." A more critical comment is confessed during her ordeal on the terrace with Charlotte when she hopes her father will look up at her and even that is just as clearly relative. "That represented Maggie's one little lapse from consistency — the sole small deflexion in the whole course of her scheme" (II, 145+101, 144, 145, 245).

But the freer evaluative discussion of her occurs at the end of Part Fifth on the assumption that our long association with her has bred familiarity and knowledge that will give proportion to such evaluation. "There had been, through life, as we know, few quarters in which the Princess's fancy could let itself loose . . ."; "she had had, as we know, her vision of the gilt bars bent . . ."; and "Maggie's provision of irony, which we have taken for naturally small, had never been so scant as now . . .". Only then does James proffer the adjectives that our long acquaintance with her romanticism can justify. Charlotte's gallery performances for the gawking visitors we learn, "made our young women, ***herself incurably dazzled***, marvel afresh at the mystery by which a creature who could be in some connexions so earnestly right could be in others so perversely wrong" (II, 280, 283, 284, 289).

Only at this point in the development of the interest does he intrude to make unequivocally clear his approval of how Maggie avoids the sentimental response to the suffering woman. "There was honestly an awful mixture in things, and it wasn't closed to her aftersense of such passages — we have already indeed in other cases seen it open — that the deepest depth of all, in a perceived penalty, was that you couldn't be sure some of your compunctions and contortions wouldn't show for ridiculous." It is in the climate of this shared history and of ironic detachment towards it that we read, a page later, the epithet he applies to her romantic concept of the self-imprisoned Amerigo's rights with his former lover: "he had a right — thought wonderful Maggie now — to so many more freedoms than he took!" The "wonderful" in her, like the "magnificent", is, for the James who here expresses wonder at both, part of her incurable dazzlement and therefore part of the mixture of things. He is far from recommending either as easy formulations of her moral position (II, 292, 294).

The scaled epithets

Such epithets have an important history during the course of the novel and they are significantly modulated to provide a context suitable for the way in which the finale may be received. They play a constant part in James's authorial game of being there without getting in the way or impeding the growing complexities. In *The Ambassadors*, the superlative from which most connotations were wrung was "wonderful"[18]; it began in social persiflage, was used ironically, suggested the "wondrous" and finally defined the protagonist of that high comedy. In *The Wings of the Dove* it consorted meaningfully among other absolutes such as "stupendous", "prodigious", "marvellous" and "splendid" to limn something of the fascination that the trio of that moving drama provokes.[19] But in *The Golden Bowl* the case is, as one might expect, markedly different. All these epithets appear but they are eclipsed by the frequency and placement of the one word "strange", by its derivatives and by a group of terms much more innately homogeneous with them than are, respectively, those in the two earlier novels.

The modulation of them is necessarily more finely controlled and they are at once a constant referent for us as we reach out for help from the non-committal author and also an index of the increasing difficulties and perplexities of moral consciousness into which he is relentlessly leading us. As James uses it, "strange", registering response, becomes the least morally committed of words. It ideally defines the quality of the interest; it suggests, eminently, the incalculable and is surely the word least likely to encourage the closing of minds. Not formulating that view of these people we share with James, it evokes a more intense awareness of its range. Permeating the text, cementing "the congruous whole", it becomes the watchword of the novel, applied to all the characters, insinuated into the consciousness of each as he or she reviews the burgeoning difficulties, and remaining always the infallible signal for us to retain that distance affording the most inclusive view.

While deliberately avoiding, in this study designed to show the qualitative values of words within their artistic context, any kind of quantitative analysis whatsoever, I offer the testimony that this group of epithets does throb with almost nagging regularity throughout the whole novel and I shall now show where and suggest why. There is at once a very clear distinction evident between the function of this whole group of words, synonymous with a perplexing oddness and unexpectedness, in the First and in the Second Book of the novel. In the three parts of the first they are used ironically; in the three parts of the second they aptly define the nature of the contemplative interest evoked there from point to point.

In Part First, for example, it is ironic that the Prince should distinguish so emphatically between the presence of "arrogance and greed" in "his race" and the absence of them in himself, when admitting "that he was somehow full of his race" and the fact is noted. "Odd enough, of a truth, was his sense of this last danger — which may illustrate moreover his general attitude toward dangers from within." His notions of what the Ververs may morally expect of him frankly alarm him: "What was singular was that it seemed not so much an expectation of anything in particular as a large bland blank assumption of merits almost beyond notation, of essential quality and value." When, at Fanny's, he itemizes his lover's charms, "it was, strangely, as a cluster of possessions of his own that these things in Charlotte Stant, now affected him . . .". When he thinks a moment later of "her strange sense for tongues" being in her case "a beauty in itself, and almost a mystery", the artistic function of such epithets is clear. James is using here "odd", "singular" and "strange" for particulars which, in these contexts, are not in the least odd, singular or strange (I, 16, 23, 46, 54).

Their irony is even clearer in Part Second when they continue to appear during our introduction to the obliging and seemingly self-effacing tycoon. "The greatest of wonders moreover was exactly in this, that so interrupted a man should ever have got, as the phrase was, should above all have got so early, to where he was." Here the incompatibilities are merely apparent; later, when we are learning of the art connoisseur, the language ensures we recognize them as real enough. It is Adam himself who interprets realities of his past and present in terms unconsciously ironic. "It was the strange scheme of things again: the years of darkness had been needed to render possible the years of light." When his guests return with Maggie and the Prince from church to the door of the billiard-room, thus relieving the siege mounted by Mrs Rance, "their appearance, as it opened to admit them, determined for Adam Verver, in the oddest way in the world, a new and sharp perception. It *was* really remarkable: this perception expanded, on the spot, as a flower, one of the strangest, might at a breath have suddenly opened." But is it really? That a widowed millionaire will be pursued by a divorcee who sees her chance is in fact no less obvious than that everyone else will recognize it: these are the norms giving life to the banter of the commentary. There is no banter but only implied ironic query, a few pages later, in James's weighing of Adam Verver's values. "Nothing perhaps might affect us as queerer, had we time to look into it, than this application of the same measure of value to such different pieces of property as old Persian carpets, say, and new human acquisitions . . .". Again, in each of these usages, the group of loosely synonymous terms is entertainingly reminding us of what we should be able to see for ourselves (I, 127, 144, 152, 196).

This continues to be the case throughout Part Three as the lovers renew their relationship. One of the terms from this group is applied to Charlotte's feelings about "the right view of her opportunity for happiness — unless indeed the opportunity itself, rather, were, in its mere strange amplitude, the producing, the precipitating cause". Another is applied to the sense she and Amerigo share as to how "they might enjoy together extraordinary freedom . . . from the moment they should understand their position aright". Both attend her expressed belief that "Nothing stranger surely had ever happened to a conscientious, a well-meaning, a perfectly passive pair: no more extraordinary decree had ever been launched against such victims than this of forcing them against their will into a relation of mutual close contact that they had done everything to avoid" (I, 246, 288, 289).

Finally, in this part, three terms from this cluster supply an ironic view of the Prince's own sense of irony, when, amid the inducements to pleasure that Matcham offers to them both, "the innermost effect of all this perceptive ease was perhaps a strange final irritation. He compared the lucid result with the extraordinary substitute for perception that presided, in the bosom of his wife, at so contented a view of his conduct and course . . .; and this wonder of irony became on occasion too intense to be kept wholly to himself." Throughout this, and the two earlier, parts of this Book First, the distance between the dramatized and the authorial values is thus persistently manifested; the recurrent terms supply for us a referent amid, even a register for, the increasing degree of the strange, but they are authorially disowned (I, 333).

What happens to this referent throughout the three parts of Book Second is that while its terms continue to be a key unlocking the *dramatic*, that same key unlocks in the *narrative* a new chamber altogether. Maggie's mounting awareness of the strange in all things is revelatory enough, but as the intensity of this sense increases and the terms register, accordingly, each degree of it, we become commensurately aware of authorial companionship in our contemplation of them. Further, our focus upon Maggie as she gropes noiselessly among the strangeness, a focus always indirectly inclusive of those others of whom she is always now even more acutely conscious, becomes one in which those others too are shown to be part of, as well as more and more aware of, precisely the same contemplated strangeness.

It is not a case of Maggie's being personally sponsored by James but of her being included among the others in the contemplation that all, including the readers, share with him. To put roughly the modulation of these key terms in the three remaining parts: in the fourth they register Maggie's discovery of what we have long known but she finds strange; in the fifth and for the first two chapters of the sixth, they register her awareness of the "strange" being fundamental to human experience and therefore perceived also by each of the others; and in the closing pages of the novel, where our long knowledge of all four principals creates "quantities" too "vast" for us possibly to call Maggie the centre either of attention or of interest, they register the only available verbal responses expressive enough for the silent stasis shared by character, author and reader (II, 361).

Throughout the whole second half of the novel, they become epithets which demonstrate that irony need not be reductive, for in the rapidly expanding consciousness of Amerigo's wife, Adam's daughter, Charlotte's rival and the Assinghams' friend, they become in fact excitingly exploratory. One of them "defines" the first of her adventurous acts — her wholly atypical resistance to Amerigo in the carriage. "Strange enough was this sense for her, and altogether new, the sense of possessing, by miraculous help, some advantage that, absolutely then and there, in the carriage, as they rolled, she might either give up or keep. Strange, inexpressibly strange — so distinctly she saw that if she did give it up she should somehow give up everything for ever" (II, 56).

She soon finds she can generalize this term. After finding "funny" the new gregariousness which the lovers studiously encourage, and deciding upon "living up to the public and popular notion" of a Princess, she is found "wondering inwardly too while she did so at that strange mixture in things through which the popular notion could be evidenced for her by such supposedly great ones of the earth as the Castledeans and their kind". Soon enough, indeed, the term becomes a barb that pierces deepest, as when she and Adam speak in Regent's Park of their original reasons for bringing Charlotte into their lives. "Maggie had gone through the form of recalling this, and the light of their ancient candour, shining from so far back, had seemed to bring back some things so strangely that, with the sharpness of the vision, she had risen to her feet." There is no rest from it for her. It now best describes routines long familiar, as well as the new services of old friends: "It was the strangest thing in the world, but it was as if Mrs Assingham might in a manner mitigate the intensity of her consciousness of Charlotte" at Fawns (II, 68, 70-71, 71, 95, 97).

When her gropings among "the whole sum of the perplexities and duplicities" are not only silent; when the intensity of this unfamiliar consciousness amounts even further and she breaks our to Fanny ("Her tone might by this time have shown a strangeness to match her smile . . ."), she enters a new phase of self-discovery. She becomes aware of "a certain queer wish that fitfully flickered up in her, a wish that usurped perversely the place of a much more natural one. If Charlotte, while she was about it, could only have been *worse*! — . . ." Along with "the different sorts of terrors" assailing her as she pursues a meaningful truth, she suddenly unearths a new response to Amerigo. "Knowledge, knowledge, was a fascination as well as a fear; and a part precisely of the strangeness of this juncture was the way her apprehension that he would break out to her with some merely general profession was mixed with her dire need to forgive him, to reassure him, to respond to him, on no ground that she didn't fully measure." For her later even more compelling sense of this imperative during the scene where the gilt cup lies in pieces, beheld by him, two of the key epithets are enhanced by a most potent figure.

> There was even a minute, when her back was turned to him, during which she knew once more the strangeness of her desire to spare him, a strangeness that had already fifty times brushed

her, in the depth of her trouble, as with the wild wing of some bird of the air who might blindly have swooped for an instant into the shaft of a well, darkening there by his momentary flutter the far-off round of sky. It was extraordinary, this quality in the taste of her wrong which made her completed sense of it seem rather to soften than to harden, and it was the more extraordinary the more she had to recognise it;. . ." (II, 108, 115, 138, 140, 185).

This imaginative understanding of others, the chief use to which she puts her adversities here in Part Fourth, finds further, and eventually extreme, play throughout the remaining parts, the narrative always keeping due notation of it. Thus she realizes that the forsaken Charlotte "could all the while only be struggling with secrets beyond any guessing. It was odd how that certainty again and again determined and coloured her wonderments of detail;. . ." After the great temptation figured by the caravan, the barbaric rejection of her sense of her responsibilities to all the others, who crowd it out of her consciousness, she notes: "It was extraordinary: they positively brought home to her that to feel about them in any of the immediate, inevitable, assuaging ways, the ways usually open to innocence outraged and generosity betrayed, would have been to give them up, and that giving them up was, marvellously, not to be thought of." The community of understanding she shares with her father during their second historic interlude of tensions on their sequestered Fawns bench is of the same order of empathy: "it was strangely as if, by this sudden arrest, by their having, in their acceptance of the unsaid, or at least their reference to it, practically given up pretending . . ." (II, 229, 237, 265).

But her imagination can reach further yet — even to the questions Charlotte must be asking of Amerigo: "and by way of a fantastic flight of divination she heard Amerigo reply . . .". By the end of Part Fifth and the ascent of Maggie's mental reach from a view of the "odd", "funny" and "strange", through a view of the "extraordinary", to a view of the "fantastic", James records his own community of understanding with us. "Marvellous the manner in which, under such imaginations, Maggie thus circled and lingered — . . ." We can endorse this opinion of the vistas revealed — endorse it without closing the distance between author and character or between both of them and ourselves. "Strange" and its derivatives and carefully graded synonyms, commit us to contemplation of the view, not to approval or any kind of uncritical acceptance of the viewers. The recurrent epithets, scaled in ascending degree, define a response which the whole antecedent narrative legitimates. The dramatic value of it, surely evident enough, is incidental to, and subsumed in, the quality and greater range of interest aroused by *all* the figures viewed at this penultimate stage (II, 282).

This distinction is vital to an understanding of the characterization and function of Maggie in the whole novel. There are limits to divination, limits, eventually, to how far, as they await final developments, she can successfully reach towards her husband. James himself remarks on her itch to discuss with Amerigo the justice of his contacting Charlotte. "Strangest of all things doubtless this care of Maggie's as to what might make for it or make against it; stranger still her lapsing at moments into a vague calculation of the conceivability, on her own part, with her husband, of some direct sounding of the subject." When, after the arrival of the telegram announcing the Ververs' visit, she does suggest such an encounter for him with the sender of it, she finds that she "troubled" and "mystified him" with "the number of ideas of which he thought her capable. They were all apparently queer for him . . .". Knowing nothing of precisely how she and her father may have arranged the departure now imminent, he is at a loss with her and her "fifty" ideas. "What renewed the obscurity was her strange image of their common offer to him, . . ." Though each now knows so much more of the other, and of their respective selves, they are clearly enough shown here towards the end to be thrown back on guessing about each other, each islanded in isolation, as my earlier account of the presentation of the Prince may have indicated. They confront, recognize and admit the incalculable — in each other and in themselves (II, 327, 344, 345).

As Maggie now takes her place in the finale as one more of the "isolates", the fact itself is underlined by the most persistent of those epithets that have affirmed the relevant interest. We learn that the "conjoined" manner of her father and his wife is for her "the strangest, once more, of all impressions . . .". We do not witness her in any form of contact with Charlotte who, she tells her father, is " 'incomparable' "; we are told only that "Nothing was stranger moreover, under the action of Charlotte's presence, than the fact of a felt sincerity in her words". Charlotte she can thus farewell; her father she can silently and indirectly relinquish; while Miss Bogle takes charge of her Principino, it is reunion with her Prince that she awaits. But that he is not only *her* Prince we learn in her response to his words: " 'See? I see nothing but *you.*' And the truth of it had with this force after a moment so strangely lighted his eyes that as for pity and dread of them she buried her own in his breast." The word that James interposes between them, now the sign of their ultimate frustration, is the word by which he has in Book First signalled the ironic interest, in Book Second shared the interest of Maggie's successive discoveries and the one by which, now, with consistency but without finality, he ceases dramatizing that interest of his own implied "in the air of the whole result" and represented by nothing less than the entire novel *The Golden Bowl* (II, 357, 356-7, 363, 369).

Her resulting view of love, pity and dread

Having taken the precautions above, of noting how some of the other "responsible agents" become "elements" in the "whole", I may now with more safety dwell on how Maggie herself arrives where she does and what knowledge she at last discovers there about love. The essence of her adventure, as distinct from those of the others, is that it is her notion of love, and of this only, that motivates her relations with all; she tries to love more comprehensively than they do and is forced to change her notion in the light of consequences, but it is always that notion alone that obsesses her. The Prince, clearly, would never originally have been interested in her without Adam's gold. Charlotte, whose love is only for the Prince, opts too for that gold and ultimately will not relinquish it even though it means banishment to the American she hates. The holder of the gold himself shares the single close tie permitted him in his limited emotional economy with a passion to build a monument to beautiful material possessions. Maggie alone remains oblivious of any material interest and continues to be impelled by her notion (that the novel reveals as so pathetically romantic, so sadly "heroic") of containing these three people in her Platonic absolute, of holding them all in what she continues to call her golden bowl even after it is shown to be a gilt, cracked cup lying in three very separate pieces (II, 214).

She is deeply challenged. The abstraction in which she refuses to differentiate, the " 'love' " that is neither of husband only nor of father only, can manifest itself as the emotion which blinded her and her father to the indulgences of their *sposi*, or as the one giving her husband such sovereign power over her, or as the one which, for her, turned her brilliant friend into a figure of anguish. Her final burying of her eyes in her husband's breast does not diminish the pain by which the differences have relentlessly claimed recognition. Her old emotion for her father strangely intensifies and the one she comes to feel for his wife is strangely distinct again, but the strangeness never asserts itself more tortuously than in the one she finally feels for her husband.

When we first meet her, such analysis is farthest from her mind: as Amerigo discovers, "any *serious* discussion of veracity, of loyalty, or rather of the want of them, practically took her unprepared, as if it were quite new to her" and so "duplicity, like 'love', had to be joked about". " 'Love' " is all. "It couldn't be 'gone into' ". Though not confident in herself (such " 'a small creeping thing' "), she is totally confident in her world in which the "rightness" of "everything" makes her father and herself so "blissful", and so her discussion with her affianced Prince of their shared relation can be only the "mere play of her joy". As passion, her feeling for him is deep, which he also discovers when she decides upon "acting up to the full privilege" of it. He realizes she is "*testifying*" to it when, on his return from Matcham, he sees the evidence of those hypothetical words which only we hear: " 'I'm as much in love with you now as the first hour; except that there are some hours — which I know when they come, because they almost frighten me — that show me I'm even more so.' " James ensures that she testifies to us, too, that this passional commitment achieves the fullest sexual consummation. She recalls how, confronted with "the fact of his reappearance and the plentitude of his presence" that "the warmly-washing wave had travelled far up the strand. She had subsequently lived for hours she couldn't count under the dizzying smothering welter — positively in submarine depths where everything came to her through walls of emerald and mother-of-pearl; . . ." (I, 15, 181, 167, 166, 8, II, 8, 19, 18, 42, 43).

That is why, when she falls within the shadow of her imagined pagoda, her resistance to his overtures in the carriage can mean such an intense conflict for her. "Yes, she was in his exerted grasp, and she knew what that was; but she was at the same time in the grasp of her conceived responsibility, and the extraordinary thing was that of the two intensities the second was presently to become the sharper." The result, after her outburst to Fanny, yet before her finding of the gilt cup, is the beginning of a more complex connection for them as they are held "together in the steel hoop of an intimacy compared with which artless passion would have been but a beating of the air". It is an intimacy in which, after the cup has appeared and been smashed, she knows "once more the strangeness of her desire to spare him"; a relation in which she is no longer the victim of "her native complacencies of so many sorts", even if still "an abjectly simple person" (II, 56, 141, 185, 192, 193).

It is a stage in a progression towards "the things [she] cannot possibly *not* know", cling though she does to her romantically imagined absolute. In her first Fawns discussion with Adam, they had innocently talked of how Charlotte's experience of unrequited love had placed her " ' "beyond everything" ' "; in her second, when she discusses with him her concept of love and jealousy, her declaration is predictable enough: " 'When however you love in the most abysmal and unutterable way of all — why then you're beyond everything, and nothing can pull you down.' " It is her sudden awareness of a loss of bearings, in what follows, that signifies how far she has yet to go. Her father is reported as reserving comment: "Mr Verver listened as if he had nothing on these high lines to oppose", then asks " 'And that's the way *you* love?' " We see how her pause reveals her present disarray in the rearguard action she is fighting against other realities. "For a minute she failed to speak, but at last she answered: 'It wasn't to talk about that. I do *feel* however beyond everything — and as a consequence of that, I dare say,' she added with a turn to gaiety, 'seem often not to know quite *where* I am.' " It is clear: the state she glibly enough imagined Charlotte experiencing through love proves to be for herself now a grimmer, more solitary one, lacking self-certitude and indeed full of care. Once, she could easily enough have known where she was if she chose, but now (to recast her own earlier formulaton) "knowledge", which had been a "fascination" was chiefly a "fear", because it is knowledge of a world quite incalculably other than the one she shared with her father (I, 188, II, 262, 263).

With Fanny only she need play no role and when that inquirer probes, "with a discretion still that fell short but by an inch", her knowledge of the feelings of each of the others and of herself, we witness her evasion.

> "I know nothing."
> "You know how *you* feel"
> But she again ***denied*** it. "I know nothing. If I did —!"
> "Well, if you did?" Fanny asked as she faltered.
> She had had enough, however. "I should die," she said as ***she turned away.*** *(II, 305).*

The feeling she is displayed as chiefly knowing is the tumult resulting from her attempt to reconcile herself to the loss of her father while deeply desiring her husband and compassionating his former mistress. " 'Love' " proves to be not compendious enough: she had not calculated on there being so many different kinds, and while she continues to reach for her romantic notion of it, she dooms herself to an inconsistency that is all her own and in no way that of the novelist who is rendering it. Thus the Maggie who has from the first of her anxiety wanted to spare Amerigo; who had been "almost moved to saying to [Charlotte]: 'Hold on tight, my poor dear — without *too much* terror — and it will all come out somehow' "; who, listening to her in the gallery, can so fully share Adam's consciousness of "the shame, the pity, the better knowledge, the smothered protest, the divined anguish even", is the same Maggie who can break out so bitterly, so simplistically, to Fanny, about Amerigo and Charlotte having been " 'the ones who are saved' " by her unexpected ability to " 'think' ", while she and Adam are " lost' ". " 'Oh yes,' Maggie ***quite lucidly*** declared, 'lost to each other really much more than Amerigo and Charlotte are; since for them it's just, it's right, it's deserved, while for us it's only sad and strange and not caused by our fault.' " Then, in the sharpest confession of her general desolation that we are ever to hear, she responds unmistakably to Fanny's facile rationalization about Adam's departure leaving her " 'more free' ".

> Maggie looked at her long. "Yes — I help him to do that."

> Mrs Assingham hesitated, but at last her bravery flared. "Why not call it then frankly his complete success?"
> "Well," said Maggie, "that's all that's left me to do" (II, 116, 284, 292, 333, 334).

While she waits with Amerigo for that leave-taking and waits, too, for the kind of reunion that both hope may then be possible for them, we see the distinct limits of her knowledge and the way she even yet redeems from the vestiges of her romanticism a form of imagining that helps her, in this last resort, to insist on " 'success' ". Her truths are indeed strangely mixed. When she speaks of her father as being " 'too great for [her]' ", adding " 'I know why I think it . . .. That's enough' ", it is the "truth" for her of her idealization of him. When she speaks of knowing " 'better than anyone what [Charlotte] won't let [her] take her for' ", it is the truth of an observed fact and of a divined motive which we can attest. When she asks him, " 'Am I to take from you then that you accept and recognize my knowledge [of the adultery]?' " and they bring up the " 'question of the quantity of truth' ", the text makes evident, a I have tried to show in my earlier account of James's presentation of the Prince, that hers is the lesser quantity, if only because she is concerned at that moment almost exclusively with the truth of her relation to him (II, 347, 349, 350).

This kind of selecting, informed by a vestigial romanticism, is what she continues to prefer when, leave-taking over, she waits while he takes the child to Miss Bogle. "It meant something for the Princess that her husband had thus got their son out of the way, not bringing him back to his mother; but everything now, as she vaguely moved about, struck her as meaning so much that the unheard chorus swelled. Yet *this* above all — her just being there as she was and waiting for him to come in, their freedom to be together there always — was the meaning most disengaged: . . ." Certainly here the chorus is unheard because silent but also because not listened to by this Princess who can still envision illusory prospects of shared freedoms. Characteristically, her imaginings at this crucial moment in her adventure echo the empty rhetoric of Polonius's advice to Laertes; they reveal her as consciously choosing from among her motives the most idealistic, filling an aloneness (that is not yet admitted as a solitude) by the most reassuring view of consequences. We, who do hear the chorus, are equipped by the novel to appraise the truth of this euphorically expressed self-knowledge, as we learn that "she stood in the cool twilight and took in all about her where it lurked her reason for what she had done. She knew as last really why — and how she had been inspired and guided, how she had been persistently able, how to her soul all the while it had been for the sake of this end" (II, 367).

It is familiar language: we heard it in her silent paean upon her father after their avowals at Fawns; we heard it, earlier, in his own reflections on himself as a Keatsian Cortez. We heard it from Charlotte earlier still on that grand staircase and from Amerigo on that grand Matcham parapet. It does not sustain Maggie for long now, however, in the face of approaching realities which she even yet couches for herself in the revealingly immature terms, drawn from it, of reward and payment. "Here it was then, the moment, the golden fruit that had shone from afar; only what *were* these things in the fact, for the hand and for the lips, when tested, when tasted — what were they as a reward? Closer than she had ever been to the measure of her course and the full face of her act, she had an instant of the terror that, when there has been suspense, always precedes, on the part of the creature to be paid, the certification of the amount." Her imagination, though, reaches further than the usual "beautiful circuit and subterfuge of [her] thought and [her] desire" as she awaits the result of her gamble: "the delay in his return . . . was like a sudden blinding light on a wild speculation" (II, 367).

Ironically, it is when she is in fact in his arms that her real solitude is affirmed, for "the full face of her act" is revealed for her in *his* face; "the truth of it" is "the measure of her course", a truth in fact measured so fully for her in his eyes, "so strangely lighted", as he professes he sees nothing but her, that "she buried her own in his breast", to the end a fugitive from such knowledge of pity and dread. Not averting our own eyes, we can now read, in the longest context of all — that of the completed novel — what she pities and what she dreads, and it is through her consciousness of Charlotte and Adam at this climatic moment that James directs our attention to the spectacle of all four solitaries. He has been at pains to show the inevitability of these emotions being so relentlessly a part of what she finally cannot not know after her battle to exercise that alleged form of love, real only in her own mind, that would comfortably contain the other three figures in her life. She now knows surely enough where she is: not beyond, but confronted with, everything (II, 367, 369, 367, 369).

Her pity is evoked most immediately for the man for whom she has long felt "the hard little passion which nothing he had done could smother"; the man who for long now, though in proximity to her, had been "in fact given over without a break to the grey medium in which he groped"; the man who was so evidently trying to love her as a newly-discovered wife while discussing with her a long-loved mistress. Her consequent burying of her eyes had been anticipated, though only in her imagination, while from her room she watched the sunrise the day she realized he was a fugitive from Charlotte's "high coerced quaver" in the gallery. "She sank to her knees with her arm on the ledge of her window-seat, where she blinded her eyes from the full glare of seeing that his idea could only be to wait, whatever might come, at her side." It is James's immediately subsequent sentence which brings out how her later real action is foreshadowed by this earlier fanciful one, its qualifying clause underlining an irony to which she is not then fully alert. "It was to her buried face that she thus for a long time felt him draw nearest; though after a while, when the strange wail of the gallery began to repeat its inevitable echo, she was conscious of how that brought out his pale hard grimace." In the later reality she is conscious enough of how their passion, for the fulfilment of which they each bade the other to " 'wait' ", cannot eclipse their knowledge, nor her love rid itself of her pity and dread (II, 281, 294, 295, 351+352+353).

This pity reaches also to Charlotte herself who, ironically, is the woman she described to Adam long before in tender terms as one who had " 'loved' " and " 'lost' ". This sentiment now has been cleansed of such sentimentality and cleansed too of the reflex sympathy that I have already mentioned in my account of the images expressing it. Maggie does imagine her own cry of " 'Hold tight, my poor dear . . .' ", just as she does imagine the golden flame, and just as she tells Fanny that she doubts whether Amerigo feels " 'how much less than [Charlotte] he pays' ". But there has been a concomitant growth in hard little reason that has progressively informed her romantically imaginative understanding of this woman (I, 185, II, 284, 332).

From the moment the bowl is smashed there is no longer unwitting reference to the cliché and commonplace her former absolute has then become. When she realizes her husband's ensuing silence to his former mistress, we learn that this fact "gave, for Maggie, altogether a new aspect to Charlotte's consciousness and condition — an aspect with which, for apprehension, for wonder, and even at moments, inconsequently enough, for something like compassion, the Princess had now to reckon". Reckon she does, as she had not heretofore, with the result that "our young woman, who had been from far back, by the habit of her nature, as much on her guard against sacrificing others as if she felt the great trap of life mainly to be set for one's doing so, now found herself attaching her fancy to that side of the situation of the exposed pair which involved for themselves at least the sacrifice of the least fortunate". But her knowledge of "pity" has much further to go even yet (II, 227, 227-28).

From the instinctive self-interest of her early misgivings she progresses to the more complex awareness of a general condition, as in that mute communion with her father in the gallery, after which we hear reasoning that is not rationalizing. "There was honestly an awful mixture in things, and it wasn't closed to her aftersense of such passages — we have already indeed in other cases seen it open — that the deepest depth of all, in a perceived penalty, was that you couldn't be sure some of your conpunctions and contortions wouldn't show for ridiculous." Some of these, inveterate in her as they are, do continue so to show, especially when she encourages Amerigo to entertain Charlotte alone on her last night in London and when she asks him if he " 'shan't . . . so much as miss her a little' ". But her earlier conviction of necessary sacrifice survives these manifestations of the "ridiculous" and though it smacks of her habitually, even yet, salvaging a "moral", she does assert to him: " 'It's as if her unhappiness had been necessary to us — as if we had needed her, at her own cost, to build us up and start us' " (II, 292, 346).

There is, however, an even deeper depth plumbed when she generalizes further still, during their talk a few moments later, of what she has yet to " 'see' " in the final visit of her former school-friend, her father's wife, her husband's mistress, who has provoked for her so much that was "strange" and "marvellous". Maggie believes she is now ready for all that there may be to come.

> "I shall see wonders, I know. I've already seen them and am prepared for them." Maggie recalled — she had memories enough. "It's terrible" — her memories prompted her to speak. "I see it's *always* terrible for women."

But she proves unprepared for what happens after that visit. The terrible knowledge abides: after the vain epithet, " 'splendid' ", which "she simply said, offering it to explain and to finish"; after her husband's patently automatic agreement with it and her final verbal gesture of salvage that "she added — to point further her moral". No words will now reach. The pity is now too clearly applicable to them all (II, 349, 368).

This pity is now inseparable from dread, and the long context which the novel provides for what the Prince finally sees, is one that provides also for that other truth from which she averts her own eyes, her sacrifice of Adam, the fourth figure caught in the great trap. Our own eyes cannot easily blink these provisions, nor the conclusions they suggest. Once her uneasiness about her father's wife and her own husband becomes an alertness, her anxiety is always as much for her father as for herself, and her decision to sacrifice him "without his dreaming what it might be for" follows hard upon his cancellation of the visit to Spain. As she prepares for their Regent's Park ordeal, the reason for his marriage sweeps over her. " 'He did it for *me*, he did it for me,' she moaned, . . ." Her passion, her love for him from that point on, bears her accepted responsibility for his happiness. Though she "could pull herself up repeatedly by remembering that the real 'relation' between her father and his wife was a thing that she knew nothing about and that in strictness was none of her concern; . . . she none the less failed to keep quiet, as she would have called it, before the projected image of their ostensibly happy isolation" at Fawns, while she herself, in London, breaks out to Fanny as to " 'what awfulness' " might be between the disturbingly protective Prince and Charlotte (II, 83, 81, 138, 107).

The dependency in her love for Adam makes it increasingly obvious that she dreads what this sacrifice will mean for herself as much as what it will mean for him. "Maggie's one little lapse from consistency — the sole small deflexion in the whole course of her scheme", we recall James telling us, is when, on the terrace of Fawns that night with Charlotte, looking with her at the card-players, she wishes that Adam would look up at her, thus discriminating in her favour. "Not yet since his marriage had Maggie so sharply and so formidably known her old possession of him as a thing divided and contested", we are then told, and as the pressures upon her continue to mount, driving home the intensity of her dependence upon him, she finds a formula for expressing her love in terms of her belief. In that final affirmation on their favoured bench in the Fawns garden, after we have listened to the extravagances of her silent paean idealizing him, we hear the last words they risk on the nature of their relation. He tells her that he will feel sacrificed by her only when she has ceased to believe in him: her reply is unequivocal.

> "I believe in you more than anyone."
> "Than anyone at all?"
> She hesitated for all it might mean; but there was — oh a thousand times! — no doubt of it. "Than any one at all." She kept nothing of it back now, met his eyes over it, let him have the whole of it; after which she went on: "And that's the way, I think, you believe in me" (II, 245, 244, 275).

After appreciating the total mutual commitment rendered in this scene, we can better appreciate Maggie's silent words to herself after her later charade with Charlotte: "Yes, she had done all". To the Charlotte whose chosen role in that charade is to call the relation between father and daughter " 'too great and too strange an ugliness' ", and to fling at her " 'You've thought *you've* known what he's worth?' ", she must pretend her sacrifice is her defeat. She is consistent. Thereafter she avoids, with everyone, approaching the subject of any painful knowledge he may possess. When Fanny, during her final colloquy, blunders towards it (" 'Your father. He knows what *you* know? . . .' "), we learn that "Maggie's silence and Maggie's eyes had in fact arrested the push of the question — . . .". We learn too that the Prince, during their discussion of " 'for whom' " Adam is " 'too great' ", "was on the very point, she judged, of asking her why she thought it. But her own eyes maintained their warning . . .". The reality of her commitment to the person, who alone embodies all she believes in, remains sacrosanct but remains too a threat that looms again during her last moments of ostensible persiflage with him on the balcony, when "she asked herself but for a few seconds whether reality, should she follow him, would overtake or meet her there". But she knows "how impossible such a passage would have been to them, how it would have torn them to pieces, if they had so much as suffered its suppressed relations to peep out of their eyes". Our memory of their mutual attestations, voiced so lucidly, at Fawns, makes clear enough the charade of their mutual protestations now, their repetition of that word " 'success' " which, as she told Fanny, is all she had left to name the parting by. When Adam, as I tried earlier to show, encourages her belief in his " 'beautiful, beautiful!' " Charlotte, on whose "*value*" he and Maggie are parting, we learn that she detects in his tone "the shade of a new note", while James tells us that though "it was all she might have wished . . .; yet it conveyed to her as nothing till now had done the reality of their parting" (II, 318, 316, 317, 334, 335, 347, 362, 366, 365).

It is in the Prince's arms that reality can no longer be held at bay. The "sustained rattle" of the play-acting over, "stillness . . . not so much restored as created", Maggie awaits him in the room itself, after "so natural, though so futile, a movement as . . . going out to the balcony again to follow with her eyes her father's departure. The carriage was out of sight — it had taken her too long solemnly to reascend, and she looked a while only at the great grey space on which, as on the room still more, the shadow of dusk had fallen." She sees nothing but the Prince, who is soon to tell her that he sees nothing but her and the immediate moment has "remarkable salience" for both. I have already suggested how part of this truth includes his awareness of the absence of Charlotte as well as his designedly reassuring gesture to the presence of his wife, and that this is in part why she buries her eyes in his breast rather than face the pity and dread she sees in his own and feels in herself. I suggest now there is a complementary meaning amid the multivalence that James's art controls through the context given these words in the whole novel: "the truth" would support Maggie's addressing the same words to him, for though deeply desiring him, she sees him only, and no longer also her father, whom she as deeply needs (II, 366).

My point may gain further credence when we recall other embraces — all of them tactically placed for emphasis — throughout the novel. They dramatize the apparent strange incompatibility, among the relationships depicted, of physical passion and spiritual belief. There is the highly sensuous rendering of how the lovers seal their "sacred" pledge. There is Maggie's resistance, in the carriage, to her husband's power that she knows to be so sovereign a one, after he embraces her at the moment when her needing to know where she is has become more important for her. There is the embrace Fanny shares with her when each pretends to believe the other after her outburst about the lovers and which ends in mutual tears. There is the Judas kiss Charlotte exacts from her while she suppresses her terror and plays her role. There is the declaration of mutual belief by father and daughter at Fawns, one the direct opposite to hers and Fanny's, for this one "was an embrace that, august and almost stern, produced for all its intimacy no revulsion and broke into no inconsequence of tears". There are the two embraces that are imminent between her Prince and herself but are prevented, the first by him and the second by her, because both wish to wait till they are free of their visitors, each of whom represents for them, respectively, the distraction of two kinds of love which seem to be mutually exclusive. When they do embrace, the novel would appear to be asserting that they find themselves still vulnerable to these distractions and it is his manifest awareness of this that she shares with a pity and a dread which she tries to shut from sight. There is now for Maggie, her persistent absolute so chastened by knowledge, much more than she can contain in her golden bowl (II, 275).

The function of the gilt cup

I must now, resumptively, turn to the physical object given that name, hoping to show how it in itself provides James with his desired "imaged resumé"[20] throughout the story which it gives a title and how for us it remains, amid all the distancing and mental circuiting, a concrete referent linking us inexorably with a real external world. It is in all its functions totally organic to the novel. It contributes vitally to all other agents which James here makes responsible in his art for "the air of the whole result": to the sequence of the scenario; to the continual disparity between the romantic and the real; to the "appeal to variety" issuing from every character's relation to it; to the "appeal to incalculability" — this most strongly and "strangely"; to the authorial efforts at distancing and detachment, yes, but also to his implied reminder of the historic, human and moral commonplace it represents; and to the "fusion" and "synthesis" that are James's expressed aesthetic goals. It contributes thus, equally, to amplitude of reference and to intensity of effect. That it is of inestimable convenience to him in his disciplining of Princess Maggie as an expressive agent is seen when these contributions are more closely examined.

I begin with its most elementary role in the story. Charlotte chances on it with the Prince in that search for Maggie's wedding gift which she makes the excuse for spending some last moments with him but though tempted, even after discovering it to be cracked, she does not buy it for her, nor will her superstitious lover accept it. It is also chanced on years later by Maggie after a visit to her husband's archives nearby and she buys it as a birthday gift for her father, unaware of its crack and paying much more for it than Charlotte could offer. But the antique dealer, capable of allowing its purchase by someone with full knowledge of its flaw, proves incapable of selling it to an ignorant, trusting Maggie and, while visiting her to retrieve it and refund her money, recognizes photographs of the lovers and tells her about their visit. She retains the bowl, placing it for her husband to see, then summons Fanny to hear her discovery. Fanny smashes it, the Prince enters and Maggie collects the three pieces, holding them together so that the breaks do not show and thereby confronting him with her implied accusation. Henceforth it is used figuratively.

Such a bare summation immediately suggests other relevant facts. The cracked gilt cup is introduced into the story in grubby Bloomsbury during a clandestine interlude in which a cosmopolitan young expatriate American woman of vague Tuscan antecedents tries with concealed desperation to elicit from the Italian nobleman, her former lover, some recognition of their earlier Roman time together. This cup, which arouses his irrational superstitions but intrigues her, is presented for their inspection by a Italian-speaking Jewish antique-dealer of indeterminate origins who, after withdrawing it from its cabinet and box as if it were a sacred chalice in a tabernacle, pursues its sale, at an extortionate price, while first concealing, then rationalizing, its flaw and while remaining throughout evasive and equivocal. It is reintroduced when the gullible daughter of a millionare American collector of antiques buys it for her father after visiting the nearby British Museum, from which her father has already bought several pieces for his art bequest, and after inspecting there the archives of the young nobleman's forebears in the original Roman time of papal corruption and ducal mercenariness. It is finally smashed, as an act of concealment by a worldly socialite who, herself an American Jewess resembling in her dress a second-hand dealer, had served as intermediary in the two marriages involving all four while concealing from the father and daughter the fact of the lovers' relationship. This, then, is the relation of the cup, as a material thing, to the material facts which are among all those given in James's presentation of the story of these people.

At an adamantine level of reality from which the whole

novel *The Golden Bowl* is basically derived, its story is of how the concealed becomes the revealed and I argue that we misread it if we see its other levels as distractions from, rather than as ramifications of, that first level. The connections which come to be made are only apparently coincidences; they are central to James's apparent notion of "the strange scheme of things" and James is evidently concerned that they are seen as central to the scheme of the novel. The incalculable perversity with which, as the cynical husband of the "*revendeuse*" says, " 'Murder will out' " is an indissoluble part of the subject, bearing no resemblance to the long arm that reaches so often through a Dickens novel but identical with the chance and accident of a Hardy one. The place where the lovers and the daughter shop is hard by the place where the father deals. That the same antiquarian would have let a knowing, hard-bargaining Charlotte buy his cup for the sceptical Italian who is obviously her lover and yet recant from having sold it to the pleasant *naif* who bought it as an intimate gift for her father is not implausible nor is it an inexplicable: it is an incalculable frankly rendered as such. The context provided for it in the novel is the insistence on precisely this kind of prevailing strangeness, already detailed above, and nowhere is there provision for explaining, much less for explaining away, any of these connections as calculable events in a determined world. As events in the Ververs' world, they are only relatively improbable anyway, and it is true that the novel is mainly occupied with their repercussions, but essentially they are seen to be central to the interest James is patently developing in our view of that world which subsumes the Ververs', the world that,ultimately, cannot be not known sooner or later and which is therefore our own world of reality, with which the persons depicted in this novel strive vainly to strike their various forms of romantic compromise and in which each comes to know solitude (I, 144, 34, II, 134).

The cracked cup, transmuted into the golden bowl only in the "beautiful circuit and subterfuge" of each character's recorded thoughts, is, in this novel involving collection and purchase, the only *morceau de musée* that enjoys a figurative as well as a literal existence, and thus, as a link between the real and the romantic, it is at once always a distancing agent and an implied authorial comment. All the characters react variously to this real cup and imagine other cups of their own. The exception is Fanny, for whom the guilt in its gilt is strongest. Predictably enough she sees it as "that complicating object", provoking her "recurrent wonder and recurrent protest"; for her it is "inscrutable in its rather stupid elegance" and she, whose "romantic" good intentions in the commerce of human beings bring her closest to "gross"[21] foolishness and stupidity, tries to smash it out of existence (II, 176, 177, 165).

The Prince, emphatically agreeing with his exquisite partner, (" 'Of course it's exquisite. That's the danger' "), confessing his superstitious dread of the flaw he recognizes in it, creates, with the alchemy of Matcham, another cup, telling her, before they visit Gloucester, " 'I feel the day like a great gold cup that we must somehow drain together' ". Reminded of the real cup, about which she had been on the earlier occasion totally pragmatic, identifying it then with her Prince as a prize that might be possessed, she accuses him of being too afraid of the cracks that she is willing to risk and, when she has risked and lost, James has her rival thus imagine her eloquent anguish at the loss of her happier relation with her lover: " 'Ours was everything a relation could be, filled to the brim with the wine of consciousness;. . .' " Adam, who never receives or even sees the real cup, tells his son-in-law shortly after the first Bloomsbury episode that he thinks of him as " 'a pure and perfect crystal' ". Not very long after our having seen the antiquarian lift such an allegedly pure and perfect crystal object from "a square box . . . covered with worn-looking leather" and after having heard him describe its gilding as " 'a lost art' ", we hear James's account of Adam Verver's limiting obsession with art. "He put into his own little glass everything he raised to his lips, and it was as if he had always carried in his pocket, like a tool of his trade, this receptacle, a little glass cut with the fineness of which the art had long since been lost, and kept in an old morocco case stamped in uneffaceable gilt with the arms of a deposed dynasty." The imagined is here juxtaposed with the actual less directly but just as relentlessly as in the lovers' instances, and all three, when added to Fanny's relation to this fact of their lives, amply provide against our thinking of the cup exclusively in reference to Maggie (I, 119, 359, II, 329, I, 138, 112, 114, 196).

James is freed, therefore, to use it fairly persistently when delineating Maggie's protracted romantic reactions against the real. Not unexpectedly, it is only she who prolongs and elaborates the figurative references to the actual bowl after it is smashed and these continue to turn the double dramatic-narrative lock in James's account of this reluctant submission to actualities. Few pages intervene between the "great gold cup" of which her husband tells his lover at Matcham and the one Maggie imagines telling him has contained her love as she has awaited his return: " ' — the cup, all day, has been too full to carry' ". Both these fanciful vessels are to contain bitter dregs. When the girl who was " 'not afraid of history' " and who found it "enlarging and inspiring" to read the Amerigo archives, discovers that the cup she bought directly afterwards " 'isn't gold' " and tells a history of its own, her habitual idealizing is checked. She becomes quiet and grim. But immediately after her cup has been smashed, she picks up the pieces and holds them together, making an apparently whole bowl again for Amerigo to see and telling him she values it even more now for the " 'truth' " it has given her about him (I, 359, II, 18, I, 9, II, 149, 177, 189).

The next time she is alone with Fanny, she begins her Procrustean effort to make this new truth fit her favoured frame. Amerigo, she says, understands what she wants.

> ". . . I want a happiness without a hold in it big enough for you to poke in your finger."
> "A brilliant perfect surface — to begin with at least. I see."
> "The golden bowl — as it *was* to have been." And Maggie dwelt musingly on this obscured figure. "The bowl with all our happiness in it. The bowl without the crack."

Assailed by her crisis of temptation during the bridge-game, she sees that "those formless fragments of her golden bowl she was trying so hard to pick up" are as "ugly" as the "terrors and shames and ruins" she could expose the players to, and the alternative is not "all happiness" but is now only some of the forms of it — "serenities and decencies and dignities" (II, 216-17, 236).

They are fragments sharp with her consciousness of how her very preserving of appearances would give Charlotte the advantage in any contest of truth they might engage in with her father. When they next do become a cup again it is "the cup of her conviction" that has "overflowed" at her recognizing, during that second Fawns session with her father, that he shares her knowledge and agrees that the consequences of it commit him to taking Charlotte to America. Typically, she becomes intoxicated by what this draught means for her saving of "the equilibrium" and ignores for a period the cost of the "sacrifice" they banter about. Ironically, it intensifies her sense of communion with him. (II, 271, 268, 267 + 269 + 272).

With Charlotte "doomed", she and her father resemble at one moment for her "a couple of sociable drinkers who sit back from the table over which they have been resting their elbows, over which they have emptied to the last drop their respective charged cups. The cups were still there on the table, but turned upside down; and nothing was left for the companions but to confirm by placid silences the fact that the wine had been good." Her use of the pluperfect is more ominous than she would then admit (II, 271, 285).

Nor, on the hot Sunday of her confrontation with Charlotte, is the wine of her consciousness the undiluted draught by which she figures that woman's passion. As she notes that Father Mitchell has become a register of the tensions of luncheon, her wonderings are all anxieties. The final cup she envisages for herself contrasts even more strongly with the first, which, while awaiting Amerigo's return from Matcham that night months before, she had thought "too full to carry", for, "just now she was carrying in her weak stiffened hand a glass filled to the brim, as to which she had recorded a vow that no drop should overflow". The first was pure love, as Charlotte's had been pure bliss; the last precariously holds the care that is soon to become pity and the fear soon to become dread. She wonders if the "cord mightn't at last have snapped between her husband and her father"; she wonders if her step-mother's flight to the garden results from similar anxieties. She knows only that "something grave had happened", and her phrase echoes importantly her much earlier one to Fanny after the antiquarian's visit: " 'Something very strange has happened . . .' " (II, 18, 298, 154).

For nowhere in the whole novel is James's usage of that familiar epithet and of others associated with it, more concentrated than in connection with Maggie and all the bowl references that suggest all she inevitably comes to know. She finds it in one of the " 'funny little fascinating' places" where, Charlotte had told her, there are "such unexpected finds". She buys it there from "a queer little foreign man". There, she tells Amerigo, she " 'came upon it, extraordinarily, through happening to go into the same shop' " as he went into with Charlotte. When her cup is said to have "turned witness — by the most wonderful of chances", it was not their sharing with her the same shop " 'that makes the strangeness of the coincidence; for don't such chances as that, in London,' " she asks Amerigo, " 'easily occur?' " She tells him the greater " 'strangeness' " was to derive from the " 'wonder' " of what the antiquarian found himself moved to tell her by his simply having liked her. She is thoroughly coherent with him on the whole matter: "she was singularly able — it had been marvellously 'given' her, she afterwards said to herself — to abide, for her light, for her clue, by her own order. 'I inspired him with sympathy — there you are! But the miracle is that he should have a sympathy to offer that could be of use to me. That was the real oddity of my chance,' the princess proceeded . . ." (II, 155, 157, 188, 163, 195, 196).

Maggie's use of all these epithets thus provides here a *coda* for the central theme of the novel as she applies them to that central object in it by which she can organize and articulate her growing knowledge and reach out through it to realities less esoteric than those she has hitherto entertained. It is a *coda* played *fortissimo*: "the vendor of the golden bowl had acted on a scruple rare enough in vendors of any class and almost unprecedented in the thrifty children of Israel . . .; . . . had given way to a whim all the more remarkable to his own commercial mind, no doubt" and "she had recognised the oddity of her adventure . . .". Maggie's ironic sense is no longer "scant" as she tells her husband about "the most extraordinary incident of all", the shop-keeper's recognition of the photographs, and "more wonderful still", his connection of the lovers with the bowl. Then James reiterates the note which more than any other in this special scale reverberates most finely now in the echoing chambers of the novel: "the connexion", Maggie's little man tells her, "must have had, mysteriously, something to do with the impulse he had obeyed" (II, 222-3, 223, 284, 224, 225).

For us there is less of the mysterious in this motive, foreshadowed long before. It was, notably, not to Maggie on this occasion, but to Charlotte on a much earlier one, that he "discriminated" when she suggested the bowl's " 'beauty was in its hardness' " and he had carefully replied to her, " 'Its beauty is in its *being* crystal. But its hardness is certainly its safety." And he then went on to tell her nothing but truth about how it could be broken (I, 116).

For Maggie, however, there is obviously a mystery that

she at last tries to confront as a whole without romantically expecting from it only happiness. The bowl has come to her incalculably and she can now try to apprehend its import without having comprehended its meaning. It comes to her in part from a man who is a stranger, intimate with the common life of London. She is later to try, without success "to explain and to finish", even "to point further her moral", to embrace its implications in the arms of the other foreigner who declares that " 'everything's terrible . . . in the heart of man' " and in whose breast she is to bury her eyes because she recognizes in his, "so strangely lighted", enough of what he at that moment sees. Certainly, with eyes thus buried, she cannot see clearly the father she idolizes even yet and who could once so complacently regard her as a nymph-nun "lost in an alien age". She knows more about that age, having been taught by her husband and her former school-friend, both of whom have so brilliantly graced it, by Fanny, in one sense, and by the Castledean set, in another, as well as by a shopkeeper in Bloomsbury. Physically sundered from her father, however, she evidently now feels even more alienated in it, even more conscious of a desolating aloneness, and she characteristically, though less inexcusably, averts her eyes from what she does see (II, 368, 349, 369, I, 187).

My suggestion as to what James might understandably expect *us* to see must wait till after my account of how he presents all his principals in the final pages of the novel; and I conclude my argument about his presentation of Maggie by relating it to those other appraisals of her with which I began it, appraisals that acknowledged subtle use of irony, imagery, comment, epithets and bowl but not their concerted impact. I need hardly protest further that the kind of interest in her to which these provisions amply attest has little to do with simple heroines or Machiavellians or outraged wives and has even less to do with unexamined goodness or indeed with any absolutes, doctrinal or romantic, that are not subjected to James's searching scrutiny. Nuhn,[22] Matthiessen,[23] Leavis,[24] Edmund Wilson,[25] Firebaugh[26] and Sears[27] must remain as dissatisfied as must Gordon,[28] Todasco,[29] Edel,[30] Lebowitz[31] and Blackmur remain misleading,[32] until they all come to terms with this evidence.

James's interest would seem, on the other hand, to have much more affinity with clues that others picked up but did not pursue far enough: with Wright's suggestions[33] about dramatic imagery, with Cargill's about the crucial duologues with Adam[34] and with Krook's about the range and variety of the characterization.[35] It is an interest of which Enck guessed there being a possibility,[36] and about which Pearson speculated, too;[37] one that Bayley saw as probable,[38] given the richness of the mode of appeal. Those who have sensed it are those who, like Chernaik[39] and Yeazell,[40] have not underestimated the radical originality given that appeal by the reach of the irony within it (as Schneider[41] has underestimated it) and who, like Reddick,[42] have appreciated the continual flux within the relationship of character and author. Fundamentally, it is an interest in the common mystery of the "naked thinking heart" (to borrow Jonson's description of Donne) and, because it is evoked for us by the soundless as well as by the sounded rendering, it explores that mystery with an eloquence that radically extends the range of the art of rhetoric in fiction.

NOTES

1. Gordon, *National Hero*, p. 46.
2. Bayley, *Characters of Love*, pp. 238, 239, 240.
3. Krook, *Ordeal*, pp. 253, 255, 258, 257.
4. Ruth Todasco, "Theme and Imagery in *The Golden Bowl*", *Texas Studies in Literature and Language* 4 (Summer 1962): 240. Hereafter *Theme and Imagery*.
5. Holland, *Expense*, p. 377.
6. Pearson, *Novel to End Novels*, p. 306. In his *Henry James: The Ibsen Years* (London: Vision P., 1972), p. 18, Michael Egan suggests that whereas "*The American* is fixed upon its canvas, *The Golden Bowl*

floats freely between narrator, spectator and actor" — a suggestion more spectral than specific. I have preferred to heed Howard Pearce's reminder in his "Henry James's Pastoral Fallacy", *PMLA* 90:5 (October 1975), p. 844, that "the architectonics of this novel are alone a warning to approach it tentatively". It was Sears in *Negative Imagination*, p. 174, n. 10, who specified the imaginary observer of Adam in the billiard-room at Fawns as a "phantom spectator", a phrase handy in any such approach.

7. Bayley, *Characters of Love*, p. 244. See also general interest in this aspect in P.S. Sita, "A Silent Morality: Non-Verbal Expression in *The Ambassadors*", *South Atlantic Bulletin* 39:ii (1974), p. 102-6 and "The Sound of Silence: Non-Verbal Expression in *The Wings of the Dove*", *Arizona Quarterly* 27:ii (Summer 1971), p. 143-50.
8. Crews, *Tragedy*, pp. 112, 113.
9. Wayne Booth, *The Rhetoric of Fiction* (Chicago: U. of Chicago P., 1961), pp. 67-86. Hereafter *Rhetoric*.
10. James, "The New Novel", *Notes on Novelists: with Some Other Notes* (London: Dent, 1914), iii, pp. 150-81.
11. Bryan Reddick, "The Control of Distance in *The Golden Bowl*", *Modern British Literature* 1:1 (Fall 1976): 46, 52, 55, 53. Hereafter *Control of Distance*.
12. Ruth B. Yeazell, "Talking in James", *PMLA* 91 (January 1976), pp. 75-76. Hereafter *Talking*.
13. Ibid., p. 76.
14. Ruth B. Yeazell, "Forum", *PMLA 91:5 (October 1976): 922, 933, 924*. Hereafter *Forum*.
15. Ibid., p. 924.
16. James, *Prefaces*, pp. 31-32.
17. Ibid., p. 328.
18. See my "Henry James and the Art of the Novel: A Study of a Developing Technique", *Diss*., Univ. of Sydney, 1958, 201-7, and agreement by Mary Kyle Michael in her "Henry James's Use of the Word *Wonderful* in *The Ambassadors*", *Modern Language Notes* 75 (February 1960): 114-17; and also by David Lodge, "Strether by the River", *Language of Fiction: Essays in Criticism and Verbal Analysis of the English Novel* (London: Routledge and Kegan Paul, 1966), pp. 189-213.
19. See my "An Attempt to Define the Meaning of *The Wings of the Dove*", *Aulla Proceedings* 2 (1962), 76-78.
20. James, *Prefaces*, p. 263.
21. Ibid., p. 67.
22. Nuhn, *Wind*, pp. 131, 136, 151.
23. Matthiessen, *Major Phase*, pp. 104, 102.
24. Leavis, *Great Tradition*, p. 168.
25. Edmund Wilson, "The Ambiguity of Henry James", *The Triple Thinkers: Twelve Essays on Literary Subjects* (London: John Lehmann, 1952), pp. 123-24.
26. Firebaugh, *Ververs*, pp. 401, 406.

27. Sears, *Negative Imagination*, p. 170.
28. Gordon, *National Hero*, p. 46.
29. Todasco, *Theme and Imagery*, p. 240.
30. Edel, *Master*, pp. 215-229.
31. N. Lebowitz, *The Imagination of Loving: Henry James's Legacy to the Novel* (Detroit: Wayne State U.P., 1965), p. 131. Hereafter *Loving.*
32. Blackmur, *Intro. GB*, pp. xx-xxi.
33. Walter Wright, "Maggie Verver Neither Saint nor Witch", *Nineteenth-Century Fiction* 12 (June 1957): 59-71.
34. Cargill, *Novels HJ*, pp. 432, 408-9, 410, 419.
35. Krook, *Ordeal*, pp. 253, 255, 258, 257.
36. Enck, *Wholeness*, pp. 227-40.
37. Pearson, *Novel to End Novels*, pp. 332-334.
38. Bayley, *Characters of Love*, pp. 238, 239, 240.
39. Chernaik, *Moralist*, pp. 105-21.
40. Yeazell, *Talking*, pp. 66-77. See also Chapter 5, note 84 below.
41. Schneider, *Divided Self*, pp. 447-60.
42. Reddick, *Control of Distance*, pp. 45-56.

5

The Congruous Whole

The final scene and "the air of the whole result", major "difficulties", revision of the rhythm of the major rhetoric, the "play of tone" and the contribution to prose fiction

The final scene and "the air of the whole result"

After arguing how James presents all his principal figures here in the finale and what is thus contributed to the total impact of their adventures, I shall continue to argue for the important newness of this impact by comparing and contrasting it with those of the earlier and later novels of this major phase and then attempt to come to grips with the distinctive rhetoric of that phase. To this end I shall resort first to the significant revision of punctuation in a passage at the heart of *The Golden Bowl* and then to that ample evidence James supplies elsewhere which illuminates the mode of appeal he makes in it, especially the function of rhythm and cadence in fusing together all those elements by which our response to the strange, incalculable mixtures in life is evoked. I then close by suggesting the contibution he thereby makes to the art of prose fiction.

The complex drama played out during the afternoon-tea of farewell is now taken up here for the last time. On each of the other occasions, I have examined the bitter nemesis it means: for the Prince, who is as conscious of Charlotte as he is of Adam's rejection of him and of the anticlimax of reunion with Maggie; for Charlotte, who now hides painful and humiliating defeat; for Adam, disillusioned with power and possession as he takes a disciplined wife into exile and farewells his daughter and grandson; and for Maggie, who has preserved a perfect surface for the golden bowl she has tried to hold together but who finds it contains not only her forms of love but also pity and dread. I must emphasize that the final impact of the novel is not the sum of all these values but the product of them that is represented by this final rendezvous. This, I repeat, is the only "discriminated occasion" in the entire scenario when all four are seen sustainedly in concert and it is the moment when they part perversely coupled.

The tone is electric and James sustains it by finger-tip control of all the agents his mode offers. Most of them have been remarked already. There is the authorial spy he describes as capable of "a lingering view, a view more penetrating than the occasion really demanded", to whom "the two noble personages" seated amid the items of the collection "might have figured as concrete attestations of a rare power of purchase". There are the lines of sparse dialogue, with their ironic backward reach, containing the "all right" and the "success" with which father and daughter try to ease realities for each other, and the "explicitly jocose" references to "failure" that he permits himself. There are the reported actions, lightly mentioned but resoundingly heard: the final embrace, the last of the many significant ones throughout the novel; and Maggie's awaiting, and response to, the Prince — "her sight of him renewed to intensity" in the same way Charlotte's sight of him was so intensely renewed after awaiting him on the staircase at the Foreign Office ball. There is Maggie's own consciousness, while earlier awaiting the Ververs' arrival, "of other occasions when she had cheated appearances of agitation with a book": on the night of the lovers' return from Matcham via Gloucester; during the bridge-game at Fawns, before being confronted by Charlotte on the terrace; carrying the correct volume to Charlotte when again dissimulating before her in the garden rotunda there; and now before issuing to her husband commands to " 'Come!' " and to " 'Go!' ". All these authorial "shifts", in two senses of that word, make their particular contributions to an expressive tension "in the air of the whole result" (II, 360, 359, 366, 361, 368, 355, 356).

James taps more general sources of it in the strongly appropriate details of time and place, as well as in the disparity between the tone of his discourse and the nature of the events occurring. These too reach back. "The time was stale, it was to be admitted, for incidents of magnitude; the September hush was in full possession at the end of the dull day, and a couple of the long windows stood open to the balcony that overhung the desolation — the balcony from which Maggie, in the springtime, had seen Amerigo and Charlotte look down together" after the Regent's Park discussion with her father that prepared the way for the departure now imminent. There are no golden bowls in sight or mind now; there is only the room "with the perfect polish of its wide floor reflecting the bowls of gathered flowers", which, together with the Prince's caged pacings, prompt from her, "a trifle grimly", " 'We're distinctly bourgeois!' ". Again the possible comment is delegated to the invoked spy: "though to a spectator sufficiently detached they might have been quite the privileged pair they were reputed, granted only they were taken as awaiting the visit of Royalty". The meanings taken from the appearances here given are ones for which any reference such as those to a "chariot", to an "august emergence", to the Prince receiving "Royalty", to Charlotte "throned" and to "the varieties of her nobler aspects" quietly sustain the ironic (II, 354-55, 354, 358, 357).

What must strike the reader long acquainted with these people is how their behaviour underlines their characteristic responses to their final situation. Adam, we are told, "had a way . . ., wherever he was, of moving about the room, noiselessly, to see what it might contain; and his manner of now resorting to this habit, acquainted as he already was with the objects in view, expressed with a certain sharpness the intention of leaving his wife to her own devices". While he and Maggie have their private moment beside the sentimentalized sacred Luini painting, the Prince and his partner have their slow, grave discourse over tea, which we last saw them taking together in that room on the occasion when they sealed their "sacred" pledge. Later, in the anti-climactic stillness of that room, while Maggie awaits her husband, we have reported for us the inveterate romantic euphoria of her ideas about "their *freedom* to be *together*" — two words much complicated through frequent application to all the principals and their couplings — and her use of "inspired", of "soul" and of "golden fruit", before the ensuing moment of climax when this language becomes no longer adequate for the realities from which she will avert her eyes (II, 358, 367).

James's language, on the other hand, could not be more uniformly low in key as he reports the devices each employs for coping with those truths they well know "would have torn them to pieces" if not suppressed beneath "the splendid effect and the general harmony" and "the right quiet lustre". There is surely no need, with so much of the explosive latent, for anything but minimal and bland statement: "the note was struck indeed; the note of that strange accepted finality of relation, as from couple to couple, which almost escaped an awkwardness only by not attempting a gloss". "Almost" and "only" alone would here justify James's faith in adverbs showing "*the* literary sense".[1] The words "real", "reality" and "truth" are there but in muted tone and intractable context, as are "right" and "good". We know the meaning that Maggie, with Adam's encouragement, will try most to disengage and the warrants she will seek to do so. Thus, on the detail vital to their parting without fear — Adam's alleged belief that he best knows his wife — James deftly, steadily and non-committally follows the words of father and daughter with a realistic account of her romantic propensity. "On which, as the warranted truth of it hung in the air — the truth warranted, as who should say, exactly by the present opportunity to pronounce, this opportunity created [by Adam] and accepted [by Maggie] — she found herself lost, though with a finer thrill than she had perhaps yet known, in the vision of all he might mean." The fullest force of the rhetoric here, amid the "vast quantities" beneath the "apparent life", is contained in James's expressive shrug in that colloquial "as who should say" (II, 362, 360, 358, 361, 362+365, 360+365, 364, 363, 364-5, 361, 365).

The "handsome wholeness of effect" here is a radically original one: it insists on our consciousness of each of these people as individuals, on our knowledge of the route by which each has reached this loneliness and on our keen awareness of the suffering it means for each. This final effect involves our appreciation of the whole of the novel and also of its wholeness, a wholeness that embodies the essence of the novel's account of the moral consciousness. The richness of context which that epithet "strange" finds awaiting it in the final sentence is multiplied by all that has happened to each of these people, and the prose now suspends the reader at precisely the right distance for appreciation of it. The reader is kept very busy. He is interested that each of these people could have served as a protagonist but was not permitted to. He knows enough about the ambivalence of their motives, their acts and the consequences of them to be able to reflect on the nature of their future relationships with each other, but he knows no more than James, and James himself ultimately implies finely attentive curiosity.

The reader thus conscious of James's control of these people, individually and collectively, should be in no doubt as to the kind of response James is trying to elicit. There has been subtlety but no evasion; there has been multivalence but no ambiguity. The full effects generated by the novel as a whole are incalculable, as are those generated in life for any sensitively imaginative intelligence, but the responses to the dénouement of the drama these people are playing out when we last glimpse them are not. The essence of the originality of this major art is that the numerous relationships are spelled out unmistakably and sounded for us in eloquent rhetoric, while having nothing to do with Fanny Assingham's kind of explication.

The greatest distance is placed between the two couples who, familially or passionally, have been closest: in terms of what happens after the novel ends, Maggie and Adam and also Charlotte and Amerigo are physicaly sundered. Clearly, *all* the relationships are variously blocked. Amerigo is at the mercy of Adam, Adam controls Charlotte by that silken rope, Charlotte loathes Maggie and Maggie hides her eyes from Amerigo's when he finally encloses her in his arms. The same holds if we examine them in the alternative sequence: Maggie pities Charlotte and pretends for her; Charlotte, to keep her wealth and position, obeys Adam's tether; Adam avoids confrontation with Amerigo; and Amerigo makes a visible effort to act as if seeing nothing but Maggie. In the depicted married relationships of Amerigo and Maggie and of Adam and Charlotte there is as little natural affinity evident as there is between Adam and Amerigo or Charlotte and Maggie. But even the figures diametrically opposed by circumstannces enjoy now only a spurious affinity. Charlotte still loves Amerigo and refuses to believe he no longer loves her; he parts from her in guilt. Maggie still idolizes her father, not really knowing him, and he continues to the end to try to bluff her into accepting as real his simulated appreciation of his wife.

In the earlier time of "felicity", the four of them so ranged together figured for Maggie as the golden bowl containing her happiness. If we see the cracked gilt cup there in their midst, we see how organically, how appropriately — in its imperfection — it links everything together, for it links all these people to the world of the shopkeeper and provides a "lingering view" of "a rare power of purchase". It becomes "a concrete attestation" of James's interest not being exclusively in either the purchasers or the purchased but in purchase. This is the strangeness yielding the manifold interest, the central incalculable that the artistic scheme here is everywhere appealing to with variety, with high refinement and with a handsome wholeness of effect. The power bestowed on the purchaser is rare indeed and is so far beyond the power Adam believed he exercised that he is now forced "to measure the wisdom of old ideas". It is a rare one too in its consequences, for the purchased seemingly can offer no resistance to it or to them. The rare strangeness does not derive from the object (for this, whether golden or gilded or cracked, may appear exquisite) but from the act of purchase itself, and when human beings buy or allow themselves to be bought, the peril is directly proportional to the power, for knowledge is always fatally limited, purity of motive is never enough, even if a possibility, and consequences are always incalculable (II, 360).

Notions such as these must be salient among the cogitations with which James from the beginning has busied the reader and they testify to that extraordinary richness of the mode of appeal that Dorothea Krook and John Bayley suggested would bear further investigation. Investigation thus justifies Judith Chernaik's belief in the function of non-reductive and thoroughly exploratory irony within the steel frame of James's control; Brian Reddick's glimpses of the fuller extent of that control; Barbara Hardy's insistence that it ruled out ambiguity and Ruth Yeazell's faith that all the language of the novel would be coherently disciplined by it. The evidence investigated suggests that the control is exercised in the interests of a much more complex vision of all the artistic values represented by all these people than that for which the above critics have argued. That vision is clearer than, but not as neat as, they evidently believed it to be. The evidence suggests that H.K. Girling, for one, might reconsider whether the context, in which the text is so assiduously disciplined and from which the control emanates, is incapable of making such multivalence of meaning ramify from the single word or phrase.

With those who cannot accept the basic premises of James's art or the demonstrated reach of his application of it here, there can be little further profitable argument; for those who cannot now see the difference in degree — making for a difference in kind — in its application to the two earlier major works, my argument upon the evidence must remain unacceptable, for my central thesis is that in the third of them he did tell us as much about his people as a coherent literary form will permit and he did therefore achieve an originality of effect in it radically different, not only from that of his other works but from those with which this third work deserves to be compared.

Major "difficulties"

It achieves its interesting distinction by being the major effort in a whole phase devoted to tackling major difficulties. These now generally derive from James's being "ridden by the law of entire expression"[2] and what he has to say about them can be instructive for any comparative view taken of the efforts made before and after it. He distinguishes between difficulties "inherent and congenital" and those " 'caught' by the wrong frequentations",[3] but most significant are his remarks on choice. "One has to choose ever so delicately among one's difficulties," he remarks in his *Prefaces*, "attaching oneself to the greatest, bearing hard on those and intelligently neglecting the others. If one attempts to tackle them all one is certain to deal completely with none; whereas the effectual dealing with a few casts a blest golden haze under cover of which, like wanton mocking goddesses in clouds, the others find prudent to retire."[4] He appears not to have always realized how his "law" limited his choice, making the tackling of some quite essential if the others were to emulate the retiring goddesses.

His major phase provides instances enough; and a glance at some of the other modes devised in it supports my claim that in *The Golden Bowl* he found his ultimate mode, speculate though we may about the unfinished projects. *The Sacred Fount*,[5] written on the eve of this phase, provides an obvious enough example of "difficulties caught by the wrong frequentation" and never effectively resolved. There the art of controlling irony is not commensurate with the comic effects apparently entertained and the conclusion is merely ambiguous. The chaos of appearances that are too much for the narrator are too much also for readers left helplessly ill-equipped for understanding, much less appreciating, the point of Mrs Brissenden's perceptions and comments. While the *donnée* rapidly "bristles", the authorial influence remains fatally hampered by the first-person narrative; the problems caught there thus remain beyond rescue by perspective or by indirections that could contribute to it. There is speculation without imagination, a cypher's cypherings, and what Thackeray can do with Barry Lyndon can hardly be attempted within the rarefied air and among the drastically foreshortened and summarized effects of the world of the later James. When stakes are so high, loss is complete.

There is in *The Ambassadors*[6] no difficulty beyond the inherent one of limiting the rendering to a report of Strether's consciousness. James, addressing himself directly to this task, achieves ironic subtleties that are never merely clever, are always cumulative, are never unattended by variety of humour and inform a whole gallery of minor figures who are ever faithfully reflected within the abiding central interest. The *donnée* is pumped "gaspingly dry"[7] by means that sustain the tone of sophisticated high comedy. There is no great artistic adventure involved. James is giving us the portrait of a gentleman with each article of a credo of fiction much sophisticated since he gave us with it *The Portrait of a Lady.* All that has to be controlled is the revelation to Strether of what we already know; nothing is explored, nothing is discovered. The rendering of his mind is no challenge. He is subtle, not devious; he is scrupulous but not obsessive; he is single-minded but not narrow; and once he loses an illusion he never tries to recapture it. Although Madame de Vionet worried her creator, he can easily enough keep the story Strether's: its scenario is straightforward, its centres of interest and of attention are one and the authorial voice speaks always from the same distance. Problems are few and with these James effectually deals. Motives and consequences, though complex, remain clear.

But the difficulties of *The Wings of the Dove*[8] — noble ones all — appear to be inherent in the conception of the subject as well as being caught by the wrong frequentations, and though the haze is as blessed and as golden after James has dealt with a few of them, the others do not retire and are in fact still clearly glimpsed within it. The final form is too simple for the conclusion apparently depicted. It does not afford us sufficient access to all the sources of interest at that point. This comes about not because Densher's has been the consciousness shared until then, but because James does not make our awareness of this consciousness compatible with our awareness of Kate's immediate one, of Milly's past one and of his own implied one. He appears too close to Densher, just as earlier he appeared too close first to Kate and then to Milly, and the transitions from the one to the other are always too abrupt because the resources of the style never keep us sufficiently aware of that constant referent which a consistently-distanced authorial presence could supply.

This is not to blame *The Wings of the Dove* for not being *The Golden Bowl* but it is to recognize how the difficulties met in the one informed James's tackling of even greater difficulties in the other. When he found a means of being more palpably omnipercipient while still not being intrusively omnipresent, there was as little risk of his appearing partial as there was of his appearing neutral. The common ground finally shared in the later novel by characters, author and reader engenders a sense of human solidarity in the face of the unanswerable; the closing pages of its predecessor leave us asking different questions of each of the three principals and looking somewhat askance at an author still busy with his difficulties. This does not make the story of Kate and Densher and Milly a less moving experience but it does make it a less luminous one. Nothing is ambiguous, but the multivalence of this major manner remains to be explored; its language does not resonate so evocatively against all that has gone before.

One index of how major this whole phase remained is that James kept restlessly seeking means for expression — as *he* understood expression — of all the notions besieging him at the turn of the century, and he explored, too, the question of how much of any of them could be expressed in *nouvelles* and in short stories. He was evidently satisfied enough with how, in the successor to *The Wings of the Dove*, he had extended the range of his control. With only some eight per cent still to write, he had described it to his agent, Pinker, as "the best book, I seem to conceive, that I have ever done". There were "developments and amplifications that have, in large part, eventually to be greatly compressed" but, secure in his artistic premises, he could serenely declare: "I have written, in perfection, 200,000 words of the G.B. — with the rarest perfection!"[9] When later dispirited by the critical reception and the sales of the New York Edition which it completed, he still acknowledged "solving" there "his artistic problems".[10]

The unfinished enterprises with their attendant new difficulties reveal him seeking new solutions. His Notebook entries and the three-tenths he had drafted of *The Ivory Tower* suggest that in rendering the moral complexities faced by Graham Fielder he could benefit from the lessons of the completed major trio, but in *The Sense of the Past*,[11] one hundred and ten pages of which had been completed before he switched to *The Ambassadors*, he was again at the frontier. In the three-quarters of the novel in text, and the note planning the final quarter, he is experimenting with the "double consciousness"[12] of Ralph Pendrel, not for the fairly predictable impact of the supernatural interest involved (there was no appeal in terror without pity, he believed)[13] but for the reach given any discourse by such a supra-consciousness. The scheme was clearly to have enjoyed also the extra dimension of Aurora Coyne's sharing in this double moral-vision that embraced not only the old transatlantic interest but also an historic span. Indeed, the possibilities glimpsed summarize James's concern, over half a century of his writing life, with "being" and "seeing", with a romantic past chastened by an actual present, with the clash of cultures, with the conflict of appearance and reality (now complicated by time), and, most of all, with the inviting difficulty of so commanding style that all this was held firm by wires of steel, visible but unobtrusive, subtle but strong. Only the war and the tribute to Rupert Brooke[14] which it wrenched him into writing with such fervour cut short his exulting in these other, private creative difficulties — in his seventy-second year.

The trio of completed works — long, elaborate and each new one more ambitious than the last — should be proof enough of James's never here entertaining difficulty for its own sake but always in the cause of his persistent inquiry into the puzzles of human freedom, love, will and knowledge. Each work offers a reward commensurate with the increasing patience of perusal it demands, as James goes further "behind" his people and exercises negative capability on their "cases". That of Madame de Vionnet clamoured for reopening, so her kind of stature, defeat and obsessional passion are more fully embodied in the study of Kate and then given "the full reign of the major"[15] in the rendering of Charlotte's ordeal. There was clearly much more to be said about Chad, who, despite his wonderful comptesse, remains merely the heir of all the Newsomes still and his kind of vulnerability and passivity were given the scrutiny of those brilliant passages evoking the weeks that Densher spends virtually alone in Venice and then studied in terms of Amerigo's final fugitive solitude.

The illusions of freedom, love and will enjoyed by romantic innocence are very much part of Strether's experience, which appears fully-enough depicted only until we share the responses of Milly Theale and until, accompanying Maggie's thoughts and feelings on these subjects, we have revealed to us a new range altogether. But the greatest difficulty of all was that faced by James in the last of the three when he sought provisions for keeping us equally conscious of all his presented "cases" and for delaying our response to them until we could share his own. Obviously, I believe that these difficulties were surmounted; the appropriate form was found and the contained coherence of James's discourse, the clear pattern of the changing relationships danced out by the partners, no more reduces its richness for the attentive reader than a crucifix reduces the mystery of God for a believer. Obviously, too, my attempts here to calculate the agents of is appeal in no way lessen the one it finally makes to incalculability.

Revision of the rhythm of the major rhetoric

I have already examined most of James's evident provisions for surmounting what he called "the difficulties inherent and congenital": his strategic manoeuvring of books, parts and chapters and his tactical deploying of scene, passage, paragraph, sentence and word to capture the interest he prized. I must now examine the smallest of all units in this assault — punctuation — provision in this case being all the more illuminating because we have also the evidence of revision. His artistry here reminds us of how justly T.S. Eliot defined it: "the example . . . offered us, was not that of a style to imitate, but of an integrity so great, a vision so exacting, that it was forced to the extreme of care and punctiliousness for exact expression".[16] It recalls, too, James's own words to Walter Besant in 1884 about "story" being "idea", integral to a novel's "organic whole", and his insistence that "in proportion as the work is successful the idea permeates and penetrates it, informs and animates it, so that every word and every punctuation point contribute directly to the expression . . .".[17] A quarter of a century later, after further searching in drama and in novel for the key that fitted both the dramatic and the narrative lock and recognizing it in the scenario principle, he had recognized in the *histrionique* of the French classical theatre a rhetorical principle appropriate to the kind of appeal he believed could be made through authorial discourse, and he massively revised the means of signalling the rhythm of this major rhetoric.

Briefly: the punctuation of a typical sentence in the original text over-provides for grammatical relationship in a manner fairly mechanical and with an effect fairly staccato; that of the revised sentence allows also for the play of inflection, cadence and tone. I choose for illustration the third sentence of the first paragraph introducing Book Second and containing Maggie's notorious pagoda figure. If I set out the original version in the manner below, going back to the margin whenever punctuation signals a syntactical unit and beginning a new line intermediately whenever a rhetorical modulation also is evident, the principle of composition yields a total of eighteen such units, thirteen of them a matter of signalled syntax, the other five of rhetorical preference.

UNITS

1. This situation had been occupying,
1 for months and months,
1 the very centre of the garden of her life,
2 but it had reared itself there
    like some strange tall tower of ivory,
  or perhaps
3   rather
      some wonderful,
1 beautiful,
1 but outlandish pagoda,
1 a structure plated with hard,
1 bright porcelain,
1 coloured and figured and adorned,
1 at the overhanging eaves,

2 with silver bells
that tinkled,
2 ever so charmingly
when stirred by chance airs.[18]

If I set the revised version out in the same manner, a different principle is immediately evident, reducing the explicit signals to five which group all eighteen units for rhetorical emphasis.

UNITS

This situation had been occupying
3 for months and months
the very centre of the garden of her life,
2 but it had reared itself there
like some strange tall tower of ivory,
or perhaps
rather
5 some wonderful beautiful
but outlandish
pagoda,
1 a structure plated with hard bright porcelain,
coloured and figured and adorned
at the overhanging eaves
with silver bells
6 that tinkled
ever so charmingly
when stirred by chance airs (II, 3).

The revisions reverse the original emphasis: the first is clear to the eye; the second is sounded, also, on the mental ear. But for James, "revision" was "re-perusal, registered"[19] and so the removal of the punctuation points makes an important difference also to emphasis upon those stages by which Maggie is led to her new idea. She is led from "the very centre of the garden of her life" to "some strange tall tower of ivory", then to "some wonderful beautiful but outlandish pagoda", upon the nature of which structure she dwells. These stages the retained punctuation still firmly expresses, just as the stages themselves express with increasing degrees of intensity her move from the familiar to the foreign and her finally confronting the incalculable in those "chance airs". This new version thus encapsulates much more movingly the essence of James's apparent concern with her throughout the novel. There is a more subtle modulation of means possible, too, within these stages. Maggie has been less at ease "for months and months" and though it would be dramatically inconsistent for this fact to be given the status of a suspicion stronger than its subordinate position within the first major group warrants, it deserves and receives more as one of three minor units there than it would as one of seventeen in the original version. "Outlandish", among merely five other units of the second group, can for the same reason achieve appropriate salience, as can each of the items in the final group, items which express with a suitably high refinement the significant pulse of her thought.

The nuance and suggestion are controlled but not by the relatively automatic apparatus of the earlier version. The rhythm of the later version — less metric, more fugal — is afforded the emphases gained by an expressive variation in pace, for the mental voice may tend to articulate each group at a speed directly proportionate to its length. Thus: the third may well move faster than the first and second, and the fifth move faster than the fourth. There is a more arresting variety of movement, in which the "strange tall tower" and the "outlandish pagoda" and the "chance airs" reiterate the central idea of incalculable mystery with the added eloquence of the soliloquizing voice, of personal meditative speech. Not surprisingly, the sentence was born and revised in dictation before being finally revised by the pen that cut the eight commas. The voice gave it its spontaneous life which the pen then significantly schematized. The result is a stylized utterance, one much more humanly revelatory of Maggie but also one that interestingly distances her. Punctuation, the smallest of the "responsible agents", has been disciplined to reinforce the effects generated by all the larger ones.

The extent to which everything does "hang together"[20] may be appreciated when we consider the fuller context provided for that carefully articulated word "outlandish", one so appropriate for Maggie's new sense of the strange that is central to the vision James finally leaves with us. Conditioned by the ironic use of that group of synonymous terms that I suggested is operating throughout Book First, its literal force here is more readily appreciated, but the form of the novel to this point presses still more closely on it. After the revised punctuation has enhanced rhythm, "outlandish" consorts more interestingly among the four other units that are its immediate neighbours and these in turn constitute one of five stages in the cumulative rhetoric of the whole sentence. That sentence is the third in a paragraph of eleven such delicately articulated ones, each at least three times as long as those in which the James of 1881 reported Isabel Archer's solitary cogitations; and the nine paragraphs of Maggie's chapter, far fewer and far more massive than those of the earlier phase of writing, further develop the "fugal" movement. Rhythm in phrase, sentence, paragraph and chapter is sounded out with the flexibility and appeal of oratory.

As well as vocabulary, syntax and composition being thus marshalled for eloquence, the intensity of figurative language is also brought to bear upon "outlandish", for this word describes a pagoda in "the garden of her life" and it was in the garden of Fawns that she and her father earlier celebrated so innocently their blissful serenity. Earlier still, her father had complacently rejoiced over his daughter's husband so resembling a Palladian church which conveniently did not disturb "the pleasant public square" of "the decent little old-time union" he shared with her. The pagoda, "plated with hard bright procelain, coloured and figured and adorned" becomes for the reader an ironic reminder of the Damascene titles her father pursued with

Charlotte just before he proposed to her. The three other characters who, with her, make up the situation which the pagoda figures, are present in the sentence that now calls that pagoda "outlandish" (II, 135).

Out-of-the-ordinary, too, are the circumstances depicted in the scene itself. Instead of waiting for her husband with her father in Eaton Square, she awaits him in her drawing room in Portland Place. We see this room as we see her, in her new dress, seated in a chair, toying with a book she fails to read, but this "discriminated occasion" among the others selected for the scenario of the novel, is distanced in time and only intermittently present to our senses as Maggie revisits it in memory, after "many days had passed", to refocus and evaluate its details. "It fell for retrospect into a succession of moments that were *watchable* still; almost in the manner of the different things done during a scene on the stage, some scene acted as to have left a great impression on the tenant of one of the stalls." Watchable even yet. It is drama made eloquent by the silent rhetoric of the authorial commentary that distances Maggie herself within it through its references to "the Princess" and to "our young woman" as well as to her name. Two of the ingredients of poetry are therefore intrinsic to this prose: it is sensitively rhythmic and it is graphically imaged. The novelistic mode provided by James ensures, also, that it will be reflectively contemplated from the vantage we have gained at this point in the whole narrative (II, 3, 11, 3, 4, 6).

The context provided for "outlandish" — all the other words of course enjoy it too — resembles a series of concentric circles. Phrase, sentence and paragraph bear upon it, as do vocabulary and figure, and so do scenario and the particular consciousness which the author is recreating and in which he reports this word. But this is only one such consciousness, read of in only one part, the fourth, and I have suggested already how the texture of the prose featuring that word recalls three other consciousnesses — those of Amerigo, Adam and Charlotte — encountered in the preceding three parts, as well as Maggie's own in all three. If we grant James's prose the "patience of perusal" he begged for it, the "finer attention" it obviously demands, our "nobler curiosity" may well be aroused. There is evidence here of its multiplicity of reference and there is provision here for the intensity of appeal generated by all the agents of tight control. This word "outlandish" which has such a lengthy family history in the novel, obeys the disciplines of composition, drama and commentary, all of which are informed by the principal of "successive indirections" and all of which are enlivened by the movement and sound of the human voice.

When we realize that the same resources being expended here for the benefit of Maggie's "case" are to continue throughout the rest of Book Second; when we realize that they have been expended, with variations of manner but never of force, upon Amerigo, upon Adam and upon Charlotte (even, relatively, upon the Assinghams) at other points which the scenario has carefully discriminated; and when we realize that the authorial voice now speaking more immediately of Maggie will not cease to evoke also our awareness of these other values in the whole scheme of his art, the richness of its mode of appeal may be appreciated. This "*best* residuum",[21] as James put it, insists that we see "one thing through another"[22] and so there is achieved the desired unity, the "synthesis", the "fusion". As a critic inquiring into it, one is not any the less "lost in the tangle of the forest", as James threatened one would be, but to identify a tree here, a flower there and some of the vines entwining both may at least make one even more aware of the density proliferating in the whole vista when, after slowly traversing it with James, we look back on it with him. We must realize then, above all, that he has provided for our rubbing shoulders with "each of the real, the deeply involved and more or less bleeding participants" in the trek.[23]

I have already quoted ample evidence, in my account of how James presents each of the principal characters, supporting my contention that the appeal each makes for empathy is as eloquent as only the above mode can guarantee, and that this is in each case enriched throughout by the ironic distancing ensured by the authorial presence, however subtle a form that presence may take. Hence, the emotion which is spontaneous in Adam and Maggie in their first garden interlude at Fawns, or in Amerigo and Charlotte on the parapet at Matcham, is made complex and poignant by the authorial check. Hence too, no matter how rhapsodically the mode communicates Adam's notion of himself as the Cortez of art treasures; or Charlotte's notion of the rightness of her status as she awaits the Prince on the staircase at the Foreign Office ball; or the Prince's notion of what befits a *galantuomo* such as he; or Maggie's notion of the "niceness" of the world on the eve of her marriage; the mode communicates too the perspective that complicates it. When, from the beginning of Book Second, the poignancy for each is intensified by the fuller consciousness each gains of himself or herself, the appeal the mode makes is sustained for each and we respond in the company of the author, who deftly ensures that the rhetoric continues to be expended equally upon all of them.

Just as James's language is untranslatable into another tongue, so too this mode is not translatable into another medium, and the reason is found in the constancy and subtlety of the authorial agent, which ensure that "picture" and "scene", commentary and drama, figure and rhythm, will reinforce one another. A radio broadcast of a script faithful to the dialogue of the novel and reproducing its pregnant pauses can suggest only intermittent breakdowns in transmission; a commentary faithful to the passage in which Maggie watches the card-players becomes a *tirade* for the blind, dramatically impotent because only heard and not heard-and-seen.[24] A televised version comes closer, because the camera can rove over a silenced or stilled scene as does the authorial attention, but the commentary must not be supplied by a character, for that fatally reduces to the partisan what James strives in the novel to keep comprehensive, curious and free of the kind of reductive irony inevitable in, say, any formulation made by Colonel Assingham.[25] Television's compromise is certainly more effective than either the attempts to present his major fiction on the stage, where it turns simplistic and bathetic for lack of his special rhetorical mode, or than James's own search for substitutes for this mode in performances of his own plays in the English theatre of his day, which merely emphasized the distance between Shaftesbury Avenue and the *Rue de Richelieu* as well as the futility of any theatre for his purposes.[26]

The "play of tone"

James asks a great deal from "the play of tone" in the final scene of his final completed novel but if we cooperate with him, as he asks, it becomes the play of tone over the context provided for this scene by the whole of that novel. What this vague phrase connotes for him is documented enough to be fairly specific. His ideal of well-toned speech, his praise of those writers who simulate it in their prose, his praise of actors who can demonstrate its resources in drama, his own speech on informal as well as formal occasions and during his dictation of his own prose[27] are all highly relevant to the kind of interest he believed latent in tone and to the nature and function of his own authorial voice. It is an ideal, in his view, exacting attention to minute detail such as only a few other writers, mainly European, have been willing to ask of themselves.

In 1888 he praises de Maupassant for the "superlative wisdom" of saying: "There is no need of the queer, complicated, numerous, and Chinese vocabulary which is imposed on us today under the name of artistic writing, ***to fix all the shades of thought; the right way is to distinguish with an extreme clearness all those modifications of the value of a word which come from the place it occupies.*** Let us have fewer nouns, verbs and adjectives of almost imperceptible sense, and more ***different phrases variously constructed, ingeniously cast, full of the science of sound and rhythm.***"[28] Certainly the queerness and complication of his own later prose result more often from abstract rather than from esoteric vocabulary and more usually from a radical re-ordering of syntax and a revising of punctuation to ensure rhetorical effect. His later examples are anticipated by his earlier precepts. In 1893 he approves Flaubert, for whom "style was made for the ear, the last court of appeal, the supreme touchstone of perfection".[29] In 1902 he writes again of Flaubert who regarded "a style without rhythm and harmony as in a work of pretended beauty no style at all", and who had claimed that these two potent forms of appeal were "most menaced by repetition — when repetition had not a positive grace". James, pursuing the same appeal, ruefully asks how the French artist would have coped with the relative pronouns and antecedents, the infinitives and auxiliaries, of English — "a medium intrinsically indocile".[30]

Again and again he stresses that this care has nothing to do with embellishment but has everything to do with the fusion that art must provide. In his 1907 preface to "The Tempest", he is even acerbically defensive on "the relation of style to meaning and of manner to motive; a matter on which, right and left, we hear such rank ineptitudes uttered. Unless it be true that these things, on either hand, are inseparable;. . . that the phrase, the cluster and order of terms, *is* the object and the sense, in as close a compression as that of body and soul", then Shakespeare "has no lesson for us".[31] There can be, in short, a vitally meaningful connotation in the cadence. Significantly, he devoted to this belief the emphatic position afforded by the final lines of his final Preface for his definitive New York edition, the earlier part of which relates to *The Golden Bowl.* They are essentially a plea to establish that his own written prose needed to be recognized, and responded to, as elaborate rhetoric. If the writer's "highest bid is addressed to the imagination, to the spiritual and the aesthetic vision, the mind led captive by a charm and a spell, an incalculable art", he says, then:

> The essential property of such a form as that is to give out its finest and most numerous secrets, and to give them out most gratefully, under the closest pressure — which is of course the pressure of the attention articulately *sounded.* Let it reward as much as it will and can the soundless, "the quiet" reading, it still deplorably "muffs" its chance and its success, still trifles with the roused appetite to which it can never honestly be indifferent, by not having so arranged itself as to owe the flower of its effect to the act and process of apprehension that so beautifully asks most from it . . .. Gustave Flaubert has somewhere in this connection an excellent word — to the effect that any imaged prose that fails to be richly rewarding in return for a competent utterance ranks itself as wrong through not being "in the conditions of life".[32]

These were the years in which the only appreciable revisions he was making to his own major prose of some dozen years earlier were clearly meant to make it more vocable, but he had been preoccupied with this effect for thrice that period. He had in 1879 admired Hawthorne "for infusing a gently colloquial tone into matter of the most unfamiliar import".[33] He had said of Daudet in 1882: "He tells his stories as a talker; they have always something of the flexibility and familiarity of conversation. The conversation, we mean, of an artist and a Frenchman; the conversation of a circle in which the faculty of vivid and discriminating speech exists as it has existed nowhere else."[34] He, who was later to describe his own prose as "*intraduisible*",[35] was sensitive in 1897 to his having to read Turgenev "in a language not his own, of not being reached by his personal tone, his individual accent".[36] The trend of his revisions tells its own story. His successive drafts of "The Real Thing", in 1891, 1892, and in 1907,[37] show James "having so arranged" his prose that by increasing attention to syntax rather than to lexis and to "the science of sound and rhythm" more than to either, the voice of the first-person narrator is manifested throughout.

The difference between early revisions and those of the works produced well within the major years is crucial to my whole argument. One is concerned with salvage, the other with enhancement, and the limits finally reached by the first are instructive. First-person narrative cannot provide the kind of context in which the tonal play becomes more richly meaningful. The voice of the graphic artist who in "The Real Thing" struggles with human and aesthetic considerations, can echo only in the chambers of his own consciousness, no matter how readily we recognize it as a voice. The authorial voice of, say, "The Beast in the Jungle", however, reverberates among all the intricate indirections in that major *novella.* The difference leads us to even more complex considerations when, on turning to a major novel, we confront the ways in which this voice can be modulated to embody most expressively the many consciousnesses that are so amply rendered in it.

We are led in fact again to the *histrionique* of the *Comédie Française*, to the notions of drama that resulted in the "divine principle of the Scenario" and to an art of formalized speech of which the supreme example for James was demonstrated by the actor Benoît-Constant Coquelin. The detail of the appreciation is illuminating. There is, to begin with, "the remarkable play and penetration of his voice, which combines the highest metalic ring with every conceivable human note". There is then its power to suggest "the finer shades of what is called character"; its "command of the effects that lie entirely in self-possession, effects of low tone, indications of inward things". But the most important profits of "so much toilsome forging and polishing of the vocal arm", are "the general finish , . . . the harmony unbroken, a regulated tone and observed propriety". There is thus a tonal constant within which the variety of other dramatic tones can safely operate. "Coquelin . . ." says James in this 1887 essay on him, "does ever so many different things, but somehow he is always the same Coquelin." This is more than a tribute to a great actor's distinctive style of utterance. It is a recognition of the way a uniform authorial voice, a constant tonal presence, contributing to "a congruous whole", can be contrived and sustained by a subtle simulation of the spoken word in the written one.[38]

The evidence is in the revision in 1915 of the original essay, the only one of some thirty of his pieces, written on the theatre in the last quarter of the century, to which he returned and in which revision all the passages quoted above are the result of further refinements. Dispirited by the critical and commercial neglect of his own definitive edition over the preceding half dozen years, he affirmed the central principle of its art by the following lengthy and emphatic addition to his original comment on the decline of the stage. "Gone at any rate are the days — if they really were with us — when any situation not grossly obvious, any interest *latent* in anything and thereby involving for its issue our finer attention and our nobler curiosity, could look for help from the play of tone, *the* great vehicle of communication. What this comes to is that histrionic lips have ceased — so far as they ever began! — to be able to tell a story worth telling or to gratify a taste worth gratifying."[39] Vital emphases: the parallels with his practice in his major fiction are obvious enough, where the interest latent surely demands the finer attention and stimulates the nobler curiosity. There, "*the* great vehicle" communicates with intensity each stage in each particular character's awareness of realities; there, too — and with an art radically original — it communicates also, with continuous relevance, the general *authorial* interest, attention and curiosity. This subsumes theirs and so what is communicated by the whole prose discourse, with this constant distancing through a non-reductive irony, is what might be described as a "spiritual [and] an aesthetic vision"[40] that includes an amply embodied, amply documented account of human beings confronting in solitude the baffling incalculability of values in life. This complex view is produced by a complex art, the chief vehicle of which is a highly sophisticated rendering in prose of the incalculably modulatable but here formally controlled human voice. If the stories worth telling are to be told in a manner gratifying the worthy taste, we are to hear them as issuing from histrionic lips.

This is how all James's own later writing was first heard by his amanuenses. Miss Theodora Bosanquet, one of the two who left the above-mentioned personal records of this process, showed to me, in 1955 in London, a typescript draft of "Within the Rim"[41] that had escaped the flames to which such material had usually been consigned by James and she kindly amplified for me the soliloquizing methods of creation that she had already sketched in her memoir:[42] the ponderous orotund delivery (with careful attention given to details of punctuation) that produced the first batch of triple-spaced quarto pages of the first draft; the use of this draft as the basis for a second, in which precision was kept compatible with euphony by the same process of deliberated utterance; and, after dictation of successive drafts, or parts of drafts, the interlinear additions by James's own pen.

In 1973, when the James Family Papers in the Houghton Library at Harvard were once again accessible to all inquirers, I examined manuscripts and such emended typescripts at greater leisure. Some one hundred and fifty holographs representing forty-three years of correspondence with his brother William reveal that the increasing complexity of James's style owes practically nothing to emendation of particular lexical detail and almost everything to general syntactical casting.[43] Between 1867 and 1910 James sophisticates the rhetoric of these personal writings so that they reflect the progressive subtlety of his thought. The idea and the language are apparently born at once.

The two emended typescript drafts[44] of the Preface James wrote for Rupert Brooke's *Letters from America* in 1915, the last writing he completed before his death early the following year, also reflect mainly the impact of locution; only in the final few afterthoughts before dispatch to the printers is there any evidence of the silent pen. In mid-course, the first dictated draft is cancelled at some points by overtyping, which indicates that this draft in fact comprises two. The kinds of additions and recastings that constitute the third process are rarely lexical, are strongly syntactical, and are the result of lengthy dictated forays in the same rhetorical mode as produced the first draft. The pen that was responsible for a stage which is in the case of this particular work a fourth, is concerned with details, always minor and, significantly, usually shifting the emphasis from the necessary minimum of grammatical punctuation towards a more sufficient rhetorical punctuation and thus ensuring a potent rhythm.

The resulting prose has more affinities with the *tirades* of the *Théâtre Française* than has been realized. James's own speech in other quarters was certainly as rhythmic. Hugh Walpole's impression of "unwinding rolls"[45] of paper is the popular one and Thomas Hardy was sceptical of the content of the "infinite sentences",[46] but for A.C. Benson they were "beautiful . . . so finished, so deliberate" and as they "shaped themselves audibly upon the air", the talk became "impassioned soliloquy" in which James's "tone, his gestures, his sympathetic alertness made instantly and abundantly clear and sparkling what on a printed page often became . . . tough and coagulated".[47] Edith Wharton related that when James read poetry, especially Whitman, he always "chanted it . . . as Poetry", would never "chatter high verse" and, "far from shirking the rhythmic emphasis, gave it full expression" as he swept forward "on great rollers of sound till the full weight of his voice fell on the last cadence".[48]

His manner in lectures, such as those he undertook during the American tour of 1905, combined a similar strict formality of demeanour with a similar emphasis upon rhythmic and deliberate declamation.[49] In one such lecture to the young ladies of Bryn Mawr he spelled out very precisely the resources he saw in the spontaneity of spoken language and the disciplining of it.

> I mean then by speaking well, in the first place, speaking with consideration for the forms and shades of our language, speaking with a consideration so inbred that it has become instinctive and well-nigh unconscious and automatic, as all the habitual, all the inveterate amenities of life become. ***By the forms and shades of our language I mean the innumerable differentiated, discriminated units of sound and sense that lend themselves to audible production, to enunciation, to intonation***: those innumerable units that have each an identity, a quality, an outline, a shape, a clearness, a fineness, a sweetness, a richness; ***that have, in a word, a value*** which it is open to us, as lovers of our admirable English tradition, or as cynical traitors to it, to preserve or to destroy.[50]

There is no article of faith in James's whole "religion of doing"[51] that is more often repeated and emphasized throughout his major phase and there is none that has wider ramifications. The chief lesson he believed he had learned by the time he revised the essay on Coquelin was "that the appliction of an art is style, and that style is expression and that expression is the salt of life",[52] and the lesson went even further still. When writing on the question of the speech of American women, he summed up the importance of this article for his entire credo in words richly edifying to anyone studying the kind of interest he appears to be generating in the products of that credo. "Everything hangs together, I say, and there's no isolated question of speech, no isolated application of taste, no isolated damnation of delicacy. The interest of tone is the interest of manners, and the interest of manners is the interest of morals, and the interest of morals is the interest of civilization . . .".[53] While he was in the midst of the immense revisory task of salvaging and enhancing these productions, he wrote understandingly of Shakespeare "that, as he passed from one application of it to another, tone became, for all its suggestions, more and more sovereign to him, and the subtlety of its secrets an exquisite interest."[54]

The contribution to prose fiction

A rhetoric deriving from the fusion of so many subtly controlled elements and making a total appeal that is highly complex is a challenge to analysis. My argument with most of those who have recently taken it up is that their methods preclude adequate acknowledgment of the fusedness, the subtlety and the totality. "Style" is for James very clearly a term comprehending all of his artistic means — is in fact synonymous with "art" and "expression" and "form" — and we do not get very far by establishing irrefutable facts about details of individual techniques or separate units of language. This is fatally true of many studies involving *The Golden Bowl*.[55] The study of rhetoric with most pertinence to that of the last major novel remains the one by Wayne Booth, for he simplifies least. Booth's notion of what constitutes authorial "obtrusion"; his recognition of how varied James's own forms of it were; his concern with the evaluations implicit in tonal variations and his insistence that these were not "something limited to the merely verbal", but included all the other agencies of expression, enable him to appreciate the nature of James's art of suasion. Much of what James can be shown to have attempted in the major years is adumbrated in Booth's remarks on authorial silence and on distancing, even if one demurs that rather than asking the reader "to reserve judgment", James is coaxing him to delay it.[56]

My disagreement with this admirable pondering of the rhetoric of fiction begins when Booth asserts: "The novelist who chooses to tell *this* story cannot at the same time tell *that* story; in centering our interest, sympathy, or affection on one character, he inevitably excludes from our interest, sympathy, or affection some other character."[57] The evidence of *The Golden Bowl* challenges this premise. Here, happily risking over-treatment, seeking sources of "multitudinous reference", speaking of "full-fed statement" and of "the imaged resumé of as many of the vivifying elements as may be coherently packed into an image at once",[58] James surely strove "to arrive, on behalf of multiplicity, at a certain science of control".[59] Image, statement, reference, allusion, as well as scene and comment, are all fully fed by the richness of their context within the whole novel. We grasp the essence of his rhetoric and the significance of the appeal he is making with it, only when we recognize how fully and constantly he provided for this feeding. If, as James said, "the divine principle of the Scenario" is a "key that, working in the same *general* way fits the complicated chambers of *both* the dramatic and the narrative lock",[60] then the power turning that key in that lock is generated by the late style.

James's contribution to the art of fiction is of course in no way limited to this final completed work but his single most distinctive one is and this has never been eclipsed. The mimetic rhetoric of Joyce, at least as great in its totally different mode and effect, does not, in its comprehensiveness, hold in suspension, for our immediate apprehension of them all, such an array of human differences. James's art is transitional to Joyce's, not least in its handling of the authorial in the reporting of consciousness, but it is not surpassed in the way it articulates several consciousnesses that are at once irrevocably locked together and sundered by their differences. Nor does the great incantatory rhetoric of Faulkner, an artist whose dramatic versatility and experimental vigour are commensurate with both, make less relevant the special use to which James finally puts his lifetime of literary trial and error.

What James learned from English and European writers, from those moral interests of George Eliot and those artistic interests of Balzac, Flaubert and Turgenev, which arrested him, was ultimately embodied in a form of fiction that proliferated the ideas, gave them human features, embedded them in the frailties of society, and traced them to motives and consequences, but, above all, kept them free of the moral over-simplifications and other treacheries for which the art of narrative had struck him as hitherto being notorious. James E. Miller Jr, thoroughly conversant with the Jamesian theory and the imaginative force of its product, sketched the contribution well when he spoke of James's showing not only "the enigma of reality" — for most great writers do this — but also "the reality of enigmas".[61] It is Patrick White, the beneficiary of all three literary traditions — English, European and American — whose vision and rhetoric, in its scope and intensity, most challenges the art which James was mastering in Rye at the turn of the century, but White's brilliant accounts of the enigma[62] cannot render otiose the incisive fullness that James gives us "in the air of the whole result" of *The Golden Bowl.*

For James had worked at his special effect for most of his writing life, re-seeing it and re-expressing it all the time. Madame de Mauves, Christopher Newman, Isabel Archer, Nanda Brookenham, and Maisie Farange, eager to heed old Lewis Lambert Strether's injunction to the beguiling Little Bilham — " 'Live all you can' "[63] — lose, renounce bitterness at the loss, eschew cynicism and emerge as idealists who are without illusions. Learning the limits of will, the challenge of knowledge, the subtleties by which the romantic poses as the real, they finally reach the quiet zone. There, Isabel, subject of manipulations benign and malign, takes possession of her own life and sets her hand to the latch, her way now straight; there, Maisie feels "the spasm within her of something deeper than a moral sense"[64] and learns to live with her loneliness by accepting human aloneness; there, Strether discovers that what is important is that he should "not, out of the whole affair, to have got anything for [himself]",[65] for that is what would make him wrong with himself; there, Kate Croy, long goaded by the dilemma of having the instinct for "being" as well as the capacity for "seeing",[66] sees with Merton Densher that, beneath Milly Theale's benedictory wings, they "will never be again as" they "were";[67] and there the four lovers ostensibly linked by a golden bowl discover they are in reality linked only by that same aloneness. The difference between the rendering of Isabel and the rendering of Maggie is the difference between explication and exploration of such a consciousness. Isabel's vigil by the fire is a review; Maggie's memories of the belated return of the Prince is a search. Isabel with her hand upon the latch knows the how and the what and the why of her past and future; Maggie with her hand on the doorknob of the Prince's study and hearing herself say " 'Wait' " is still piecing out the past of the quartet of which she is a member, is still feeling her way through the present and is soon to discover in the Prince's arms the strangeness of their future. Her consciousness is both part of James's point and part of his means, for depicted in it are three more variations on that point.

Joseph Conrad and Graham Greene read the major manner sympathetically enough to detect the importance of its difficulty but we may now be able to argue more reasonably with their responses. Not, certainly, with the former's belief that the deviser of it "never attempts the impossible"; nor with his impression of the "sense of life still going on" and "the subtle presence of the dead" being felt in the "silence . . . when the last word is read"; but with his more famous statement, for James would seem to be less notable as "the historian of fine consciences"[68] than as that of the fine consciousness in which they are given trenchancy and perspective. With the latter's choice of the fragment from *The Ivory Tower* about "the black and merciless things behind the great possessions"[69] we can hardly quarrel at all.

So, too, is it hard to argue with the poets who pronounced upon this massive fable. We have seen the forms of "violence and chaos" that Stephen Spender told us lurk under its "golden display".[70] We have seen how W.H. Auden's "poet of the difficult"[71] exercised his stern proconsulship over provinces innately intractable without regimenting or diminishing them. But with the other famous statement, the one by T.S. Eliot, about James's mind being too fine to be violated by an idea and about his "mastery over, his baffling escape from, Ideas",[72] we may have a quibble. There is escape from their reductive doctrines, just as there is mastery over their indulgent proliferation, but the great escape is from their generalizing abstractions and the great mastery is seen in his perception, refinement and marshalling of them and his keeping them free of that capital letter. In short, "Max", the unerring parodist of both manner and fable, would seem to have been justified in his belief that this "very conscious and very devoted artist may be trusted, he especially, to have followed the right line of progress — to have got the logical development of his own peculiar gifts".[73]

The controversy about *The Golden Bowl* may thus be considerably reduced and the important issues more fully realized when that novel is seen to be radically original. For this, his most ambitious work, James provides an artistic scheme that resolves the difficulties he entertains in his major phase and enables him to explore his notions of love, power, will and knowledge as comprehensively as is compatible with a coherent literary form. The result is neither ambiguous nor even only ambivalent but richly and distinctively multivalent.

All the agents responsible for rendering James's final vision here with such amplitude and intensity are manifestly operating far more variously and subtly than he himself noted they might and recorded they had. Their concerted effects allow him to sustain a controlling omnipresence that is never an obtruding omniscience. His strategic use of a total structure based on an adroitly arranged sequence of discriminated scenes makes each of them resemble a transparent sheet whereon key details achieve a fuller significance only when superimposed on earlier sheets, each contributing progressively to an ironic perspective.

This strategy is reinforced by the linguistic tactics apparent in the whole discourse. Though discreetly subdued, the authorial voice remains a constant referent among the many shifts of dramatic focus. As the unfolding of motives and consequences proceeds with glacial gradualness, we are coaxed to share with James a relationship with each character of distanced-empathy which holds our imaginative attention while postponing our moral judgment and which complicates our moral consciousness of all that has been and is being shown and said. We are shown developments in the consciousness of each of the characters as well as all their mutual involvements: the radical originality of James's attempt is that he is evidently using these indirections to keep us as aware as the art of narrative can keep us of all of them all the time. Narrative thus approaches the expressiveness of that other temporal art, music, where harmonies and dissonances are sounded by chord rather than by context.

The cooperative reader, denied the luxury of any authorial guarantees amid the ramifying moral problems, is kept busy responding to a dialectic of imagery, to recurrent and carefully scaled epithets and to candid authorial avowals of a shared curiosity in the whole spectacle. Image, phrase, word and comment, enjoying the context supplied by the narrative antecedent to the point where they occur, lead us even deeper into the revealed dilemmas. James is using a poet's figurative intensity and dramatist's familiar immediacy at a novelist's leisure; this sophisticated mode ensures we remain at precisely the vantage point from which all the difficult knowledge can be seen to be accumulating.

The appeal of this formidable mode of fiction remains a highly eloquent one, for James exploits throughout it the resources of a rhetoric closely allied to the declamatory and histrionic tradition of the French classical theatre. By simulating in his own authorial report of scenes its expressive use of tableau, gesture and silence, he achieves his ambition of having them hypothetically acted; by simulating also the flexibility of spoken language throughout his discourse upon the consciousness of each character from point to point, he ensures that to the potency of emotion and to the interest of questing thought are deftly added those verbal hints which insist that both share the prevailing ironic perspective. James's distinctive language, a perpetual agent of unity, determines that the final effect of the novel involves not only the whole of it but our sense of its organic wholeness. The continual appeal it makes to a faithfully life-like incalculability of effect thus remains a firmly controlled one.

The Golden Bowl thus radically reduces the gap between *homo fictus* and *homo sapiens* by depicting ultimate human problems more complexly, more variously, more penetratingly and more comprehensively than they had hitherto been depicted.

There are still many questions about this novel that remain unanswered and if, as Adeline R. Tintner rightly suggests in her survey, they are to be asked about specifics,[74] we must still beware of reductive inferences. For though it matters little whether Waddesdon Manor is the model for Fawns and even less which of the Rothschild vases are evoked by Charlotte's commentary in the gallery,[75] it matters much that we ponder what is evoked by the date "1713" (I, 159) carved on the gate through which Adam and his daughter serenely pass on the way to their bench in the garden of their rented Eden. Is James reminding us of that other impermanent Augustan peace, purchased by Marlborough's power abroad? As Short said, "Everything counts:. . ."[76] and, despite Wells, this formidable novel manifestly *is* "continuously relevant".[77] That is why, in this case, critical discussion also needs to strive for more of the specific than terms such as "spatial form"[78] can supply. If, too, we are to be enjoined to consider Jungian archetypes, as we may well need to be, they should take us further than does Lisa Appignanesi's notion of Maggie as a "Cinderella figure",[79] which really returns us to the kind of fairy-tale Princess so popular with earlier critics such as Lebowitz.[80] There is more, not less, still to be found in this golden bowl which is as fully capacious a vessel as James believed the novel form itself to be when he likened that to an altogether different vessel.[81] If, as Mark Krupnick asserts,[82] there is nothing in it at all, he will need many more pages in which to argue his case; as indeed will John Halverson to demonstrate the "stylistic fatuities" of the whole late manner, in which, allegedly, "James's complexity is indiscriminate".[83] Much more relevant is Yeazell's kind of investigation into James's later notions of knowledge and forms of language and into the tensions between speech and figure, even though she still sees the purport of these primarily in terms of Maggie.[84]

The title of the final fable brings us back to Blake and to Ecclesiastes, against whose use of this phrase James's choice is inevitable seen. The story of Maggie and Adam and Charlotte and the Prince contains its own elaborate negative to Blake's rhetorical question as to whether wisdom can be held in a silver rod or love in a golden bowl and would seem to emphasize that the silver and gold decrease rather than enhance the possibility. All four characters could at the last reply gravely to the question preceding this in Thel's Motto: "Does the eagle know what is in the pit / Or wilt thou go ask the mole?"

But their story would seem to have less affinity with retorts to Blake and much more with response to the grim and resonant voice from the Old Testament that speaks of the vanity of desire, of the bafflement of human kind, of how irrevocably dust will return to the earth and the spirit return to the god who gave it, once the silver cord is loosed and the golden bowl is broken.[85] They all have to come to terms with "the element of staleness in all the freshness and of freshness in all the staleness", as well as with that of "innocence in the guilt and of guilt in the innocence" (II, 354). They know well enough the strangeness of the alloy, "the close connexion of bliss and bale", "the awful mixture of things" and their "strange mystery". Theirs is a world "terribly mixed", one where life is seen "bringing people together who would be at least more correctly separate; keeping people separate who would be at least more correctly together".[86] The rhythm and cadence of James's voice provide a significant *obbligato* to the ancient one that speaks of the sacred vessel at the heart of faithful relationships and of the moral absolutes that became part of the Puritan heritage and eventually informed the Verver idealism.

How then can James's characteristic final view be defined? If we approach the task negatively we on the one hand glimpse none of the fury with which Hardy shakes his fist at an indifferent or malign universe after showing us his baffled Jude and Sue or his crucified Tess; and on the other hand none of the unqualified zest with which Joyce celebrates his Molly Bloom's affirmation of each scrap of living. Nor is there that same sombre pride that Conrad displays in the way the best of the human crew can hang on by hanging together; or indeed any of the tremulous excitement with which White fulfils his "desire of raising other men into a perception of the infinite".[87] There is in place of these visions that same lingering view, that same "finer attention" and "nobler curiosity" that James persistently invites us to share with him from the beginning to the end of his narrative. It is an attention and curiosity that are comprehensive, compassionate, clear and free, facing quietly the ironic in life's awful mixtures and strange mysteries, attending it finally in silence, a silence that the narrative has made meaningful, authoritative and every bit as penetrating as the occasion demands. James himself was of course quite specific about "the 'amusement' of the chronicle in question — by which, once more, I mean the gathered cluster of all *kinds* of interest"; for him "absolutely *no* refinement of ingenuity or of precaution need by dreamed of as wasted in that most exquisite of all causes the appeal to variety, the appeal to incalculability, the appeal to a high refinement and handsome wholeness of effect".[88] Such a cluster of them is in its complexity and intensity unique and I agree with A.J.A. Waldock that its "rigours are worthwhile".[89]Above all, its final effect is to inform us with a sense of grave wonderment at the incalculable appeal and baffling elusiveness of life with value.

There is another golden bowl, the actual one several friends of Henry James gave to him in tribute on his seventieth birthday,[90] ironically enough in 1913, the year before civilization as he had known it was irrevocably broken. Nearly a decade had passed since the novel had first appeared and there was irony too in the bewilderment that thereafter became part of its history, for James, as the opening quotation to this study recalls, had later challenged the critics with the words, " 'My mixture has only to be perfect literally to bewilder you . . .'." My account of it may suggest that he did " 'consummately shake' " its values into an indissoluble oneness that is unique for nevertheless keeping sharp to the taste the distinctness of each. This account is offered half a century later as an evaluation informed by an exegesis of his provisions.

Towards the end of his life, we recall, he wrote to Edith Wharton that one must "*go through the movements* of life"; that is, "of the immediate and apparent life", in full knowledge of "the deeper and darker and unapparent, in which things *really* happen to us". He told her "to live it all through, every inch of it . . . but live it ever so quietly; and . . . waitingly!"[91] That I believe is the way we may best read *The Golden Bowl*, which can then be seen as holding together, in a mode as unbreakable as it is radically original, the perfect surface of civilized appearances and "the shame, the pity, the better knowledge, the smothered protest, the divined anguish even" (II, 292) of realities, full consciousness of which each of us endures in an isolation, ever incalculably enforced, permitting freedom of reach "only through the beautiful circuit and subterfuge of our thought and our desire".[92]

NOTES

1. *Letters* (Lubbock), II, 222.
2. James, *Prefaces*, p. 144.
3. Ibid., p. 302.
4. Ibid., p. 173.
5. James, *The Sacred Fount* (New York: Scribner's, 1901).
6. James, *The Ambassadors* (London: Methuen, 1903).
7. James, *Prefaces*, p. 114.
8. James, *The Wings of the Dove* (London: Constable, 1902).
9. *Letters* (Lubbock), II, 15, letter dated May 20 1904.
10. Ibid., II, 514.
11. James, *The Sense of the Past* (London: Collins, 1917).
12. James, "Notes for *The Sense of the Past*", *Sense of the Past*, p. 289.
13. James, *Notebooks*, p. 364; "Notes for *The Sense of the Past*", p. 320; *Prefaces*, p. 72.
14. *Letters from America*, by Rupert Brooke, with a Preface by Henry James (London: Sidgwick & Jackson, 1916), pp. ix-xiii.
15. James, *Prefaces*, p. 311.
16. T.S. Eliot, "A Prediction in Regard to Three English Authors", *Vanity Fair* (February 1924). Quoted here from *Critical Essays*, p. 56.
17. James, "The Art of Fiction", *Partial Portraits*, p. 400.
18. James, *GB* (Methuen), p. 289.
19. James, *Prefaces*, pp. 338-39.
20. Ibid., p. 204.
21. Ibid., p. 141.
22. Ibid., p. 154.
23. Ibid., p. 328.
24. British Broadcasting Corporation, Third Programme (London, 7 October 1955). Adapted for radio by Mary Hope Allen.
25. British Broadcasting Corporation, Channel 2 (London, 10 August 1973).
26. To see a provincial repertory performance of a dramatization of *The Wings of the Dove* within weeks of seeing the *Comédie* perform "Phèdre" in the *Théâtre Française* is to realize James's failure to understand "theatre" and how fatally he divorced it from "drama". William Archer, A.B. Walkley and George Bernard Shaw, among others who reviewed his own "Guy Domville", recognized this quickly enough. See *The Complete Plays of Henry James*, ed. Leon Edel (London: Hart-Davis, 1949), pp. 479-82. See also his letter to his brother William (29 December 1893) with its significant plea: "If the drama could only be theoretically or hypothetically

acted,. . ." *Letters* (Lubbock), 1, pp. 216-17. For James's later explicit recognitions of the "theatric" being the "outward" and the "universal" being the "inward", see "Edmond Rostand", *Cornhill Magazine* 39 (November 1901): 577-98. My argument about the significant deficiencies of the stage and television versions of the later work is supported by James Thurber, "The Wings of Henry James", *New Yorker* 35 (7 November 1959): 184.

27. James, Theodora Bosanquet, *Henry James at Work* (London: Hogarth, 1924). Hereafter *HJ at Work.*
28. James, "Guy de Maupassant", *Fortnightly Review* 49 (March 1888): 364-86. Quoted from *Partial Portraits*, pp. 262-63.
29. James, "Gustave Flaubert", *Macmillan's Magazine* 67 (March 1893): 332-43. Quoted here from *Henry James: Selected Literary Criticism*, ed. Morris Shapira (London: Heinemann, 1963), p. 152. Hereafter *Selected Literary Criticism.*
30. James, "Critical Introduction" to an English translation of *Madame Bovary* (London: Heinemann, 1902). Quoted here from *Selected Literary Criticism*, ed. M. Shapira, p. 238.
31. James, "Special Introduction" to "The Tempest" in Vol. XVI of *The Complete Works of William Shakespeare*, ed. Sidney Lee (New York: Sproule, 1907). Hereafter *Tempest.* Quoted here from *Selected Literary Criticism*, ed. M. Shapira, p. 303.
32. James, *Prefaces*, pp. 346-47.
33. James, *Hawthorne* (London: Macmillan, 1879), p. 120.
34. James, "Alphonse Daudet", *Atlantic Monthly* 49 (June 1882): 846-51. Quoted here from *Literary Reviews and Essays, by Henry James, on American, English and French Literature*, ed. Albert Mordell (New York: Grove, 1957), p. 183. Hereafter *Literary Reviews.*
35. *Selected Letters of Henry James*, ed. Leon Edel (London: Rupert Hart-Davis, 1956), p. 136. Letter dated 7 September 1913.
36. James, "Ivan Turgenieff", *Library of the World's Best Literature, Ancient and Modern*, ed. Charles Dudley Warner, XXV (New York: Peale & Hill, 1896-1897). Quoted here from *The House of Fiction: Essays on the Novel by Henry James*, ed. Leon Edel (London: Rupert Hart-Davis, 1957), p. 171.
37. See Appendix A.
38. James, "Coquelin", *Century Magazine* 33 (January 1887): 407-13. Revised and reprinted, as "Introduction" to *Constant Coquelin, Art and the Actor* (New York: Dramatic Museum of Columbia University, 1915), pp. 1-36. This revised version quoted here from *Henry James: The Scenic Art: Notes on Acting and Drama*, ed. Allan Wade (London: Hart-Davis, 1949), pp. 202, 204, 205-6, 201, 204. Hereafter *Scenic Art.*
39. Ibid., p. 209.
40. James, *Prefaces*, p. 346.
41. James, *Within the Rim and Other Essays 1914-1915* (London: Collins, 1919).
42. Bosanquet, *HJ at Work.*

43. Holographs of Correspondence between Henry James and William James. Letters from 10 May 1867 to 13 November 1907. MS. Am. 1092. Houghton Library, Harvard University.
44. See Appendix B.
45. Hugh Walpole, "Henry James, A Reminiscence", *Horizon* (February 1940). Quoted in *The Legend of the Master: Henry James.* Compiled by Simon Nowell-Smith (London: Constable, 1947), p. xxi. Hereafter *Legend.*
46. Florence Emily Hardy, *The Life of Thomas Hardy 1840-1928* (London: Macmillan, 1962), p. 181.
47. Benson, *Legend*, ed. Nowell-Smith, p. 12.
48. Edith Wharton, *A Backward Glance* (London: Constable, 1972), p. 185.
49. M.P. Harris, "Henry James Lecturer", *American Literature* 23 (November 1951): 305. See also D.H. Dunbar, "Henry James as a Lecturer", *The Critic* 57 (July 1905): 24-25 and W.C. France, "Henry James as a Lecturer", *Bookman* 21 (March 1905): 71-72.
50. "The Question of Our Speech", *Appleton's Booklover's Magazine*, 6 (August 1905): 203. Lecture delivered, 8 June 1905.
51. James, *Prefaces*, p. 347.
52. James, *Scenic Art*, p. 200.
53. "The Speech of American Women", *Harper's Bazar* [sic] 41 (January-February 1906), p. 115.
54. James, *Tempest*, p. 303.
55. I refer to such dissertations as the following: J.L. Thomas, "The Technical Synthesis of Henry James: A Study of the Method of 'the Major Phase' ", *DAI* 32 (1971), 4027A (N.Y.U.); E.A. Sklepowich, "The Play of Tone: Henry James and the Concept of Social Artifice", *DAI* 32 (1971), 4633A-34A (Virginia); B.B. Aswad, "The Crucible of Conversation: A Study of Jamesian Dialogue", *DAI* 34 (1973), 1890A (S.U.N.Y., Binghampton); F.X. Gillen "The Relationship of Rhetorical Control to Meaning in the Novels of Henry James, Virginia Woolf and E.M. Forster", *DAI* 30 (1969), 1525A (Fordham); K.O. Lauer, "The Interior Monologue in *The Ambassadors* and *The Golden Bowl*", *DAI* 31 (1970), 6015A (Michigan State); and B.P. Tracy, "Henry James's Representation of Inner Consciousness in Meditation Scenes from the Late Novels", *DAI* 32 (1971), 1533A (Michigan State). Thomas's study of the synthesis of dramatic, poetic and novelistic modes in each of the three major novels and of how "the narrative portions suggest the spoken language" remains more ambitious than is compatible either with full description or with precise definition. Similarly, Sklepowich considers "play of tone" only in relation to "social artifice", and Aswad remains concerned only with what the characters are saying to each other and not also with what James is telling us about all of them. Gillen stresses how James plays on "the reader's response to traditional roles" instead of how he plays on our knowledge of the antecedent narrative at any

point and on the context by which it so richly conditions all responses. Lauer dwells tantalizingly on "the creation of an individual consciousness" and Tracey tries to quantify the means by which this is distinguished from the "omniscient creator consciousness". The more substantial conclusions about *The Golden Bowl* remain beyond these reaches, if only because it is here lumped with kith and kin to whom it has little to say, even if its language were the same as theirs. Among the more direct attacks upon the problem of the major language, too, there has been much quantitative analysis in the way Louis T. Milic and other "stylisticians" recommend in *Style and Stylistics: An Analytical Bibliography* (N.Y.: Free P., 1967). R.G. Johnson, "A Study of the Style of Henry James's Later Novels", *DAI* 32 (1971), 2092A (Bowling Green); S.B. Purdy, "The Language of Henry James with Emphasis on His Diction and Vocabulary", *DAI* 21 (1960), 626 (Wisconsin); L.S. Wilson, "The Stylistics of Henry James: A Linguistic Analysis of Selected Early and Late Novels", *DAI* 35 (1974), 7896A (Florida State); J.B. Goldenthal, "Henry James and Impressionism: A Method of Stylistic Analysis", *DAI* 35 (1974), 2967A (N.Y.U.); Seymour Chatman, *The Later Style of Henry James* (Oxford: Blackwell, 1972); S.R. Crowl, "The Beholder's Eye: Romantic and Critical Perspectives through Style in James's 'Turn of the Screw', *The Wings of the Dove* and *The Golden Bowl*", *DAI* 31 (1970), 5357A (Indiana); S.M. Greenstein, "The Negative Principle and the Virtuous Character: Undercutting in the Work of Richardson, Austen and James", *DAI* 35 (1974), 4521A (Indiana); and William Veeder, *Henry James — the Lessons of the Master: Popular Fiction and Personal Style in the Nineteenth Century* (London: U. of Chicago P., 1975), p. 229. Again the difficulty with the undeniable piecemeal truths offered in these linguistic descriptions is their severely limited value when one wants to interpret the aesthetic function of such units. Even the zealous coverage by Chatman of the agents of the late style results in a cataloguing of a descriptive kind and there is once more insufficient appreciation of the nature of the respective congruous wholes wherein the agents function. Veeder's attempt to define James's "personal style" as a "transformation" of usages within popular fiction becomes unconvincing the further Veeder travels from *The Portrait of a Lady*, his chief study. In the later years James's words were dancing to tunes the extreme opposite of those once popular or then current; and when the tunes of his contemporaries were brought to his notice, he invariably re-orchestrated them. The three studies more suggestive of principles operating within the late language are those by Barry Menikoff, "Punctuation and Point of View in the Late Style of Henry James", *Style* 4 (1970): 29-47; by H. Watanabe, "Past Perfect Retrospection in the Style of Henry James", *American Literature* 34 (1962): 165-81 and, in particular, Ruth Yeazell's own dissertation, "The Late Style of

Henry James: A Study of the Novel", *DAI* 32 (1972) 7016A (Yale), the basis of her subsequent patient sorties into the Jamesian forest.

56. Booth, *Rhetoric*, pp. 67-86, 74, 77.
57. Ibid., pp. 78-9.
58. James, *Prefaces*, p. 263.
59. Ibid., p. 231.
60. James, *Notebooks*, p. 188.
61. James E. Miller Jr, "Henry James in Reality", *Critical Inquiry* 2:3 (Spring 1976): 601.
62. I refer chiefly to Patrick White's *The Eye of the Storm* (London: Cape, 1973), my appreciation of which is to be found in " 'The Splinters of a Mind Make a Whole Piece', Patrick White's *The Eye of the Storm*", *Studies in the Recent Australian Novel*, ed. K.G. Hamilton (St. Lucia, Queensland: Univ. of Queensland P., 1978), pp. 61-83.
63. James, *The Ambassadors*, 2 vols. XVII and XVIII. *The Novels and Tales of Henry James* (New York: Scribner, 1907-1909), I, 217.
64. James, *What Maisie Knew*. XI, 354. *The Novels and Tales of Henry James* (New York: Scribner, 1907-1909) p. 354.
65. James, *Ambassadors*, p. 326.
66. James, *Wings of the Dove*, I, 33.
67. Ibid., II, 405.
68. Conrad, *Notes*, pp. 23, 21.
69. James, *Ivory Tower* p. 287. Quoted by Greene in *Collected Essays*, p. 39.
70. Spender, *Question*, p. 125.
71. Auden, *Collected Poetry*, p. 125.
72. *Question*, ed. Dupee, p. 125.
73. *Critical Essays*, ed. Edel, p. 24.
74. Adeline R. Tintner, "Henry James Criticism: A Current Perspective", *American Literary Realism* 7 (Spring 1974): 155-68.
75. Adeline R. Tintner, "*The Golden Bowl* and Waddesdon Manor", *Apollo* 104 (August 1976): 108-9).
76. Short, *Images*, p. 949.
77. *HJ and Wells*, ed. Edel and Ray, p. 246.
78. Alan Rose, "The Spatial Form of *The Golden Bowl*", *Modern Fiction Studies* 12:1 (Spring 1966): 103-16.
79. Lisa Appignanesi *Femininity and the Creative Imagination: A Study of Henry James, Robert Musil and Marcel Proust* (London: Vision, 1973), p. 72.
80. Naomi Lebowitz, "Magic and Metamorphosis in The Golden Bowl", *Sewanee Review* 73 (January-March 1965): 59-60; re-emphasized in *Loving*, p. 131.
81. James, "Emile Zola", *Atlantic Monthly* 92 (August 1903): 193-210; rpt. *Selected Literary Criticism*, p. 242.
82. Mark Krupnick, "*The Golden Bowl*: Henry James's Novel About Nothing", *English Studies* 57 (December 1976): 540.

83. John Halverson, "Late Manner, Major Phase", *Sewanee Review* 79 (1971): 214-31.
84. Ruth B. Yeazell, *Language and Knowledge in the Late Novels of Henry James* (Chicago: Univ. of Chicago P., 1976). Other recent studies preserving the redemptive Maggie in a basically optimistic novel include Granville H. Jones in *Henry James's Psychology of Experience: Innocence, Responsibility and Renunciation in the Fiction of Henry James* (Hague: Mouton, 1975), who writes on p. 185 of a bowl containing "more sweet than bitter"; and Manfred Mackenzie in his *Communities of Love and Honor in Henry James* (Cambridge, Mass: Harvard U.P., 1976), who argues on p. 179 for a Maggie who must "initiate and conclude the general rectification". Dale E. Peterson, on the other hand in his *The Clement Vision: Poetic Realism in Turgenev and James* (Port Washington, N.Y.: Kennikat P., 1975), p. 134, continues the tradition of James the "visionary realist" involved in a more complex and "human struggle to liberate the aesthetic consciousness from the oppressive guardianship of the ethical consciousness". All these studies are recognizable as the latest refinements of critical stances falling within the three groups I earlier mentioned. But, in "Henry James and the Comedy of Love: The Golden Bowl", *Erasmus Review* 1:i (1971): 47-62 and in *Henry James and the Comic Form: A Study of the Major Novels* (Ann Arbor: Univ. of Michigan P., 1975), Lee J. Richmond and Ronald Wallace, respectively, strive towards a view of the later James that is novel rather than new and is achieved only by a usage of "comic" which distorts the term as well as the fiction.
85. This affinity is substantiated by Ian Sibley in his doctoral dissertation, "Imagination and Moral Integrity in Henry James's Major Phase: An Exegetical Study of Three Major Novels and Seven Related *Nouvelles*, Emphasizing Ultimate Correspondences with Dante and Ecclesiastes", submitted to the University of Queensland, 1980.
86. James, *Prefaces*, p. 143.
87. Patrick White is quoting Blake in the epigraph to his *Riders in the Chariot* (Eyre & Spottiswoode, 1961).
88. James, *Prefaces*, p. 329.
89. A.J.A. Waldock, *James, Joyce and Others* (London: Williams and Norgate, 1937), p. 26.
90. Now among the James Family Papers and memorabilia in the Houghton Library, Harvard. (The gold christening bowl presented by George the First to the original owners of Lamb House is clearly of biographical interest, with little of the artistic or philosophical relevance Edel attributes to it in *Master*, p. 215).
91. Quoted in Leyburn, *Alloy*, p. 171.
92. James, *Prefaces*, p. 32.

Appendixes

APPENDIX A[1]

The history of "The Real Thing" is of interest to this study in two ways. Firstly, it shows James trying to rescue a story from the disadvantages of first-person narration by teaching the narrator to talk Jamesese. The dilemma of the illustrator who depicts gentlefolk and whose cockney and Italian models, Miss Churm and Oronte, suit better his artistic purposes than do the suddenly-impoverished Major Monarch and his wife who appeal to his compassion, is not nearly as interesting as is the dilemma of the later James trying to invest with his characteristic mature powers a tale originally designed for quick sale in a magazine. Secondly, having been first written and revised on the eve of the major phase and then revised again at the heart of it, the texts illuminate the essential difference between his hand-written and his dictated prose.

The magazine version[2] is a compromise between his professed intention and his uneasiness about it: ". . . I shall probably find there is much more to be done with this than the compass will admit of. Make it tremendously succinct — with a very short pulse of rhythm — and the closest selection of detail — in other words *summarize* intensely and keep down the lateral development". It does summarize neatly enough with its "very brief treatment" the original *donnée.*[3] It is fairly crisp in the laconic vernacular of the narrator. When James tries to put it into better shape for its book-form[4] the following year, he accentuates the artist's dilemma by showing more equally the totally different demands made on him by the two sets of models and by stressing his consciousness of the artistic issues.

Unlike the even later revisory process, this one proceeds not by interpolation of phrases, clauses and sentences but by substitution of vocabulary. Miss Churm, who originally was "quite adequate" and gave "a kind of regular performance" is now "fully adequate" and gives "a capital performance". Oronte, who was originally "my insinuating visitor" with "*lazzarone* habits", now is, more attractively, "my bright adventurer" with "native exuberance". The plight of their competitors the Monarchs is now balanced fairly against them. Their "means", formerly "extremely small", are now "dreadfully small". Whereas Mrs Monarch formerly "recalled" that she used to sketch a little, we are now told she "hinted" this fact; instead of having "lady-like airs" she is given "a lady-like air"; rather than sitting "dull and silent" she sits "vague and silent". We are told of her husband, whose boring preoccupation with railway timetables and bird-shooting, made him, originally, "a mixture of the station-master and the ornithologist" that "he managed to interweave the station-master with the ornithologist"; his conception of Oronte as "a little Neapolitan cad" is toned down: Oronte becomes for him "a scrap of a *lazzarone*". For the narrator's fellow-artist, Jack Hawley, both Monarchs were "a blighting apparition" but they become for him merely "a ridiculous pair" (pp. 51, 57, 60, 62, 46, 45, 56, 58, 55, 60, 65).

For the artist himself, caught between both pairs, the alternative diction insists on the challenge to execution. The pair so incontrovertibly "the real thing" but so disastrously "always the same thing" are for him now not just "rather irritatingly stiff" but "insurmountably stiff". It is not a question of "how far they took one" but "how far they could lead the pencil". Jack, who in the first version, "was unable to recognize that I had gone much further" when confronted by the products of the Monarchs' modelling, is now in this version "disappointed by the exhibition" and concludes not that " 'there's a muddle somewhere' " but that " 'there's a big hole somewhere' ". The revisory pen thus digs at linguistic detail. Apart from three consecutive sentences excised — clearly because they were an irrelevant aside by the artist upon the unreliability of any person's estimate of a portrait made of them — the changes involve lexis rather than syntax[5] (pp. 56, 56, 56, 62, 63).

The revisory voice reverses this emphasis. There are in the dictated third version[6] twice as many alterations involving a more radical recasting of the rhythm of a sentence than such minor changes in diction and there are frequent interpolations in which we hear, in an essentially "major" tone, the artist's confessions of the impact the Monarchs have on him professionally and humanly. Mrs Monarch's "tinted oval mask showed friction as an exposed surface shows it"; now it shows "waste as an exposed surface shows friction" — which suggests more sharply the artist's eye and the man's feelings. Similarly, "the hand of time had played over her freely but only to simplify" becomes "but to an effect of elimination", which acknowledges a painful human process and dwells on its aesthetically uninteresting result. Other new phrasings throw further emphasis upon relationships: the one between the Monarchs and the resulting united appeal they make to the artist. Whereas the lady returns from the brief parading of her figure, "her fluttered eyes on her husband", she now returns with "her fluttered eyes on the partner of her appeal". In both the second and the third versions she insists on her ability to remain quiet during the "sitting" by saying to the Major: "I'm not a nasty fidget am I?' "; but in the third, James now has the artist rhythmically add: "it was going to wring tears from me, I felt, the way she hid her head, ostrich-like, in the other broad bosom". Again, when he tells them of his need for "a certain amount of expression" from them and they chorus " 'Of course!' " there is added: " — and I had never heard such unanimity". The rhetorical resources now involve phrase rather than word, sentence rather than phrase (pp. 44, 44, 47, 47, 48).

Lumbered with the first-personal, James clearly makes a virtue of necessity by more deliberately placing the pronoun. "Their friends liked them but didn't like to support them" is changed to "their friends liked them, I made out, without liking to support them"; and "I liked them — they were so simple" is changed to "I liked them — I felt, quite as their friends must have done — they were so simple". His consciousness of their pathetic remoteness from realities is underlined when, telling them they will need to wear costumes that had served their time "a hundred years ago on living world-stained men and women", he now adds the highly-rhythmical aside: "on figures not perhaps so far removed, in that vanished world, from *their* type, the Monarchs, *quoi*! of the breeched and bewigged age"; and this gives extra ironic force to the Major's solemn response — " 'We'll put on anything that fits!' ". The sentence describing the Major's perpetual state of sitting and waiting, either in lodgings, with or without his partner, or in the studio, is recast from "so he simply sat and waited when I was too absorbed in my work to talk" to "so when I was too absorbed in my work to talk he simply sat and waited", giving the poignantly revelatory word the more emphatic position. In the 1893 text, the artist directly continued: "but I liked to make him talk — it made my work, when not interrupting it, less sordid, less special"; this is altered in the 1907 text to the much gentler "I liked to hear him talk" and a much more sympathetic relation is suggested when "sordid" is replaced by "mechanical" (pp. 49, 35, 51, 54, 55-56).

What this final version attends to most closely is the paradox of "the real thing" always turning out in art as "the same thing" and therefore never becoming for art "the ideal thing". Thus: "I was oppressed by the serenity of [Mrs Monarch's] confidence that she *was* the Real Thing" is strengthened to "I rather writhed under the serenity . . .". Jack Hawley's response after scrutinizing the drawing made from the Monarchs is made in terms just as colourfully idiomatic but much more precise and pertinent — " 'Well, there's a screw loose somewhere' " — which, unlike his earlier use of "muddle" and "hole", pinpoints the problem as being one central to the creative act. But this mysterious process is now given the context of the conditions of life itself, in which there is a general baffling complexity. Once the artist begins facing the fact that his human scruple and his artistic integrity are apparently incompatible, he finds there are other facts to face. So, "I saw that at this rate I shouldn't get the other books to do" becomes "I had to face the fact that at this rate I shouldn't get the other books to do"; and where he tells us in earlier drafts that the Monarchs finally "reappeared together, three days later, and under the circumstances there was something tragic in the fact", he now tells us: "given all the other facts, there was something tragic in that one". The mode becomes less merely narratory, more amply reflective (pp. 67, 56, 63, 66, 67).

This is the closest that the later James can approach to simulating, in his successive revisions of his first-personal rendering of this artist's consciousness, his own consciousness of how such a *donnée* so much more thickly bristles with eloquent suggestion. In its final form the story's symmetrical scheme, wherein the characters could so easily resemble cyphers and the whole effect could become one too neat for truth, is ameliorated; the events that, the artist tells us in conclusion, became such a lambent memory, are given temporal perspective by suitable phrasing ("... as I often had in those days ..."). His voice never develops the resonance of James's own, more habitual, third-personal authorial manner, but the breath of the incalculable is now intermittently felt in the final, more sensitively oratorical, narration (p. 69).

Notes

1. This summary is based on my paper "Henry James's Three Versions of 'The Real Thing' ", delivered at a postgraduate seminar conducted by Dr David Lodge in the Department of English, University of Birmingham, 29 October 1973.
2. *Black and White*, 16 April 1892, pp. 502-7.
3. James, *Notebooks*, p. 104.
4. James, *The Real Thing and Other Tales* (London: Macmillan, 1893), pp. 1-40. This text is reproduced in *Henry James: Selected Short Stories* (London: Penguin, 1963), pp. 43-69 and as this later printing is the one more readily available for the appreciation of context, I cite all page references from it.
5. Other studies stressing this first kind of revision of other work by James include: Theodora Bosanquet, "The Revised Version [of *The American*]", *The Little Review* 5 (August 1918): 56-62; Violet Dunbar, "The Revisions of 'Daisy Miller' ", *Modern Language Notes* 65 (May 1950) 311-17; Leon Edel, "Henry James's Revisions for *The Ambassadors*", *Notes and Queries* n.s. 2 (January 1955): 37-38; Charles Fish, "Form and Revision: the Example of *Watch and Ward*", *Nineteenth-Century Fiction* 22 (September 1967): 173-90; A.F. Gegenheimer, "Early and Late Revision in Henry James's 'A Passionate Pilgrim' ", *American Literature* 23 (May 1951): 233-42; R.A. Gettmann, "Henry James's Revision of *The American*", *American Literature* 16 (January 1945): 279-95; S.M. Humphreys, "Henry James's 'Revisions for *The Ambassadors*' ". *Notes and Queries* n.s. 1 (September 1954): 397-99; Helene Harvitt, "How Henry James Revised *Roderick Hudson*", *PMLA* 39 (March 1924): 202-27; R.D. Havens, "The Revision of *Roderick Hudson*", *PMLA* 40 (June 1925): 433-34; S.J. Krause, "James's Revisions of the Style of *The Portrait of a Lady*", *American Literature* 30 (1958): 67-88; B.R. McElderry, Jr, "Henry James's Revision of *Watch and Ward*", *Modern Language Notes* 67 (November 1952): 457-61; F.O. Matthiessen, "The Painter's Sponge and Varnish Bottle: Henry James's Revisions of *The Portrait of a Lady*", *American Bookman* 1 (1944): 49-68; J.C. Maxwell, "The Revision of *Roderick Hudson*" *English Studies* 45 (June 1964): 239; I. Traschen, "Henry James and the Art of Revision". *Philological Quarterly* 35 (January 1956):

39-47; Charles Vandersee, "James's 'Pandora': The Mixed Consequences of Revision", *Studies in Bibliography*, 21 (1968): 93-108; and Sister Stephanie Vincec, "A Significant Revision of *The Wings of the Dove*", *Review of English Studies* 23 (1972): 58-61. These studies are either defensive or sceptical rather than exploratory and even when not concerned only with the early and middle periods in James's development they singularly neglect the impact of dictation.

6. *The Novels and Tales of Henry James.* Vol. XVIII (New York: Scribner, 1907-9), pp. 307-46.

APPENDIX B

The glimpse we are given of James wrestling with language in the preliminary drafts[1] of his introductory essay on Brooke is of manifold relevance to my study. Between the first draft of it and the first version of "The Real Thing", his language had been influenced by twenty years of dictation to amanueses and the draft that finally saw print is his last finished and coherent work. The controversial "last dictation"[2] of which Leon Edel took a copy before the original was, apparently, destroyed, shows the incoherence of the dying man whose mind was then crumbling into Napoleonic illusions. On a page attached to the copy of the Brooke essay that went to the printer, there has been appended in a hand not James's, the statement that it was finished by James in November 1915 and is certainly his last literary work. Within three months of completing it he was dead.

It is extremely difficult to read because each of the apparent motives for writing it put such pressure upon James. Five months earlier, he had adopted British citizenship and so the essay afforded him one more occasion for a tribute to those ideals which he believed the English way of life embodied and which were then being threatened by the war that in a very real sense hastened his own death. To this intense feeling, must be added his personal response to the English poet he had met at Cambridge in 1909 and in London again only weeks before that young man's promising life ended. But even deeper was the feeling of the older man — "lover and interpreter of the fine amenities, of brave decisions and generous loyalties"[3] — for this ultimate example of the loser, the sacrificed, the victim of forces incalculably malign. The prose made to bear all these demands does need to be "articulately *sounded*",[4] or to be given at least a patient and careful imagined articulation.

This prose achieves its effects by evoking neither the voice of any imagined artist nor that of the author who finds sentences for filtering the thoughts of the imagined Prince Amerigo but by rendering the most deeply personal voice of James himself, the voice heard in the letters to his brother William and — more eloquent even than that one — the voice of the artist talking-to-himself-on-paper in the *Notebooks* he believed would remain private. The first sentence of the essay can be shown to be preserving continuity amid the amplitude of nuances — and thus winning the unity that bestows coherence — by the sensitive pulse of its rhythm. When this sentence that is so thoroughly representative of all that follow it is set out in the same way I earlier set out Maggie's "pagoda" sentence and the same is done for one from the *Notebooks*, the exercise is instructive.

First, the opening words of the essay:

Nothing more generally
3 or more recurrently
solicits us,
1 in the light of literature,
1 I think,
1 than the interest of our learning how the poet,
1 the true poet,
and above all the particular one
with whom we may
4
for the moment
be concerned,
1 has come into his estate,
asserted
3 and preserved
his identity,
2 worked out his question of sticking to that
and to nothing else;
*and has so been able to reach us
3 and touch us
as a poet,
in spite of the accidents
3 and dangers
that must have beset this course.[5]

There is in this case little need to dwell on the changes made between this version and the first, which has in fact four more of such units in it, which places the fifth — the interpolated "I think" — as the fourth one, and again very slightly refines the beat by omitting an "in fine" originally interpolated at the asterisk

The final punctuation provides for eleven syntactic units, eight of which end with a reference, direct or indirect, to the idea of the Poet *per se* that is being elaborated in it: the additional twelve units, all minor rhetorical ones I attribute to it, are "placed" so as to "sound" this idea not only with variation of diction but also with variation of pace and cadence. Thus we hear of "the poet", of "the true poet", of "the particular one", of "his estate", of "his identity", of "his question of sticking to that", "*as* a poet", and of "this course". But we hear of this persistent notion, as it is elaborated, in a tone which modulates among a variety of inflections and which develops a rhythm, subtle and strong — subtle for precision and strong for cohesion. The idea is spun finely but it is also spun clearly and eloquently. The total impact of it becomes part of its import, for even here at the beginning of what is virtually James's personal funeral oration for Brooke, the fervency is manifest, is "heard", as it were, in the mind's ear. Essentially the same effect was achieved in the first draft of it.

The point of critical interest lies not on the differences between drafts — as it did in the case of "The Real Thing" — but in the similarities between this dictated sentence and one from a famous passage jotted into a Notebook five years earlier in silence. It occurs where James is reflecting on his addiction to "the dramatic way".

1 Momentary sidewinds —
1 things of no real authority —
break in
3 and yearningly
to put their inferior little questions to me;
1 but I come back,
1 I come back,
1 as I say,
I all throbbingly
1 and yearningly
and passionately,
1 oh,
1 *mon bon*,
come back to this way
that is
5 clearly
the only one
in which I can do anything now,
and that will open out to me
more and more
5 and that has overwhelming reasons pleading
all beautifully
in its breast.[6]

Again there are eleven syntactic units — even though James's confident conviction that this jotting would never be made public precludes any possibility, as well as any evidence, of revision, and again I can with consistency attribute twelve more minor rhetorical units that convey the modulations, the inflections and the cadences of the implied voice just as faithfully as, in the essay sentence, they faithfully recreated the pulse of the dictating one. Written ten years after the habit of dictation began, the jotting reveals a mode of expression that has become instinctual. The language of both essay and jotting catch the thought as it flies and convey the act of the catching. The wider implications of this now lead us to three other statements by James that are illuminated by them.

Discussing in his Preface to *The Portrait of a Lady* the finer forms of attention a reader must supply if a writer is to develop the finer forms of interest, James breaks out: "The artist may of course, in wanton moods, dream of some Paradise (for art) where the direct appeal to the intelligence might be legalized; for to such extravagances as these his yearning mind can scarce hope ever completely to close itself. The most he can do is to remember they are extravagances."[7] Some seven years later, he is commending Compton Mackenzie for how "the fineness" of his "appeal to our interest" derives from his "positively caring for his expression as expression, positively providing for his phrase as a fondly foreseeing parent for a child, positively loving it in the light of what it may do for him — meeting revelations, that is, in what it may do, and appearing to recognize that ***the value of the offered thing, its whole relation to us, is created by the breath of language***, that on such terms exclusively, for appropriation and enjoyment, we know it, and that any claimed independence of 'form' on its part is the most abject of fallacies".[8] Both statements recall one made on the eve of the major phase when, in the 1893 essay on Flaubert, he directly followed the assertion "the finish of his prose was the proof of his profundity" by the words: "If you pushed far enough into language you found yourself in the embrace of thought."[9]

All three statements describe very well where James's own late style took him. The direct appeal to the intelligence is a wanton dream but the direct revelation of words in the act of embracing a thought can take the later James excitingly close to the realization of that artistic Paradise. That act is rendered most faithfully when "created by the *breath* of language", for, any register less human and less delicate than the questing voice — whether sounded or silent or simulated — will embrace less of what the mind of the artist is exploring. James's final use of language, sustaining coherence even while straining finely-interested attention almost to the point where that coherence is imperilled, reveals, in its mode of conception and in its refinement of that mode, the immerse amount of linguistic territory he profitably traversed during his long pursuit of his artistic ideal. The introspective novelist sought and found a poet's intensity of expression in the soliloquizing voice so dear to the dramatist and invaluable to any literary artist who makes the more adventurous raids on the inarticulate.

Difficult but not obscure, mannered but eschewing mannerism, James's prose keeps pace with the demands he makes upon it. For each raid, he sophisticated his equipment and (to paraphrase T.S. Eliot even further) he disciplined the squads of emotion by his mastery of rhythmic utterance. Just as *The Golden Bowl* reduced, thus, the gap between literature and life, so, too, twelve years later, his style was further reducing the gap between the language of his literature and the language of his thought, between the calculability of art and the incalculability of life. Indeed, even while the fire was being extinguished, the Absolute fusion was being sought still in "the crucible of the imagination".[10]

Notes

1. "First Copy", pp. 1-47, minus pp. 36-38 and p. 44. "Second Copy", pp. 1-48, signed "Henry James". *James Family Papers*, Houghton Library, Harvard University.
2. "Henry James's Last Dictation", *Times Literary Supplement*, 2 May 1968 and Edel, *Master*, pp. 580, 553-57. See also Montgomery Hyde on this document in *Times Literary Supplement*, 9 May 1968, p. 481; 23 May 1968, p. 529; 30 May 1968, p. 553; 6 June 1968, p. 597; and 18 June 1968, p. 621.
3. From the Chelsea Old Church memorial tablet, shattered in the same later world war in which, also, one of the two bombs to fall on Rye demolished the summer-house in the garden of Lamb House, the "Temple of the Muse" where the "Priestess of the Remington" typed while James paced and dictated. Vindicating his faith in English valour, the Chelsea parishioners collected the shards and restored all tablets.
4. James, *Prefaces*, pp. 346-47. See also M. LaRoche, "Reading Henry James Aloud", *Mark Twain Quarterly* 5 (Spring 1943) 8.
5. "Rupert Brooke", *Letters from America* by Rupert Brooke (London: Sidgwick and Jackson, 1916, rpt. 1923), p.ix.
6. James, *Notebooks*, p. 348.
7. James, *Prefaces*, p. 54.
8. "The New Novel", 1914; quoted from *Selected Literary Criticism*, ed. Shapira, p. 341.
9. "Gustave Flaubert", *Selected Literary Criticism*, ed. Shapira, p. 153.
10. *HJ and Wells*, ed. Edel and Ray, p. 128.

Bibliography

A more comprehensive list of works relevant to this study is to be found in my dissertation "The Radical Originality of Henry James's Ultimate Mode: *The Golden Bowl.* An Exegesis of His Artistic Provisions", University of Queensland, 1978. The following briefer list includes all items appearing in the foregoing chapter notes, plus those of relevance published since Leon Edel's and Dan H. Laurence's *A Bibliography of Henry James* (London: Rupert Hart-Davis, 1957) and Beatrice Ricks's *Henry James: A Bibliography of Secondary Works,* (Metuchen, N.J.: Scarecrow, 1975), as well as those which, though already listed in Ricks but not in my notes, proved to be of pertinence to my interests in James's major phase.

PRIMARY SOURCES: WORKS BY HENRY JAMES

The Ambassadors. London: Methuen, 1903.

The Ambassadors. Vols. XXI and XXII. *The Novels and Tales of Henry James.* New York: Scribner's, 1907-9.

"The Art of Fiction". *Longman's Magazine* 4 (September 1884) 502-21.

"The Art of Fiction". *Partial Portraits.* London: Macmillan, 1888, pp. 375-408.

The Art of the Novel: Critical Prefaces by Henry James. Introd. Richard P. Blackmur. New York: Scribner's, 1950.

The Complete Plays of Henry James. Ed. Leon Edel. New York: Lippincott, 1949.

The Complete Tales of Henry James. Ed. and introd. Leon Edel. 12 vols. London: Hart-Davis, 1962-64.

"Coquelin". *Century Magazine* 33 (January 1887) 407-13.

"Critical Introduction to an English Translation of *Madame Bovary*". *Madame Bovary*, by Gustave Flaubert. London: Heinemann, 1902, pp. v-xliii.
"Emile Zola". *Atlantic Monthly* 92 (August 1903) 193-210.
The Finer Grain. New York: Scribner's, 1910.
French Poets and Novelists. London: Macmillan, 1878.
The Future of the Novel. Essays on the Art of Fiction. Ed. and introd. Leon Edel. New York: Vintage, 1956.
The Golden Bowl. London: Methuen, 1905.
The Golden Bowl. Vols. XXIII and XXIV. *The Novels and Tales of Henry James.* New York: Scribner's, 1907-9.
Hawthorne. London: Macmillan, 1879.
Henry James: The American Essays. Ed. and introd. Leon Edel. New York: Vintage, 1956.
Henry James and H.G. Wells: A Record of their Friendship, their Debate on the Art of Fiction, and their Quarrel. Ed. and introd. Leon Edel and Gordon N. Ray. London: Hart-Davis, 1959.
Henry James: Letters: Vol. I, 1843-1875. Ed. Leon Edel. Cambridge: Harvard University Press, Belknap Press, 1974.
Henry James: The Scenic Art: Notes on Acting and the Drama: 1872-1901. Ed. with introd. and notes by Allan Wade. London: Hart-Davis, 1949.
Holographs of Correspondence between Henry James and William James. Letters dated from 10 May 1867 to 13 November 1907. MS Am 1092. James Family Papers, Houghton Library, Harvard University.
The House of Fiction: Essays on the Novel by Henry James. Ed. and introd. Leon Edel. London: Hart-Davis, 1957.
"Introduction". *Constant Coquelin, Art and the Actor.* New York: Dramatic Museum of Columbia University, 1915, pp. 1-36. Rpt. as "Coquelin, 1887-1915", *Henry James: The Scenic Art*, pp. 198-218.
"Ivan Turgenieff". *Library of the World's Best Literature, Ancient and Modern* Ed. Charles Dudley Warner. New York: Peale and Hill, 1896-97, XXV, 15057-62.
The Ivory Tower. London: Collins, 1917.
The Letters of Henry James. Sel. and ed. Percy Lubbock. 2 vols. London: Macmillan, 1920.
Letters to An Editor. London: privately printed by Clement Shorter, 1916.
Letters to Benson and Monod. Introd. E.F. Benson. New York: Scribner's, 1930.
Letters to Joseph Conrad. London: First Edition Club, 1926.
Letters to Walter Berry. Paris: Black Sun Press, 1928.
Literary Reviews and Essays by Henry James on American, English and French Literature. Ed. Albert Mordell. New York: Grove, 1957.
"London Notes". *Harper's Weekly* 6 February 1897, pp. 134-35.
The Middle Years. London: Collins, 1917.
"The Mind of England at War". *New York Sun*, 1 August 1915, p. v, col. 3.
A Most Unholy Trade. London: The Scarab Press, 1923.

"Mr Henry James on England". Letter to the Editor. *The Observer*, 18 April 1915, p. 14, col. 3.

"The New Novel". *Notes on Novelists: With Some Other Notes*. London: Dent, 1914, pp. 150-81.

"Note on Literary Form". *The Art of Authorship. Literary Reminiscences: Methods of Work, and Advice to Young Beginners, Personally Contributed by Leading Authors of the Day.* Comp. and ed. George Bainton. London: Clarke, 1890, p. 208.

The Notebooks of Henry James. Ed. F.O. Matthiessen and Kenneth B. Murdock. New York: O.U.P., 1947.

Notes and Reviews. With Preface by Pierre de Chaignon La Rose. A Series of Twenty-five papers Hitherto Unpublished in Book Form. Cambridge, Massachusetts: Dunster House, 1921.

"Notes for *The Ivory Tower*". *The Ivory Tower.* London: Collins, 1917, pp. 263-348.

"Notes for *The Sense of the Past*". *The Sense of the Past.* London: Collins, 1917.

Notes of a Son and Brother. New York: Scribner's, 1914.

Notes on Novelists. London: Dent, 1914.

"The Novel in 'The Ring and the Book' ". *Browning's Centenary.* London: Asher, 1912, pp. 21-50.

"The Novels of George Eliot". *Atlantic Montly* 18 (October 1866) 479-92.

The Novels and Tales of Henry James. 24 vols. New York: Scribner's, 1907-9.

The Painter's Eye: Notes and Essays on the Pictorial Arts by Henry James. Sel. and ed. with introd. John L. Sweeney. London: Hart-Davis, 1956.

Partial Portraits. London: Macmillan, 1888.

Picture and Text. New York: Harper, 1893.

The Portrait of a Lady. New York: Houghton, Mifflin, 1881.

"The Question of Our Speech". *Appleton's Booklover's Magazine* 6 (August 1905) 199-210.

The Question of the Mind: England at War. An Essay issued by the Central Committee of National Patriotic Organizations, London: 1915.

"The Real Thing". *Black and White* iii 16 April 1892, pp. 502-7.

"The Real Thing". (Revised.) *The Real Thing and Other Tales.* London: Macmillan, 1893, pp. 1-40.

"The Real Thing". (Further revised.) *The Novels and Tales of Henry James.* Vol. XVIII. New York: Scribner's, 1907-9, pp. 307-46.

"The Real Thing". (Text of the 1893 version.) *Henry James: Selected Short Stories.* Ed. and introd. Michael Swan. London: Penguin, 1963, pp. 43-69.

"Robert Louis Stevenson". *Henry James and Robert Louis Stevenson: A Record of Friendship and Criticism.* Ed. and introd. Janet Adam Smith. London: Hart-Davis, 1948, pp. 123-60.

"Rupert Brooke". *Letters from America.* By Rupert Brooke. 1916, Rpt. London: Sidgwick and Jackson, 1923, pp. ix-xlii.

'Rupert Brooke". Two amended typescript drafts of James's introduction to *Letters from America.* New York: Scribner's, 1916, pp. ix-xlii. Both dictated to Miss Bosanquet: the First, pp. 1-47, minus pp. 36-38, 44; the Second, pp. 1-48. James Family Papers. Houghton Library, Harvard University.

The Sacred Fount. New York: Scribner's, 1901.

Selected Letters of Henry James. Ed. and introd. Leon Edel. London: Hart-Davis, 1956.

The Sense of the Past. London: Collins, 1917.

A Small Boy and Others. New York: Scribner's, 1913.

"Special Introduction". *The Tempest.* In Vol. XVI of *The Complete Plays of William Shakespeare.* Ed. Sidney Lee. New York: Sproule, 1907, pp. ix-xxxii.

"The Speech of American Women". *Harper's Bazar* [sic] 40 (November-December 1906) 979-82, 1103-06; 41 (January-February 1907) 17-21, 113-17.

Theatre and Friendship. With a commentary by Elizabeth Robins. London: Cape, 1932.

Views and Reviews. Coll. and introd. Le Roy Phillips. Boston: Ball Publishing Company, 1908.

The Wings of the Dove. London: Constable, 1903.

The Wings of the Dove. Vols. XIX and XX. *The Novels and Tales of Henry James.* New York: Scribner, 1907-9.

Within the Rim and Other Essays, 1914-1915. London: Collins, 1919.

"Within the Rim". Typescript draft in the possession of Miss Theodora Bosanquet, "Arlington", Piccadilly, London, W.I., 1955.

SECONDARY SOURCES: WORKS ABOUT HENRY JAMES

Allott, M. "*Romola* and *The Golden Bowl*". *Notes and Queries* 198 (March 1953) 124.

——— "Symbol and Image in the Later Work of Henry James". *Essays in Criticism* 3 (July 1953) 321-26.

Anderson, Quentin. *The American Henry James.* New Brunswick, N.J.: Rutgers University Press, 1957.

——— "The Golden Bowl as a Cultural Artifact". *The Imperial Self: An Essay in American Literary and Cultural History.* New York: Knopf, 1971, pp. 201-44.

——— "Henry James and the New Jerusalem". *Kenyon Review* 8 (Autumn 1946) 515-66.

Appignanesi, Lisa. *Femininity and the Creative Imagination: A Study of Henry James, Robert Musil and Marcel Proust.* New York: Harper & Row, 1973.

Aswad, Betsy B. "The Crucible of Conversation: A Study of Jamesian Dialogue". *Dissertation Abstracts International* (Hereafter *DAI*) 34 (1973) 1890A (S.U.N.Y., Binghampton).

Auchinloss, Louis. *Reading Henry James.* Minneapolis: University of Minnesota Press, 1975.

Auden, W.H. "At the Grave of Henry James". *Partisan Review* 8 (July-August 1941) Poem, 266-70.

______ *The Collected Poetry of W.H. Auden.* New York: Random House, 1945.

Babb, Howard S., ed. *Essays on Stylistic Analysis.* New York: Harcourt, Brace, Jovanovich, 1972.

Bayley, John. "Love and Knowledge: *The Golden Bowl*". In his *The Characters of Love: A Study in the Literature of Personality.* New York: Basic Books, 1961, pp. 203-62.

Beach, J.W. *The Method of Henry James.* 1918. Rpt. Philadelphia: Albert Saifer, 1954.

Beerbohm, Max. *Around Theatres.* London: Rupert Hart-Davis, 1930.

______ "The Guerdon". [1916] In his *A Variety of Things.* London: Heinemann, 1928. Rpt. in *Parodies: An Anthology from Chaucer to Beerbohm and After.* Ed. Dwight Macdonald. London: Faber, 1964, pp. 147-49.

______ "The Mote in the Middle Distance". In his *A Christmas Garland.* New York: O.U.P., 1936, pp. 3-10. Rpt. in *The Question of Henry James*, ed. F.W. Dupee, pp. 40-43.

Bell, Millicent. "Jamesian Being". *Virginia Quarterly Review* 51 (1975) 115-32.

Bellringer, Alan W. "*The Ivory Tower:* The Cessation of Concern". *Journal of American Studies* 10 (August 1976), 241-55.

Bender, Bert. "Henry James's Late Lyric Meditations upon the Mysteries of Fate and Self Sacrifice". *Genre* 9 (1976) 247-62.

Besant, W. *The Art of Fiction.* London: Chatto and Windus, 1902. Lecture to Royal Institution, 25 April 1884.

Bewley, M. *The Complex Fate: Hawthorne, Henry James and Some Other American Writers.* London: Chatto & Windus, 1952.

Blackmur, R.B. Introduction to *The Art of the Novel: Critical Prefaces by Henry James.* New York: Scribner's, 1950.

______ Introduction to *The Golden Bowl.* New York: Dell, 1963.

______ Introduction to *The Golden Bowl.* New York: Grove, 1952, pp. v-xxi.

Booth, Wayne. *The Rhetoric of Fiction.* Chicago: University of Chicago Press, 1961.

Bosanquet, Theodora. *Henry James at Work.* London: Hogarth Press, 1924.

______ "The Revised Version [of *The American*]". *The Little Review* 5 (August 1918) 56-62.

Bowden, E.T. *The Themes of Henry James: A System of Observation through the Visual Arts.* New Haven, Connecticut: Yale University Press, 1956.

Brooke, Rupert. *Complete Poems of Rupert Brooke.* London: Sidgwick and Jackson, 1936.

Brooks, Van Wyck. *The Pilgrimage of Henry James.* New York: Dutton, 1925.

Burde, Edgar J. "The Double Vision of Henry James: An Essay on the Three Late Novels". *DAI* 31 (1970) 1753A (Claremont).
Cargill, O. *The Novels of Henry James.* New York: Macmillan, 1961.
Chapman, Sara S. "Stalking the Beast: Egomania and Redemptive Suffering in James's 'Major Phase' ". *Colby Library Quarterly* 11 (1975) 50-66.
Chatman, Seymour. *The Later Style of Henry James.* Oxford: Blackwell's, 1972.
———, ed. *Literary Style: A Symposium.* London: O.U.P., 1971.
Chernaik, Judith. "Henry James as Moralist: The Case of the Late Novels". *The Centennial Review* 16 (1972) 105-21.
Colby, Frank Moore. "In Darkest James". In his *Imaginary Obligations.* New York: Dodd, Mead Co., 1904, pp. 321-35.
Colling, Patricia, ed. *Dissertation Abstracts International. A. The Humanities and Social Sciences,* Vols. XXIV-XXVIII. Ann Arbor, Michigan: Greenway, 1964-77.
Conrad, J. *Notes on Life and Letters.* London: Dent, 1925, pp. 13-23.
Cox, C.B. "James, Conrad, and the Language of Criticism". *Sewanee Review* 85 (Spring 1977) 351-60.
Crews, F.C. *The Tragedy of Manners: Moral Drama in the Later Novels of Henry James.* New Haven, Conn.: Yale University Press, 1957.
Crowl, Susan R. "The Beholder's Eye: Romantic and Critical Perspective Through Style in James's 'Turn of the Screw', *The Wings of the Dove,* and *The Golden Bowl*". *DAI* 31 (1970) 5357A (Ind.)
Crowley, Francis E. "Henry James's *The Beast in the Jungle* and *The Ambassadors*". *Psychoanalytical Review* 62 (1975) 154-63.
Davis, Sara de Saussure. "The Female Protagonist in Henry James's Fiction, 1870-1890". *DAI* 35 (1975) 7862-63A.
Dean, S. "James's *The Golden Bowl*". *Explicator* 35 (Summer 1977) 8-9.
Dunbar, O.H. "Henry James as a Lecturer". *The Critic* 57 (July 1905) 24-25.
Dunbar, V.R. "The Revision of Daisy Miller". *Modern Language Notes* 65 (May 1950) 311-17.
Dupee, F.W., *Henry James.* London: Methuen, 1951.
———, ed. *The Question of Henry James: A Collection of Critical Essays.* London: Wingate, 1947.
Durkin, Sister Mary Brian. "Henry James's Revisions of the Style of *The Reverberator*". *American Literature* 33 (1961) 330-49.
Edel, Leon, Ed. and introd. with headnotes *The Complete Plays of Henry James.* Philadelphia: Lippincott, 1949.
——— *Henry James: A Biography.* 5 vols.
Vol. I *The Untried Years, 1843-1870.* London: Rupert Hart-Davis, 1953.
Vol. II. *The Conquest of London, 1870-1883.* London: Rupert-Hart Davis, 1962.
Vol. III. *The Middle Years, 1884-1894.* London: Rupert Hart-Davis, 1963.
Vol. IV. *The Treacherous Years, 1895-1901.* London: Rupert Hart-Davis, 1969.

Vol. V. *The Master, 1901-1916.* London: Rupert Hart-Davis, 1973.

______ Ed. and introd. *Henry James: A Collection of Critical Essays.* Englewood Cliffs, N.H.: Prentice-Hall, 1963.

______ "Henry James's Last Dictation". *Times Literary Supplement* 2 May 1968, pp. 459-560.

______ "Henry James's Revisions for *The Ambassadors*". *Notes and Queries* n.s. II (January 1955) 37-38.

______ and Ray, Gordon N. *Henry James and H.G. Wells: A Record of their Friendship, their Debate on the Art of Fiction, and their Quarrel.* London: Hart-Davis, 1959.

Edelstein, Arnold S. "The Triumph of Fantasy: Ambiguity and Ambivalence in the Fiction of Henry James". *DAI* 33 (1972) 271A-72A (Calif. Berkeley).

Edgar, P. *Henry James: Man and Author.* 1927. Rpt. New York: Russell and Russell, 1964.

Eliot, T.S. "In Memory of Henry James". *The Little Review* (August 1918) 44-53.

______ "A Prediction in Regard to Three English Authors". *Vanity Fair* 21:6 (February 1924) 29, 98.

Elton, O. "The Novels of Mr Henry James". *Living Age* 240 (January 1904) 1-14.

Enck, John J. "Wholeness of Effect in *The Golden Bowl*". *Wisconsin Academy of Sciences, Arts and Letters* 47 (1958) 227-40.

Ferguson, F. "The Drama in *The Golden Bowl*". *Hound and Horn* 7 (April-June 1934) 407-13.

______ "*The Golden Bowl* Revisited". *Sewanee Review* 63 (Winter 1955) 13-38.

______ "James' Idea of Dramatic Form". *Kenyon Review* 4 (1943) 495-507.

Firebaugh, J.J. "The Ververs". *Essays in Criticism* 4 (October 1954) 400-410.

Fish, Charles. "Form and Revision: The Example of *Watch and Ward*". *Nineteenth-Century Fiction* 22 (September 1967) 173-90.

Forster, E.M. *Aspects of the Novel.* 1927: Rpt. London: Arnold, 1949.

Fowler, Roger, ed. *Essays on Style and Language: Linguistic Approaches to Literary Style.* London: Routledge & Kegan Paul, 1966.

France, W.C. "Henry James as a Lecturer". *Bookman* 21 (March 1905) 71-72.

Furbank, P.N. "Henry James: The Novelist as Actor". *Essays in Criticism* 1 (October 1951) 404-20.

Gale, R.L. *The Caught Image: Figurative Language in the Fiction of Henry James.* Chapel Hill: University of North Carolina Press, 1964.

Gard, A.R. "Critics of *The Golden Bowl*". *Melbourne Critical Review* 6 (1963) 102-109.

______, ed. *Henry James: The Critical Heritage.* London: Routledge & Kegan Paul, 1968, pp. 55-74.

Garner, F.A. "Henry James's Use of Architecture". *DAI* 35 (1975) 5342A (Tennessee).

Gegenheimer, A.F. "Early and Late Revision in Henry James's 'A Passionate Pilgrim' ". *American Literature* 23 (May 1951) 233-42.

Geismar, M. *Henry James and the Jacobites.* Boston: Houghton Mifflin, 1963.

Gervais, David. "James's Reading of *Madame Bovary*". *Cambridge Quarterly* 7:1 (1976) 1-26.

Gettmann, R.A. "Henry James's Revision of *The American*". *American Literature* 16 (January 1945) 279-95.

Gillen, F.X. "The Relationship of Rhetorical Control to Meaning in the Novels of Henry James, Virginia Woolf, and E.M. Forster". *DAI* 30 (1969) 1525A (Fordham).

Girling, H.K. "The Function of Slang in the Dramatic Poetry of 'The Golden Bowl' ". *Nineteenth-Century Fiction* 2 (September 1956) 130-47.

——— "On Editing a Paragraph of *The Princess Casamassima*". *Language and Style* 8 (1975) 243-63.

The Golden Bowl. Adapted for radio by Mary Hope Allen. British Broadcasting Commission, Third Programme, 7 October 1955.

The Golden Bowl. Adapted for television. British Broadcasting Commission Two, 10 August 1973.

Goldenthal, J.B. "Henry James and Impressionism: A Method of Stylistic Analysis". *DAI* 35 (1974) 2967A (N.Y.U.)

Gordon, Caroline. "Mr Verver, Our National Hero". *Sewanee Review* 63 (Winter 1955) 29-47.

Gornto, E.F. "A Study of the Influence of the Fairy Tale in the Fiction of Henry James". *DAI* 34 (1974) 7754A (Illinois, Urbana-Champaign).

Green, Eleanor. Letters to author. 1950-1967.

——— "Some Impressions to Introduce Henry James". *Henry James.* Sydney: Wentworth Press, 1960, pp. 5-21.

Greene, G. "Henry James: The Private Universe". 1936. Rpt. in *Collected Essays of Graham Greene.* London: Bodley Head, 1969, pp. 111-22.

Greene, Mildred S. "*Les liaisons dangereuses* and *The Golden Bowl*: Maggie's 'Loving Reason' ". *Modern Fiction Studies* 19 (1973-74) 531-40.

Greenstein, S.M. "The Negative Principle and the Virtuous Character: Undercutting in the Work of Richardson, Austen and James". *DAI* 35 (1974) 4521A (Indiana).

Hall, M.L. "Consciousness and the Unconscious: Henry James and Jungian Psychology". *DAI* 35 (1975) 6097A.

Hall, W.F. "The Meaning of *The Sacred Fount*: Its Own Little Law of Composition". *Modern Language Quarterly* 32 (June 1976) 168-78.

Halperin, J. *The Theory of the Novel: New Essays.* New York: O.U.P., 1974.

Halverson, John. "Late Manner, Major Phase". *Sewanee Review* 79 (1971) 214-31.

Happy, R.L. "The Function of the Ending in the Later Novels of Henry James". *DAI* 35 (1974) 1046A (Mo. Columbia).

Hardy, Barbara. *The Appropriate Form: An Essay on the Novel.* London: Athlone Press, 1964.

Hardy, Florence Emily. *The Life of Thomas Hardy. 1840-1928.* London: Macmillan, 1962.

Harris, M.P. "Henry James, Lecturer". *American Literature* 23 (November 1951) 302-14.

Hartsock, M.E. "Another Way to Heightened Consciousness". *Humanist* 37 (July 1977) 26-30.

______ "Dizzying Summit: James's 'The Altar of the Dead' ". *Studies in Short Fiction* 11 (1975) 371-79.

______ "The Most Valuable Thing: James on Death". *Modern Fiction Studies* 22 (Winter 1976-77) 507-24.

______ "Time for Comedy. The Late Novels of Henry James". *English Studies* 56 (April 1975) 114-28.

______ "Unintentional Fallacy: Critics and *The Golden Bowl*". *Modern Language Quarterly* 35 (September 1974) 272-88.

Harvitt, H. "How Henry James Revised *Roderick Hudson*". *PMLA* 39 (March 1924) 202-27.

Hatch, E.K. "Henry James and the Aesthetic Movement". *DAI* 35 (1975) 5405A (Virginia).

Havens, R.D. "The Revision of *Roderick Hudson*". *PMLA* 40 (June 1925) 433-34.

Helder, J. "The Commedia Dell 'Arte Tradition and Three Later Novels of Henry James". *DAI* 35 (1974) 1047A (Bowling Green State).

Hoag, Gerald. "The Death of the Paper Lion". *Studies in Short Fiction* 12 (1975) 163-72.

Hocks, Richard A. *Henry James and Pragmatistic Thought: A Study in the Relationship between the Philosophy of William James and the Literary Art of Henry James.* Chapel Hill: University of North Carolina Press, 1974.

Hoile, Christopher. "Lambert Strether and the Boaters — Tonio Kröger and the Dancers: Confrontation and Self-Acceptance". *Canadian Review of Comparative Literature* 2 (1975) 243-61.

Holder, A. *Three Voyages in Search of Europe: A Study of Henry James, Ezra Pound and T.S. Eliot.* Philadelphia: University of Philadelphia Press, 1966.

Holder-Barell, A. *A Development of Imagery and Its Functional Significance in Henry James's Novels.* Cooper Monographs on English and American Language and Literature No. 3 Bern; Francke, 1959.

Holland, Laurence Bedwell. *The Expense of Vision: Essays on the Craft of Henry James.* Princeton, N.J.: Princeton University Press, 1964.

Holland, L.B. "*The Wings of the Dove*". *English Literary History* 26:4 (December 1959) 549-75.

Howard, Richard. "Letters of a Master". *Yale Review* 64 (1975) 594-97.

Humphreys, S.M. "HJ's Revisions for *The Ambassadors*". *Notes and Queries* n.s. 1 (September 1954) 397-99.

Hyde, H. "Henry James at Home". *Essays by Divers Hands* 35 (1975) 58-77.

Hyde, H. "Henry James's 'Last Dictation' ". *Times Literary Supplement*, 9 May 1968, p. 481; 23 May 1968, p. 529; 30 May 1968, p. 553; 6 June 1968, p. 597; 18 June 1968, p. 621.

Jefferson, D.W. *Henry James.* London: Oliver and Boyd, 1960.
Jeffrey, David K. "On Henry James". *Scholia Satyrica* 1:i (1975) 13-18.
Johnson, Robert G. "A Study of the Style of Henry James's Late Novels". *DAI* 32 (1971) 2092A (Bowling Green).
Jones, Granville H. *Henry James's Psychology of Experience: Innocence, Responsibility, and Renunciation in the Fiction of Henry James.* In *De Proprietatibus Literarum.* The Hague: Mouton, 1975.
Kimball, J. "Henry James's Last Portrait of a Lady: Charlotte Stant in *The Golden Bowl*". *Nineteenth-Century Fiction* 28 (January 1957) 449-68.
Kleinberg, Seymour. "Ambiguity and Ambivalence: The Psychology of Sexuality in Henry James' *The Portrait of a Lady*". *Markham Review* 5 (May 1969), 2-7.
Krause, S.J. "James's Revisions of the Style of *The Portrait of a Lady*". *American Literature* 30 (1958) 67-88.
Krook, D. "*The Golden Bowl*". *Cambridge Journal* 7 (September 1954) 716-37.
——— "Intentions and Intentions: The Problem of Intention and Henry James's *The Turn of the Screw*". In *Theory of the Novel: New Essays.* Ed. John Halperin. New York: O.U.P., 1974, pp. 353-72.
——— "The Madness of Art: Further Reflections on the Ambiguity of Henry James". *Hebrew University Studies in Literature* 1:i (1973) 25-38.
——— "The Method of the Later Works of Henry James". *London Magazine* 1 (July 1954) 55-70.
——— *The Ordeal of Consciousness in Henry James.* Cambridge: University Press, 1962.
——— "The Wings of the Dove", *Cambridge Journal* 7 (August 1954) 671-89.
Krupnick, Mark L. "*The Golden Bowl*: Henry James's Novel About Nothing". *English Studies* 57 (December 1976) 533-40.
Labrie, E.R. "The Good and the Beautiful in Henry James". *Greyfriar: Siena Studies in Literature* 16 (1975) 3-15.
La Roche, M. "Reading Henry James Aloud". *Mark Twain Quarterly* 5 (Spring 1943) 8.
Lauer, K.O. "The Interior Monologue in *The Ambassadors* and *The Golden Bowl*". *DAI* 31 (1970) 6015A (Mich. State).
Layard, Austen Henry. *The Italian Schools of Painting: Based on the Handbook of Kugler.* Part 2. London: Murray, 1907.
Leavis, F.R. "George Eliot, IV: 'Daniel Deronda' and 'The Portrait of a Lady' ". *Scrutiny* 14 (December 1946) 102-31.
——— *The Great Tradition: George Eliot, Henry James, Joseph Conrad.* London: Chatto and Windus, 1948.
Lebowitz, N. *The Imagination of Loving: Henry James's Legacy to the Novel.* Detroit: Wayne State University Press, 1965.
——— "Magic and Metamorphosis in *The Golden Bowl*". *Sewanee Review* 73 (January-March 1965) 58-73.
Lee, B. *The Novels of Henry James: A Study of Cultural Consciousness.* London: Edward Arnold, 1978.

Leitch, T.M. "The James Tradition: An Investigation in Literary History". *DAI* 37 (1976) 4369A (Yale University.)

Leyburn, Ellen D. *Strange Alloy: The Relation of Comedy to Tragedy in the Fiction of Henry James.* Foreword W.T. Stafford. Chapel Hill: University of North Carolina Press, 1968.

Liberman, T.R. "The Open Ending in the Later Novels of Henry James". *DAI* 37 (1976) 4370A (Case Western Reserve University).

Ling, Amy. "The Pagoda Image in Henry James's *The Golden Bowl*". *American Literature* 46 (1974) 383-88.

Littré, Emile. *Diction de la Langue Française.* Tome 2. Paris: Jean-Jacques Pauvert, 1956.

Lodge, David. "Strether by the River". In his *Language of Fiction: Essays in Criticism and Verbal Analysis of the English Novel.* London: Routledge and Kegan Paul, 1966, pp,. 189-213.

Lohmann, C.K. "Jamesian Irony and the American Sense of Mission". *Texas Studies in Literature and Language* 16 (Summer 1974) 329-47.

Louvre, A.W. "The Limits of Living in Style". *DAI* 34 (1974) 7238A (Cornell).

Lubbock, Percy. *The Craft of Fiction.* New York: Scribner's, 1921.

Luxford, Ansel F., Jr. "Henry James's Forgotten Phase: A Critical Analysis of the Late Fiction". *DAI* 32 (1972) 4518A (Va.).

Mackenzie, Manfred. *Communities of Love and Honor in Henry James.* Cambridge, Massachusetts: Harvard University Press, 1976.

MacNaughton, William R. "The Narrator in Henry James's *The Sacred Fount*". In *Literature and Ideas in America: Essays in Memory of Harry Hayden Clark.* Athens: Ohio University Press, 1975, pp. 151-81.

McElderry, B.R., Jr. "Henry James's Revision of *Watch and Ward*". *Modern Language Notes* 67 (November 1952) 457-61.

McGinty, Sister M.C., C.S.J. "The Jamesian Parenthesis: Elements of Suspension in the Narrative Sentences of Henry James's Late Style". *DA* 24 (1964) 4193 (Catholic University).

McIntyre, C.F. "The Later Manner of Henry James". *PMLA* 20 (March 1905) 26-39.

Maini, Darshan Singh. *Henry James: The Indirect Vision. Studies in Themes and Techniques.* Bombay and New Delhi: Tata McGraw-Hill, 1973.

______ "The Style of Henry James". *Indian Journal of English Studies* 9 (1968) 18-29.

Margalioth, D.Z. "Taste and Morality: A Study of the Works of Henry James". *DAI* 35 (1974) 6721A (Columbia University).

Marks, Sita P.S. "A Silent Morality: Non-Verbal Expression in *The Ambassadors*". *South Atlantic Bulletin* 39:ii (1974) 102-6.

______ "The Sound and the Silence: Non-Verbal Patterns in *The Wings of the Dove*". *Arizona Quarterly* 27:ii (Summer 1971) 143-50.

Matthiessen, F.O. *The Major Phase.* New York: O.U.P., 1946.

______ "The Painter's Sponge and Varnish Bottle: Henry James's Revisions of *The Portrait of a Lady*". *American Bookman* 1 (1944) 49-68.

Maves, Carl. *Sensuous Pessimism: Italy in the Work of Henry James.* Bloomington: Indiana University Press, 1973.

Maxwell, J.C. "The Revision of *Roderick Hudson*". *English Studies* 45 (June 1964) 239.

Menikoff, Barry. "Punctuation and Point of View in the Late Style of Henry James". *Style* 4 (1970) 29-47.

——— "The Subjective Pronoun in the Late Style of Henry James". *English Studies* 52 (1971) 436-41.

Merrill, Robert. "What Strether *Sees*: The Ending of *The Ambassadors*". *Bulletin of the Rocky Mountain Modern Language Association* 27 (1973) 45-52.

Meserole, Harrison T., et al., comps. *MLA International Bibliography.* New York: MLA, 1958 to 1977.

Michael, M.K. "Henry James's Use of the Word *Wonderful* in *The Ambassadors*". *Modern Language Notes* 75 (1960) 114-17.

Michaels, W.B. 'Writers Reading: James and Eliot". *Modern Language Notes* 91 (October 1976) 827-49.

Milic, Louis T. *Style and Stylistics: An Analytical Bibliography.* New York: Free Press, 1967.

Miller, James E., Jr. "Henry James: A Theory of Fiction". *Prairie Schooner* 45 (1971) 330-56.

——— "Henry James in Reality". *Critical Inquiry* 2:3 (Spring 1976) 585-604.

———, Ed. and introd. *Theory of Fiction: Henry James.* Lincoln: University of Nebraska Press, 1972.

Minnick, Thomas L. " 'The Light of Deepening Experience' in the Major Novels of Henry James". *Rendezvous: Journal of Arts and Letters* 10:ii (1975) 37-51.

Monteiro, George. " 'The Items of High Civilization': Hawthorne, Henry James and George Parsons Lathrop". *Nathaniel Hawthorne Journal* (1975) 146-55.

Mooney, Stephen L. "James, Keats, and the Religion of Consciousness". *Modern Language Quarterly* 22 (December 1961) 399-401.

Moore, Harry T. *Henry James and His World.* New York: Viking, 1974.

Mori, Mihoko. "Meian to *The Golden Bowl*". *Eigo Seinen* 121 (1975) 212-13.

Morrison, Peggy Ann R. "The Connoisseur in the Novels of Henry James". *DAI* 33 (1973) 2660A (Brandeis).

Mull, Donald L. *Henry James's "Sublime Economy": Money as Symbolic Centre in the Fiction.* Middletown, Connecticut: Wesleyan University Press, 1973.

Mulqueen, James E. "Perfection of a Pattern: The Structure of *The Ambassadors, The Wings of the Dove,* and *The Golden Bowl*". *Arizona Quarterly* 27:2 (1971) 133-42.

Murakami, F. "The Creation of *The Golden Bowl*". *Jimbun Kenkyu* 10 (July 1959) 117-31.

Murray, Peter and Linda. *Dictionary of Art and Artists.* London: Thames and Hudson, 1965.

Naik, M.K. "The Draught from the 'Golden Bowl' ". *Journal of the Karnatak University* 7 (1963) 199-217.

Nance, W. " 'The Beast in the Jungle': Two Versions of Oedipus". *Studies in Short Fiction* 13 (Fall 1976) 433-40.

Nowell-Smith, Simon, ed. *The Legend of the Master: Henry James.* London: Constable, 1947.

Nuhn, Ferner. *The Wind Blew from the East: A Study in the Orientation of American Culture.* New York: Harper, 1942.

O'Connor, D.L. "Henry James and the Language World of Renunciation". *DAI* 36 (1975) 3697A (Cornell University).

Owen, E. "The 'Given Appearance' of Charlotte Verver". *Essays in Criticism* 13 (October 1963) 364-74.

Pearce, Howard. "Henry James's Pastoral Fallacy". *PMLA* 90:5 (October 1975) 834-47.

Pearson, Gabriel. "The Novel to End All Novels: *The Golden Bowl*". In *The Air of Reality: New Essays on Henry James.* Ed. John Goode. London: Methuen, 1972, pp. 301-62.

Perrin, E.N. "*The Golden Bowl*". *Essays in Criticism* 5 (April 1955), 189-90.

Petersen, Dale E. *The Clement Vision: Poetic Realism in Turgenev and James.* Port Washington, New York: Kennikat Press, 1975.

Pingree, E.E., ed. *Humanities Index.* Vols. I-IV. New York: Wilson, 1974 to 1977.

Pound, Ezra. *The Literary Remains of Ezra Pound.* Ed. and introd. T.S. Eliot. London: Faber, 1954.

Powers, Lyall H. *Henry James: An Introduction and Interpretation.* New York: Holt, Rinehart and Winston, 1970.

Purdy, S.B. "Henry James and the *Mot Juste*". *Wisconsin Studies in Literature* (1969) 118-25.

______ "Henry James, Gustave Flaubert, and the Ideal Style". *Language and Style* 3 (1970) 163-84.

______ "Henry James's Use of *Vulgar*". *American Speech* 42 (1967) 45-50.

______ "The Language of Henry James with Emphasis on His Diction and Vocabulary". *DAI* 21 (1960) 626 (Wis.).

Putt, S.G. "Henry James, Radical Gentleman". *Massachusetts Review* 18 (Spring 1977) 179-86.

Raunheim, John P. "A Study of the Revisions of the Tales of Henry James Included in the New York Edition". *DAI* 33 (1972) 733A (N.Y.U.).

Reddick, Bryan. "The Control of Distance in *The Golden Bowl*". *Modern British Literature* 1:1 (Fall 1976) 46-56.

Review of *The Golden Bowl. Times Literary Supplement*, February 1905, p. 47.

Review of *The Wings of the Dove. Times Literary Supplement*, September 1902, p. 263.

Richmond, Lee J. "Henry James and the Comedy of Love: *The Golden Bowl*". *Erasmus Review* 1:i (1971) 47-62.

Rimmon, Shlomith. *The Concept of Ambiguity: The Example of James.* Chicago: University of Chicago Press, 1977.

Roberts, M. "Henry James's Final Period". *Yale Review* 37 (September 1947) 60-67.

Rose, Alan. "The Spatial Form of *The Golden Bowl*". *Modern Fiction Studies* 12:i (Spring 1966) 103-16.

Rowe, John Carlos. "The Deceptive Symmetry of Art in *The Golden Bowl*". In his *Henry Adams and Henry James.* Ithaca, New York: Cornell University Press, 1976.

Samuels, Charles T. *The Ambiguity of Henry James.* Urbana: University of Illinois Press, 1971.

Schneider, Daniel J. "The Divided Self in the Fiction of Henry James". *PMLA* 90:3 (May 1975) 447-60.

——— *Symbolism: The Manichean Vision: A Study in the Art of James, Conrad, Woolf and Stevens.* Lincoln: University of Nebraska Press, 1975.

Scott, Arthur. "A Protest Against the James Vogue". *College English* 13 (1952) 194-201.

Sears, Sallie. *The Negative Imagination: Form and Perspective in the Novels of Henry James.* Ithaca, N.Y.: Cornell University Press, 1968.

Sebouhian, George. "The Transcendental Imagination of Merton Densher". *Modern Language Studies* 5:ii (1975) 35-45.

Segal, Ora. *The Lucid Reflector: The Observer in Henry James' Fiction.* New Haven: Yale University Press, 1970.

Shahane, V.A. "Formative Influences on E.M. Forster, Henry James — A Study in Ambivalence". *Osmania Studies in English* 1 (1961) 39-53.

Shapira, M., ed. *Selected Literary Criticism.* Introd. F.R. Leavis. London: Heinemann, 1963.

Sharp, Sister M. Corona, O.S.U. *The Confidante in Henry James: Evolution and Moral Value of a Fictive Character.* Notre Dame, Indiana: University of Notre Dame Press, 1963.

Shipley, John B., gen. ed. *Abstracts of English Studies.* Vols. I to XX. Illinois: National Council of Teachers of English, 1958 to 1977.

Short, R.W. "Henry James's World of Images". *PMLA* 68 (September 1954) 943-60.

——— "The Sentence Structure of Henry James". *American Literature* 18 (May 1946) 71-88.

Sibley, Ian. "Imagination and Moral Integrity in Henry James's Major Phase. An Exegetical Study of Three Major Novels and Seven Related *Nouvelles*, Emphasizing Ultimate Correspondences with Dante and Ecclesiastes". Ph.D. *DISS.* Submitted to University of Queensland.

Sklepowich, E.A. "The Play of Tone: Henry James and the Concept of Social Artifice". *DAI* 32 (1971) 4633A-34A (Va.).

Spender, Stephen. *The Destructive Element: A Study of Modern Writers and Beliefs.* London: Jonathan Cape, 1935.

——— "*The Golden Bowl*". *The Question of Henry James.* Ed. F.W. Dupee. New York: Henry Holt, 1945, 236-45.

——— *Love-Hate Relations: A Study of Anglo-American Sensibilities.* London: Hamish Hamilton, 1974.

Stafford, W.T. "Henry James". *American Literary Scholarship: An Annual* (1973) 116-34.

Stein, W.B. "*The Wings of the Dove*: James's Eucharist of *Punch*". *The Centennial Review* 21:3 (Summer 1977) 236-60.

Stevenson, Elizabeth. *The Crooked Corridor*. New York: Macmillan, 1949.

Stewart, J.I.M. "Henry James". In his lecture on "Modern English Literature" delivered for The British Council, at the Holywell Music Room, Oxford, 21 August 1955.

Sturge-Gretton, M. "Mr Henry James and His Prefaces". *Contemporary Review* 101 (January 1912) 69-78.

Tanner, Tony. "*The Golden Bowl* and the Reassessment of Innocence". *The London Magazine* 1:2, n.s. (November 1961) 38-49.

Theobald, J.R. "New Reflections on *The Golden Bowl*". *Twentiety-Century Literature* 3 (April 1957) 20-26.

Thomas, J.L. "The Technical Synthesis of Henry James: A Study of the Method of 'The Major Phase' ". *DAI* 32 (1971) 4027A (N.Y.U.).

Thomas W.B. "The Author's Voice in *The Ambassadors*". *Journal of Narrative Technique* 1 (1971) 108-21.

Thurber, James. "The Wings of Henry James". *New Yorker* 7 November 1959, pp. 184-97.

Tilford, John E. "James the Old Intruder", *Modern Fiction Studies* 4 (Summer 1958) pp. 157-64.

Tintner, Adeline R. "*The Golden Bowl* and Waddesdon Manor". *Apollo* 104 (August 1976) 106-13.

______ "Henry James Criticism: A Current Perspective". *American Literary Realism* 7 (Spring 1974) 155-68.

______ "Maggie's Pagoda: Architectural Follies in *The Golden Bowl*". *Markham Review* 3 (1973) 113-15.

______ "Sir Sidney Colvin in *The Golden Bowl*: Mr Crichton Identified". *Colby Library Quarterly* 10 (1974) 428-31.

Todasco, R.T. "Theme and Imagery in *The Golden Bowl*". *Texas Studies in Literature and Language* 4 (Summer 1962) 228-40.

Tracy, Bruce P. "Henry James's Representation of Inner Consciousness in Meditation Scenes from the Late Novels". *DAI* 32 (1971) 1533A (Mich. State).

Traschen, I. "Henry James and the Art of Revision". *Philological Quarterly* 35 (January 1956) 39-47.

______ "James's Revisions of the Love Affair in *The American*". *New England Quarterly* 29 (March 1956) 43-62.

Trilling, L. "The Jameses". *Times Literary Supplement*, 20 October 1972, p. 1257.

Ullmann, Stephen. *Style in the French Novel*. Cambridge: University Press, 1957.

Unrue, Darlene, H. "Henry James's Extraordinary Use of Portraits". *RE/Artes Liberales* 1:ii (1975) 47-53.

Vandersee, Charles. "James's 'Pandora': The Mixed Consequences of Revision". *Studies in Bibliography* 21 (1968) 93-108.

Veeder, William. *Henry James — the Lessons of the Master: Popular Fiction and Personal Style in the Nineteenth Century.* Chicago: University of Chicago Press, 1975.
Vincec, Sister Stephanie. "A Significant Revision of *The Wings of the Dove*". *Review of English Studies* 23 (1972) 58-61.
Waldock, A.J.A. *James, Joyce and Others.* London: Williams and Norgate, 1937.
Wallace, Ronald. *Henry James and the Comic Form: A Study of the Major Novels.* Ann Arbor: University of Michigan Press, 1975.
Ward, J.A. "The Ambiguities of Henry James". *Sewanee Review* 83:1 (January-March 1975) 39-60.
______ "Evil in *The Golden Bowl*". *Western Humanities Review* 14 (1960) 47-59.
______ *The Imagination of Disaster: Evil in the Fiction of Henry James.* Lincoln: University of Nebraska Press, 1961.
______ *The Search for Form: Studies in the Structure of James's Fiction.* Chapel Hill: University of North Carolina Press, 1967.
Warren, A. "Myth and Dialectic in the Later Novels". *Kenyon Review* 5 (Autumn 1943) 551-68.
Watanabe, H. "Past Perfect Retrospection in the Style of Henry James". *American Literature* 34 (1962) 165-81.
Waterlow, S.P. "The Work of Mr Henry James". *Independent Review* 4 (November 1904) 236-43.
Watt, Ian. "The First Paragraph of *The Ambassadors.* An Explication". *Essays in Criticism* 10 (1960) 250-74.
Wegelin, Christof. "The 'Internationalism' of 'The Golden Bowl' ". *Nineteenth-Century Fiction* 2 (December 1956) 161-81.
Weiner, R.B. "The Terrible Algebra: Images of the Self in Henry James". *DAI* 35 (1974) 3016A (Boston College).
Weinstein, Philip M. *Henry James and the Requirements of the Imagination.* Cambridge: Harvard University Press, 1971.
Welsh, Alexander. "Allegory of Truth in English Fiction". *Victorian Studies* 8:3 (September 1965) 7-28.
West, Rebecca. *Henry James.* London: Nisbett, 1916.
Wharton, Edith. *A Backward Glance.* 1934. Rpt. London: Constable, 1972.
______ *The Writing of Fiction.* New York: Scribner's, 1925.
White, Patrick. *Riders in the Chariot.* London: Cape, 1973.
______ *The Eye of the Storm.* Eyre & Spottiswoode, 1961.
Wilds, N.G. "Rhetorical Strategy in Early Twentieth-Century Fiction: Studies in Henry James, Ford Madox Ford, and James Joyce". *DAI* 36 (1975) 3706A (University of South Carolina).
Wilson, E. "The Ambiguity of Henry James". In his *The Triple Thinkers: Twelve Essays on Literary Subjects.* London: John Lehmann, 1952, pp. 89-128.
Wilson, L.S. "The Stylistics of Henry James: A Linguistic Analysis of Selected Early and Late Novels". *DAI* 35 (1974) 7896A (Florida State).

Wilson, R.B.J. "Ambiguity and Eloquence in *The Golden Bowl*". *Henry James*. Sydney: Wentworth Press, 1960, pp. 23-37.

——— "An Attempt to Define the Meaning of *The Wings of the Dove*". Paper delivered at the Biennial Conference of the *Australian Universities Language and Literature Association* in Canberra, Australian Capital Territory, August 1962.

——— "Henry James and the Art of the Novel: A Study of a Developing Technique". *Diss.* University of Sydney, 1958.

——— "Henry James and 'The Note Absolute' ". *English Studies* 23 (1966) 31-35.

——— "Henry James's Three Versions of 'The Real Thing' ". Paper delivered at postgraduate seminar conducted by Dr David Lodge in the Department of English, University of Birmingham, 29 October 1973.

——— "The 'refinement' of Strether's 'supreme scruple' and his renunciation of Maria". 30pp. Paper delivered at post-graduate seminar, conducted by Dr Barbara Hardy, Birkbeck College, University of London, 5 July 1965. In author's possession.

——— "The Splinters of a Mind Make a Whole Piece, Patrick White's *The Eye of the Storm*". *Studies in the Recent Australian Novel.* Ed. K.G. Hamilton, St. Lucia, Queensland: University of Queensland Press, 1978, pp. 61-83.

Wilson, W. "Henry James on 'Newspaper English' ". *Current Literature* 39 (August 1905) 155.

Woolf, V. "Mr Henry James's Latest Novel". *The Guardian*, 22 February 1905, p. 339, cols. 2-3.

Wright, Walter. "Maggie Verver: Neither Saint Nor Witch". *Nineteenth-Century Fiction* 12 (June 1957) 59-71.

Yeazell, Ruth B. "Forum". *PMLA* 91:5 (October 1976) 422-24.

——— *Language and Knowledge in the Late Novels of Henry James.* Chicago: University of Chicago Press, 1976.

——— The Late Style of Henry James: A Study of Style in the Novel". *DAI* 32 (1972) 7016A (Yale).

——— "The New 'Arithmetic' of Henry James". *Criticism* 16 (Spring 1974) 109-19.

——— "Talking in James". *PMLA* 91 (January 1976) 66 77.

Index

DATE DUE

AUG 2 8 1986			
MAY 2 0 1989			
GAYLORD			PRINTED IN U.S.A.